THE SYMBOLIC SCENARIOS OF ISLAMISM

The Symbolic Scenarios of Islamism initiates a dialogue between the discourse of three of the most discussed figures in the history of the Sunni Islamic movement – Hasan al-Banna, Sayyid Qutb and Osama bin Laden – and contemporary debates across religion and political theory. In the wake of the Arab Spring, the dramatic vicissitudes of Egypt, Syria, and Iraq, and the return of the 'Islamist threat' in Europe, this book provides a crucial foundation upon which to situate current developments in world politics.

Redressing the inefficiency of the terms in which the debate on Islam and Islamism is generally conducted, the book examines the role played by tradition, modernity, and transmodernity as major 'symbolic scenarios' of Islamist discourses, highlighting the internal complexity and dynamism of Islamism. By uncovering forms of knowledge that have hitherto gone unnoticed or have been marginalised by traditional and dominant approaches to politics, accounting for central political ideas in non-Western sources and in the Global South, the book provides a unique contribution towards rethinking the nature of citizenship, antagonism, space, and frontiers required today.

While offering valuable reading for scholars of Islamic studies, religious studies and politics, it provides a critical and important perspective for academics with an interest in discourse theory, post-colonial theory, political philosophy, and comparative political thought.

Contemporary Thought in the Islamic World

Series Editor: Carool Kersten, King's College London, UK

Contemporary Thought in the Islamic World promotes new directions in scholarship in the study of Islamic thinking. Muslim scholars of today challenge deeply ingrained dichotomies and binaries. New ideas have stimulated an upcoming generation of progressive Muslim thinkers and scholars of Islam to radically rethink the ways in which immediate and emergent issues affecting the contemporary Islamic world are to be assessed. Central in these new discourses are notions such as cosmopolitanism, exile, authority and resistance. This series aims to take the field beyond the usual historical-philological and social science-driven approaches, and to insert the study of Islam and the Muslim world into far wider multi-disciplinary inquiries on religion and religiosity in an increasingly interconnected world.

Also published in this series

Alternative Islamic Discourses and Religious Authority
Edited by Carool Kersten and Susanne Olsson

The Sociology of Islam
Collected Essays of Bryan S. Turner
Edited by Bryan S. Turner and Kamaludeen Mohamed Nasir

The Symbolic Scenarios of Islamism

A Study in Islamic Political Thought

ANDREA MURA
The Open University, UK and University of Exeter, UK

ASHGATE

© Andrea Mura 2015

All rights reserved. No part of this publication may be reproduced, stored in a retrieval system or transmitted in any form or by any means, electronic, mechanical, photocopying, recording or otherwise without the prior permission of the publisher.

Andrea Mura has asserted his right under the Copyright, Designs and Patents Act, 1988, to be identified as the author of this work.

Published by
Ashgate Publishing Limited
Wey Court East
Union Road
Farnham
Surrey, GU9 7PT
England

Ashgate Publishing Company
110 Cherry Street
Suite 3-1
Burlington, VT 05401-3818
USA

www.ashgate.com

British Library Cataloguing in Publication Data
A catalogue record for this book is available from the British Library

The Library of Congress has cataloged the printed edition as follows:
Mura, Andrea.
  The symbolic scenarios of Islamism : a study in Islamic political thought / By Andrea Mura.
     pages cm
  Includes bibliographical references and index.
  ISBN 978-1-4724-4389-2 (hardcover) -- ISBN 978-1-4724-4390-8 (ebook) --
ISBN 978-1-4724-4391-5 (epub) 1. Islamic fundamentalism. 2. Islam and politics.
3. Banna, Hasan, 1906-1949. 4. Qutb, Sayyid, 1906-1966. 5. Bin Laden, Osama, 1957-2011.
I. Title.

BP166.14.F85M865 2015
320.55'7--dc23
                                                                    2015007103

ISBN 9781472443892 (hbk)
ISBN 9781472443908 (ebk – PDF)
ISBN 9781472443915 (ebk – ePUB)

Printed in the United Kingdom by Henry Ling Limited,
at the Dorset Press, Dorchester, DT1 1HD

To Laura and our becomings

Contents

List of Figures ix
About the Author xi
Acknowledgements xiii

Introduction 1

PART I

1 Approaching Islamism 13

2 Modernity and Tradition: Discursive Genealogies 31

3 Globalisation and Transmodernity 73

PART II

4 The Discourse of Hasan Al-Banna: A Territorial Trajectory 97

5 The Discourse of Sayyid Qutb: A Transitional Trajectory 131

6 The Discourse of Osama bin Laden: A Transterritorial Trajectory 167

Conclusion 193

Bibliography 217
Index 239

List of Figures

2.1	An inclusive model: Territoriality	63
2.2	An exclusionary model: Territory	64
5.1	Qutb's normative vision	148
5.2	Qutb's descriptive vision	158

About the Author

Andrea Mura is a Lecturer at the Institute of Arab and Islamic Studies at the University of Exeter, and a visiting academic at the Centre for Citizenship, Identities and Governance at The Open University, where he previously contributed to the *Oecumene: Citizenship after Orientalism* project. He has published widely in the fields of political philosophy, psychoanalysis, and comparative political thought, inquiring into the influence that political-theological questions have traditionally exerted upon ideas of power, justice, and economy in different traditions.

Acknowledgements

The theoretical terrain in which this unpretentious study is set, its methodological proceeding, its action and ethos owe a large intellectual debt to Ernesto Laclau. One of his recommendations to earlier PhD students was included in my doctoral thesis, which was the first inspiration for this book, and pointed me towards what I saw as a fundamental task that I hoped to carry out in the spirit of that time: 'The discourse of philosophy cannot be constituted without some "accidental" assumptions. To show these assumptions is to de-centre the discourse of Philosophy vis-à-vis itself – i.e., vis-à-vis its ambitions to constitute a ground. The kind of exercise that I am suggesting proposes, consequently, that each thesis – whether it refers to South Africa, Islam, the military regime in Argentina or the black politics in Britain – should be a contribution to the radical deconstruction of the dichotomies through which the metaphysics of presence constitutes itself' ('Intellectual Strategies', University of Essex, 1991). I am also indebted to Moya Lloyd, who patiently and creatively guided me in the years of doctoral study at the Loughborough University's Department of Politics, History and International Relations, which I gratefully acknowledge for funding my early research. I would like to thank all those colleagues who contributed with suggestions and encouragement to the various reworkings of this book, in particular Yannis Stavrakakis, Andrea Teti and Simona Guerra – all of whom offered invaluable comments and enduring friendship.

The research leading to these results has received funding from the European Research Council under the European Union's Seventh Framework Programme (FP7/2007-2013) / ERC grant agreement no. 249379. This work could never be accomplished without the support and stimulating academic environment of the Open University, and the opportunity to develop my ideas as Postdoctoral Researcher at the 'Oecumene: Citizenship after Orientalism' project. Nothing would have been possible without the treasured support, generous friendship and ongoing intellectual engagements with my marvellous colleagues in the Oecumene team. Special thanks go to Engin Isin who led me during this journey, enriching my intellectual perspective in many ways. Daniel Ryburn and Angela Duthie also deserve special thanks for having contributed in different degrees to improving the style of discourse of this book. I also wish to thank

David Shervington at Ashgate and Carool Kersten, who directs Ashgate's book series Contemporary Thought in the Islamic World, for their priceless support and assistance with this project.

Several parts of the book have drawn material from previously published work, which I wish to acknowledge: 'The Inclusive Dynamics of Islamic Universalism: From the Vantage Point of Sayyid Qutb's Critical Philosophy', *Comparative Philosophy*, 5/1 (2014): 30–55; 'A Genealogical Inquiry into Early Islamism: The Discourse of Hasan al-Banna', *Journal of Political Ideologies*, 17/1 (2012): 61–85; 'The Symbolic Function of Transmodernity', *Language and Psychoanalysis*, 1 (2012): 67–86; (with Andrea Teti) 'Sunni Islam and Politics', in Jeff Haynes (ed.), *Routledge Handbook of Religion and Politics* (London: Routledge, 2009). Excerpts from various publishers and online sources offering accurate translations of original documents in Arabic have been reproduced in this study for the purposes of criticism and argumentation. Every effort has been made to trace copyright holders.

The most special thanks go to my beloved family, friends and adored new nephews: Isabel, Elian, Zeno, Mariam and Samuel.

Failings are all mine.

Introduction

Since the publication of Marx and Engels's *Communist Manifesto*, the famous formula, 'a spectre is haunting Europe – the spectre of communism', has been subject to all kind of variations, adapting to different contexts and political visions. In one of the most successful alternatives after the fall of the Berlin Wall, it is 'Islamism' that plays the controversial role of the new spectre of Europe. Although this substitution has gained special force and visibility over the last two decades, the spectral presence of Islamism is not new. Well before the beginning of the millennium, discourses appealing to 'Islam' as the centre of political and social life had been populating the political scene of the ex-colonial world, having an impact on world politics beyond domestic boundaries. But the international context of the second half of the twentieth century was still dominated by the two blocks of the Cold War and by the powerful counter-hegemonic appeal of 'communism'. The irruption of Islamism as a 'new' spectre at a global level occurred at a moment when the end of the Cold War had allowed neo-liberal discourses to emerge as the triumphant narrative of the *End of History*, and the sole testimony of reality in the face of a defeated communism. The spectrality of Islamism consisted first and foremost in the irruption of an obstacle to the neo-liberal fantasy of 'Western' absolute control, mastery and representation of reality. Its irruption cracked the 'post-ideological' illusion of a cosmopolitan future of harmony, peace and prosperity, where social and international tensions could be accommodated by way of consensus-seeking procedures, which would render conflict unnecessary and ideological divisions obsolete. *Islamist* discourses emerged then as modes of political representation that held a mirror to the dramatic events marking the beginning of the new millennium. From terrorist attacks by Islamist groups in New York, London, Madrid, Paris, and cities in Asia and the Middle East, to the persisting instability and violence in the Israeli–Palestinian arena, and the first major conflicts of the twenty-first century: the military campaigns in Iraq and Afghanistan where security, economic and political considerations have kept merging together in what George W. Bush called 'the war on [Islamic] terror', and Barack Obama rephrased, with decaffeinated language, 'overseas contingency operations' against the 'terrorist [Islamic] threat'.

We have placed the term 'Islamic' in brackets, not only in acknowledgement of the fact that the 'war on terror' was launched in response to the *Islamic religious fanaticism* responsible for the 11 September attacks but also because despite its media visibility, Islam remained for many an invisible presence, a spectral entity. Since 9/11, 'Islamic' phenomena have been the phantasmatic catalyst of Western innermost fears, a source of anxiety and a threat to the sense of security and stability of the West only recently eclipsed by emergence of a new global threat hovering over Western lives: 'the financial crisis'. The conceptual imprecision that equates terms such as 'Islamic', 'Islamist', 'Muslim', 'obscurantism', 'terrorism', 'intolerance', has given form to a phantom 'Islam' that continues to pervade the language of the media, politicians, and ordinary citizens. In the immediate aftermath of 9/11, bin Laden and the Taliban were often taken to epitomise Islam as such, and to constitute undeniable proof of a structural incompatibility between Islam and democracy. Ten years later, it was with some embarrassment that critics welcomed the eruption of the Arab Spring and had to admit that some sort of democracy could ultimately be achieved in the Middle East and North Africa. This however was largely put down to the Arab Spring being a secular and un-Islamic 'revolt', a clear demonstration that a lay, modernised and Westernised youth had finally taken control over its own destiny. After all, as most media coverage portrayed it, the Arab Spring was nothing but a product of the technological revolution set in motion by Facebook. So, after early remarks in the vein of 'The Arab Spring, who would have predicted it?',[1] questions arose about 'the role of Twitter and Facebook in Arab Spring uprising'.[2]

Needless to say, this required once again a bracketing of Islam and Islamism: disregarding the role of Islamist movements such as the Tunisian *al-Nahda* or the Egyptian Muslim Brotherhood in catering to the needs of a democratic society in pre-revolutionary times; neglecting, in the early days of the Egyptian revolution, the mobilising role of assertive 'young' Muslim Brothers vis-à-vis their dismissive leaders who were mostly unsympathetic to the possibility of a general insurrection; or ignoring the force of religious feeling among demonstrators in

---

[1] Roger Cohen, 'When Fear Breaks', *New York Times*, 9 June 2011, available at http://www.nytimes.com/2011/06/10/opinion/10iht-edcohen10.html?_r=1; Clemens Breisinger, Olivier Ecker and Perrihan Al-Riffai, 'Economics of the Arab Awakening: From Revolution to Transformation and Food Security', IFPRI Policy Brief 18 (May 2011); F. Gregory Gause III, 'Why Middle East Studies Missed the Arab Spring', *Foreign Affairs*, July/August 2011.

[2] Mishal Husain, 'How Facebook Changed the World: The Arab Spring', BBC documentary, available at http://www.bbc.co.uk/programmes/b014l2ck; John Pollock, 'Streetbook', *Technology Review*, September/October 2011, available at http://www.technologyreview.com/web/38379.

the streets of Tunisia, Egypt, Syria, Libya and more recently in Turkey. Thus, this phantom Islam continued to haunt the West, not only in the form of a 'denial' but also as a fear, the risk for the Arab Spring being that al-Qaeda and the like will ultimately gain control of the transitional process in these countries, or that post-revolutionary elections might reveal that the Arab Spring was not so lay and secular after all. Hence, tensions in the media concerning the role of the Muslim Brotherhood in Egypt, or the sweeping success of *al-Nahda* during the 2011 elections in Tunisia. These events were praised as positive examples of a potential harmony between Islamism and secularism,[3] while, at the same time, more critical observers pointed to them as the 'ominous model for where these uprisings will end' ('the road to the Caliphate').[4] This position has been lately fuelled in the West by a resurgent anxiety for the rapid and successful advance of DAIISH (acronym of *Al-Dawla al-Islamiya fi al-Iraq wa al-Sham*, internationally referred to as ISIS or ISIL), and the recent attacks in Paris, with the result that, right when the ghost of al-Qaeda seemed to be ready to leave, clearing the space for new anxieties in the West, Islam's haunting presence kept reviving all the old fears, manifesting its immortal 'zombie' attributes, rising from its own ashes as a proper 'Arabian' phoenix.

Understandably, in the last decade, the need to confront this spectre has also spawned attempts to enrich academic 'knowledge' of Islam and Islamic issues in general. Islam and Islamism have become increasingly hot topics for a number of Western scholars in fields as disparate as, for instance, international relations or political sociology. The result has been a proliferation of books and articles concerning the social composition and the strategies of Islamist groups, the political significance of Islam in world politics, its impact on state security, its compatibility with democratic institutions, and its effects on social integration and citizenship.

This book initially found inspiration in this fervent intellectual climate. The ambition from the outset was to confront the Islamic 'spectre', thereby contributing to the theoretical debate on Islam and Islamism within this fundamental historical conjuncture. But, rather than produce more fissures, the

---

[3] Editorial Board Opinion, 'Tunisia Again Points the Way for Arab Democracy', *Washington Post*, 25 October 2011, and Farrag Ismail, 'Egypt Needs to Learn from the Revolutionaries in Tunisia', *al-Gomhuria*, 31 October 2011, translated in *Al Arabiya* on 1 November 2011, available at http://english.alarabiya.net/views/2011/11/01/174864.html.

[4] Raymond Ibrahim, 'Tunisian Elections and the Road to the Caliphate', *Jihad Watch*, 27 October 2011, available at http://www.jihadwatch.org/2011/10/raymond-ibrahim-tunisian-elections-and-the-road-to-the-caliphate.html.

aspiration here was to overcome some of the tensions that have characterised the contemporary academic debate on Islamism.

As we shall discuss in the following pages, one of the key sources of division in the current debate has been an old and classic 'Orientalist' tendency to treat Islamism as a monolithic phenomenon. The opposing camp hardly fares better, with alternative theoretical approaches over-emphasising internal differentiation within Islamic discourse. Moreover, while scholars have mainly focused either on broad geopolitical strategies or socio-economic differences among Islamist groups, a theoretical differentiation between Islamist modes of representing space and subjectivity is yet to be fully developed in the field of political theory. In the last years, for instance, particular attention has been given to the relation between globalisation and Islamism, highlighting the manner in which a number of Islamist organisations have increasingly adapted to a deterritorialised context, thereby privileging a transnational view.[5] This tendency has certainly been reinforced post-9/11 with the coming into prominence of Islamist organisations such as al-Qaeda and DAIISH on the stage of world politics. The quantity of literature here has mushroomed to tackle in particular the global dimension of jihad and political violence.[6] On the other hand, alternative views have pointed to a sort of 'nationalisation' of the Islamist project. In their influential work, for instance, prominent scholars such as Gilles Kepel and Olivier Roy first detected the adoption of a national agenda by Islamist movements as the result of the progressive erosion of their original ideological and anti-secularist vision.[7] This transition was the consequence of a long political experience marked by a number of drawbacks, including the difficulties in translating an ideological platform into a practical policy adequate to the needs imposed by the international arena, the economic bankruptcy and repressive attitudes following early seizure of

---

[5] Significant examples include Oliver Roy, *Globalized Islam: Fundamentalism, Deterritorialization and the Search for a New Ummah* (London: Hurst & Company, 2004); Peter G. Mandaville, *Global Political Islam* (New York: Routledge, 2007); and *Transnational Muslim Politics: Reimagining the Umma* (London: Routledge, 2001); Simon Murden, *Islam, the Middle East, and the New Global Hegemony* (Boulder, CO: London: Lynne Rienner, 2002).

[6] Cf. Fawaz A. Gerges, *The Far Enemy: Why Jihad Went Global* (Cambridge: Cambridge University Press, 2005); Devin R. Springer et al., *Islamic Radicalism and Global Jihad* (Washington, DC: Georgetown University Press, 2008).

[7] Gilles Kepel, *Jihad: The Trail of Political Islam* (London: I.B. Tauris, 2002); and Olivier Roy, *The Failure of Political Islam* (London: Tauris, 1994). Interestingly, Roy differentiates the analytical object of enquiry, linking the destiny of Islamism to this nationalised path alone, while using the term 'neo-fundamentalism' to refer to the global tendencies that a number of new militant groups have expressed in the last decades.

power in Afghanistan and Sudan (two Islamic states that have been, respectively, under the Taliban regime in Afghanistan and the ideological influence of Hasan al-Turabi's *National Islamic Front* in Sudan), and, in the long term, the 'failure' of an Iranian Islamic revolution more and more sensitive to the needs of a nationalist *raison d'État*. All these factors indicate that 'the Islamist movement may have generated the conditions of its own obsolescence'.[8]

According to Kepel, political failure has compelled Islamist movements to undertake a process of political 'normalisation', adapting to a political language increasingly characterised by assimilation to a democratic, human rights-centred vocabulary.[9] It is true that the process described above has long been accompanied by a 'mainstream' tendency among Islamist organisations, movements and parties to focus on domestic politics, and to achieve a national outlook. According to Malise Ruthven: 'far from being counter-nationalist in the sense of opposing the "secular" national states imposed on the Islamic world since decolonization, Islamism in practice mostly reveals itself as an alternative variety of nationalism whose political focus is cultural and religious rather than primarily economic'.[10]

In the Shi'a context, the death of Khomeini heralded the rising influence of national interest vis-à-vis Islamic ideology. This development could be seen in the Iranian support for Christian Armenia instead of a Shi'a country like Azerbaijan or in the accommodating attitude undertaken in the late 1990s towards the conservative Arab regimes in the Gulf in order to minimise the pressure put on the region by American forces. The 'discreet support' of the US operation Enduring Freedom in 2001 aimed at overthrowing the regime of the Taliban and the contention with international institutions and Western powers over Tehran's strategic nuclear programme have also reflected the weight of nationalist considerations by the regime.

This was the context that gave rise to the first source of inspiration for this book, revealing a need to highlight the discursive complexity of Islamism and the way both global and national perspectives have cohabited within the Islamist galaxy. Against Roy and Kepel, however, we contend that Islamism has reflected modern and national characteristics since its very inception. Nationalisation was not the outcome of years of failure, but the result of the inner discursive tendencies that had already been developed, as we will see in the second part of

---

[8] Gilles Kepel, 'Islamism Reconsidered: A Running Dialogue with Modernity', *Harvard International Review*, 22/ 2 (2000): 26.
[9] Kepel, *Jihad: The Trail of Political Islam*, p. 368.
[10] Malise Ruthven, *Fundamentalism: The Search for Meaning* (Oxford: Oxford University Press, 2004), p. 150.

the book, by Hasan al-Banna, the founder of the first Islamist organisation of modern times, the Muslim Brotherhood.

While the focus of the afore-mentioned literature has been on historical events, geopolitical strategies, sociological aspects, and organisational factors, the speculative implications of this tension between global and national outlooks have remained largely unexplored. What does it mean to acknowledge that several Islamist actors have been pursuing a national agenda or adopting a globalised perspective from a political theory standpoint? What does this shift involve in terms of imagining community, identity, and territoriality? What are the political implications of such twists in the construction of the other/outside? To put it another way, which kinds of spatial representations and subjective formations are implicated in the national or global strategies that many scholars have detected? It is this range of questions that this book will try to answer.

In the continental tradition, only a few political theorists have attempted to investigate notions of subjectivity in relation to Islamism. Sometimes these approaches have suffered from a degree of abstraction and reductionism producing 'neo-orientalist' patterns.[11] A case in point is Alain Badiou's criticism of 'political Islamism' as 'nothing but one of the subjectivated names of today's obscurantism': a form of 'generic fascism' negating the 'universalist subject of emancipation', or the *subject faithful to the event* in his thought.[12] When considering the New York attacks, the 'formal traits' of this political formation are to be found in its inescapably 'nihilist character: the sacralization of death; the absolute indifference to the victims; the transformation of oneself and others into instruments'.[13] Even when the thesis of 'generic fascism' is contrasted with this characterisation, the many nuances diversifying the Islamist matrix are blatantly neglected to be reduced to a core of political tenets which simply reproduce familiar 'Occidentalised' conventions of political thought:

> When its genesis was coeval with that of progressive subject, the obscure subject of Islamism did indeed crush anything that could have given body to a generic emancipatory subject, but it did not, contrary to what Badiou seems to intimate, erase all traces of the founding tenets of emancipatory politics. On the contrary, its tactic, largely effective against a left deluded by its own populism and strategic

---

[11] On this topic, see the remarkable critique of Ian Almond, *The New Orientalists: Postmodern Representations of Islam from Foucault to Baudrillard* (London: I.B. Tauris, 2007).
[12] Alain Badiou, *Logiques des mondes* (Paris: Éditions du Seuil, 2006), p. 68.
[13] Alain Badiou, *Infinite Thought: Truth and the Return of Philosophy* (London: Continuum, 2003), p. 120.

ineptitude, was to adopt and hypostasize the key principles of emancipation, making out as if their secular, communist version was merely a degenerate form of an archaic and eternal Islamic politics, with its submissive organicist egalitarianism. In this sense, the obscure subject [Islamism] is more a thief of the present than simply its destroyer.[14]

In this context, philosophical reflections on Islamism have suffered from the essentialist 'inability to see beyond the abstract idea of Islam to its actual particularities'.[15]

The aim of this book is to make a case for including a theoretical differentiation of Islamist notions of space and subjectivity within the space of a speculative analysis of Islamism. The book will attempt to overcome most of the clichés and essentialisms that are commonly coupled with the notion of Islamism, highlighting its internal complexity and vitality. This, however, will be done without abdicating to the ability of Islamism to figure as a unitary and 'abstract idea'; that is, attention will also be given to the aspiration of Islamism to play its hegemonic function as a comprehensive *discursive universe* which embodies conceptual and practical differences. Such an analysis, in turn, will permit the reader to interpret some of the crucial manifestations of contemporary world politics.

In the attempt to highlight the internal complexity of Islamism, analytical focus will be placed on three distinct *symbolic scenarios* playing a central role in the differentiation of Islamist discourses: tradition, modernity and transmodernity. A *discourse-centred* reading of these analytical categories in Part I will be used, then, to analyse, in the second part of the book, three exemplary trajectories (discourses) of Islamist political thought: the discourse of, respectively, Hasana al-Banna, Sayyid Qutb, and Osama bin Laden.

Before leaping into the main body of this book, however, a few caveats are needed in respect to the limits framing this intellectual endeavour. It should be stressed that although the book contains references to a multiplicity of geographical contexts in order to acknowledge the complexity of Islamism, the main focus will be on the Middle Eastern region, with special emphasis on Egypt. These settings offer empirical cases that exemplify certain modalities of engaging with tradition, modernity and transmodernity. Egypt, in particular,

---

[14] Alberto Toscano, 'The Bourgeois and The Islamist, or, The Other Subjects of Politics', *Cosmos and History: The Journal of Natural and Social Philosophy*, 2/1–2 (2006): 36.
[15] Nathan Coombs, 'Christian Communists, Islamic Anarchists?: Part 2', *International Journal of Žižek Studies*, 3/3 (2009): 3, available at http://zizekstudies.org/index.php/ijzs/article/view/193.

best represents the discursive intricacy that this book aims to expose, offering a clear picture of the linguistic battle at stake. It is in Egypt in fact that Islamism first emerged as a mass political movement. The foundation of the Society of The Muslim Brothers in 1928 revealed in highly discernible ways the competition that colonial interference enacted between traditional and modern discourses. It is by looking precisely at this competition that we isolate the main features constituting a 'territorial trajectory' in the discourse of Hasan al-Banna (Chapter 4). It is again in Egypt that a 'transitional trajectory' can be identified with the theoretical elaboration of Sayyid Qutb in the 1960s (Chapter 5) and his attempt to recover and revalorise a traditional vocabulary. Finally, the Egyptian historical context since the 1970s – with the defeat in the 1967 Arab–Israeli War, Anwar al-Sadat's presidency, the Camp David Accords and the massive impact of globalisation over the following years – was crucial in fostering the emergence of a global jihadist movement. That is, the transition from the discourse of Sayyid Qutb to the 'transterritorial trajectory' of Osama bin Laden (Chapter 6), where tradition is now combined with the imaginary of a transmodern vocabulary. In this sense, the Middle East also offers a paradigmatic context from which to examine new changes of Islamism in the post-Arab Spring, the strengthening of old discursive trajectories or the emergences of new ones.

Of course, the emphasis on the above-mentioned discourses entails that a specific attention be put on Sunni Islam. This means that the Shi'a brand of Islamism (e.g., the discourse of key twentieth-century figures such as Ruhollah Mousavi Khomeini, Ayatollah Morteza Motahhari or Ali Shariati) will not be considered here, although some reference to it will be made in the conclusion. To concentrate on a homogeneous sub-universe of Islamism will permit highlighting more clearly the way in which, even in a similar context (Sunni, Arab, Middle Eastern background), Islamist discourses differentiate vis-à-vis tradition, modernity and transmodernity.

The following chapters account for all these levels addressing the role of these symbolic scenarios in the construction of Islamist discourses. Chapter 1 tackles some of the main tensions affecting the debate on Islamism over the past years. A brief introduction to Ernesto Laclau's approach to discourse theory is also provided in this chapter, as this theoretical perspective has offered important analytical tools to the kind of discourse analysis proposed in this book. Chapter 2 pursues a discourse-centred reading of tradition and modernity, leaving to Chapter 3 the task to examine the discursive structure of transmodernity. This order will help highlight the genealogical context informing the discursive articulations examined in this study. From a broad historical perspective, in fact, modernity and tradition provide the symbolic background of the first Islamist discourse, the discourse of Hasan al-Banna, which will be examined in Chapter 4. Transmodernity figures here as a symbolic context whose articulatory dynamics emerged more recently in conjunction to the massive transformations that occurred in the last decades on a global scale, thereby providing a later contribution to the internal differentiation of Islamism. Apart from this chronological aspect, however, a selected focus on tradition and modernity in Chapter 2 serves also to expose a different discursive function of these two realms. In pointing to the genealogical role of tradition and modernity, two discourses will be examined in particular, which are central for an insight into Islamist political thought: 'Islamic universalism' and 'nationalism'. These discourses, which pertain respectively to the traditional and the modern reservoir, express with particular clarity the structural dynamics of *dualism* and *inclusivity*, two major paradigms organising Islamist representations of space and subjectivity. It will be the task of Chapter 3, instead, to examine the symbolic function of transmodernity, highlighting particularly the relation between key desedimenting effects of globalisation, such as spatial displacement, virtuality and fragmentation, and the emergence of discourses like 'globalism', 'universalism' and 'virtualism' at the core of the transmodern scenario. Part II will then consider the political thought of the three above-mentioned leading figures of Islamism: Hasan al-Banna in Chapter 4; Sayyid Qutb in Chapter 5; and Osama bin Laden in Chapter 6. This will permit differentiating between distinct ways of imagining community and territoriality.

While contributing to the current debate on Islam and Islamism, it is our hope that this approach can bring a new perspective to analytic inquiries into other discursive formations and discourse theory in general, offering a new angle from which to consider controversial analytical categories such as tradition, modernity and so-called postmodernity.

In the following chapter, the reader will be introduced to the main body of this book. We will trace here some of the limits and possible solutions that we encounter when approaching the discourse of 'Islamism.' This entails unveiling the symbolic function of 'Islam' at the centre of the Islamist universe: its ability to figure as the discursive and imaginary horizon upon which everyday life rests, and political and social action can be envisioned.

PART I

Chapter 1
Approaching Islamism

In the incipit of this book 'Islamism' has been described as a complex 'discursive universe'. Before assuming a discourse theory perspective and expounding the theoretical implications of such a definition, it is useful to provide the reader with a suitable context for this conceptualisation.

In general terms, Islamism can be taken to denote the religious and political project of self-professing *al-Islamiyyun*, a term translated in English as 'Islamists'. This term shares with 'Muslims', *al-Muslimun,* the common root 'Islam' (*s-l-m*). 'Muslims', however, are those who profess the fundamental declaration of Islamic creed (i.e., *shahada*): 'There is no god but God, and Muhammad is the Messenger of God'. *Islamists* would rather refer to those Muslims who strive to restore the primacy of Islam in the social and political order. From this perspective, Islamism stands as a 'revivalist' trend aimed at 'reviving' Islam not only in the personal life of believers but also in the social and political dimensions of the community in general. The term 'revival' suggests the idea of religion currently being practised as a nominative rather than as a substantial intimate experience.[1] It implies that 'Islam' is perceived as absent or 'dormant' within a context in which it is claimed to have played a previous major and active role for individuals as well as for societies. Unlike other revivalist trends (e.g. as so-called 'fundamentalism') however, Islamism does not only endeavour to 're-vive' religious feelings by ascribing to them a substantial role in providing believers' life with meaning and a sense of horizon. The peculiarity of this revivalist trend is that 'Islam' itself becomes the foundation stone of the political and social order.

But how to approach this complex universe made up of ideas, pamphlets, organisational and legislative provisions, as well as single adherents, social movements, institutions, parties, etc.? A number of tensions have characterised the literature on Islamism in this regard. For instance, scholars have put different analytical emphasis on Islamism according to their privileging a conception

---

[1] Melvin E. Dieter, *The Holiness Revival of the Nineteenth Century* (Lanham, MD: The Scarecrow Press, 1996); Joel A. Carpenter, *Revive Us Again: The Reawakening of American Fundamentalism* (Oxford: Oxford University Press, 1997); for an analysis of this concept in Islamic contexts, see Shireen T. Hunter (ed.), *The Politics of Islamic Revivalism: Diversity and Unity* (Bloomington, IN: Indiana University Press, 1988).

of it mainly as an ideology or a social movement. The first tendency has been particularly popular since the early decades of Islamism – the first Islamist movement, the Muslim Brotherhood, was founded in 1928 – up until the late 1980s. At that time, the Islamist ideology was for the most part considered through the lens of modernist theories and interpreted as an anti-modern, obscurantist and anti-imperialist ideology.[2] In the last three decades, increasing attention has been put on Islamism as a 'modern' mass social movement. A re-interpretation of Islamist 'movements' has highlighted the innovative character of their organisation and propaganda tools, focusing on those socio-economic parameters that explained their ability to mobilise entire sections of society.[3] Naturally, contemporary analyses of Islamism reflect this variety of approaches, with some scholars emphasising the set of ideas and ideals which inform the political action of Islamism, and others tackling organisational and socio-economic factors.[4] As we shall see briefly, these diverse approaches supply a tension between ideas and organisation as well as between modernist and anti-modernist interpretations that a discourse theory approach might be able to overcome.

Before pointing to this fundamental theoretical knot, however, it is useful to stress a second level of tension informing approaches on Islamism. A reference has to be established to the canonical debate arising from the crucial critique

---

[2] See, for instance, the literature on the Brotherhood in these early decades: James Heyworth-Dunne, *Religious and Political Trends in Modern Egypt* (Washington, DC: The author, 1950); Christina Phelps Harris, *Nationalism and Revolution in Egypt: The Role of the Muslim Brotherhood* (The Hague: Mouton and Co., 1964); and Robert Mitchell, *The Society of the Muslim Brothers* (London: Oxford University Press, 1969).

[3] By assuming, again, the example of the Muslim Brothers, see Branjar Lia, *The Society of the Muslim Brothers in Egypt: The Rise of an Islamic Mass Movement 1928–1942* (London: Ithaca Press/Garnet Publishing, 1998).

[4] On the ideological and theoretical vision of Islamist movements, see for instance Azza Karam, *Transnational Political Islam: Religion, Ideology and Power* (London: Pluto Press, 2004); Ibrahim M. Abu-Rabi', *The Contemporary Arab Reader on Political Islam* (Edmonton, AB: University of Alberta Press, 2010). For more recent analyses on the ideological platform of Islamism, with focus on the link between ideology and political violence, see Meghnad Desai, *Rethinking Islamism: The Ideology of the New Terror* (London and New York: I.B. Tauris, 2007); Mary R. Habeck, *Knowing the Enemy: Jihadist Ideology and the War on Terror* (New Haven, CT: Yale University Press, 2006). Interesting examples of social movement approaches include Salwa Ismail, *The Popular Movement Dimensions of Contemporary Militant Islamism: Socio-Spatial Determinants in the Cairo Urban Setting* (Cambridge: Cambridge University Press, 2000); and Quintan Wiktorowicz (ed.), *Islamic Activism: A Social Movement Theory Approach* (Bloomington, IN: Indiana University Press, 2004).

posed by Edward Said in *Orientalism*.[5] In his ground-breaking work, Orientalism is conceived as the systematic depiction of Oriental societies and cultures from a Western perspective, fostered by a long-standing production of political, literary and anthropological literature on the Orient. Such a mode of orientalist interpretation methodically merged forms of power and knowledge based on binary divisions and essentialist reductions into a practice functional to Western colonial expansion. Orientalism did not reflect an intentional rationalisation of colonialism aimed at justifying the colonial enterprise of the West, but rather epitomised the *forma mentis* through which Western powers had exerted their control over colonial territories.

Said conceived of such a mindset as being ruled mostly by a binary logic, which was functional not only to the colonial enterprise per se but also to the very definition of European identity (and modern subjectivity in general). Since the 'other' was to be conceived as uncivilised, emotional, cruel and despotic, European identity was constructed in terms of its opposite; that is, as civilised, rational, democratic and free. At the same time, this reductionist approach – legitimised by the principle that Western knowledge knows the nature of the other better than the other knows itself – was used as a powerful tool of political and cultural exclusion.

In this context, Islam seemed to play a major role being that it epitomised the Orient itself. By deploying a dualistic perspective, Islam was represented in the West as a monolithic ontological entity whose essential features were furthermore grasped as atemporal in the way that they were supposed to be substantially 'immune to change by historical influences'.[6] This representation masked the very plurality of manifestations constituting Islam in accordance with its cultural and temporal context of reference. Resulting from this, Islam stood as a discourse whose ultimate reference had to be found in literary texts and never in an ontological 'other'.

The pivotal critique posed by Edward Said in '*Orientalism*' led to a major impasse in the understanding of the status of Islam and the epistemological approach that could better provide an adequate description of it. As Bobby Sayyid put it:

> If Islam is constituted by orientalism, what happens when orientalism dissolves? What, if any, kind of Islam will remain? Said's main concerns are with the struggle

---

[5] Cf. Edward Said, *Orientalism* (Harmondsworth: Penguin, 1978).
[6] Yaha Sadowski, 'The New Orientalism and Democracy Debate', *Middle East Report*, No. 183 (1993): 19.

against intellectual and cultural imperialism. He illustrated the hostility of imperialism against Islam, his 'counter-writing' is directed towards neglecting orientalism, but 'the negation of Orientalism is not the affirmation of Islam'. This has the effect of turning Said's negation of orientalism into a negation of Islam itself.[7]

On the one hand, defenders of a possible 'orientalist' approach tried to re-affirm the substantial truth of Islam as a 'cluster of essential attributes' which may be singled out and posed as its ultimate ontological foundation.[8] To this end, as mentioned in the Introduction, even philosophical reflections on Islamist subjectivity by contemporary thinkers might suffer from a certain degree of essentialism. Ian Almond, for one, has recently pointed to a sort of *neo-orientalist pattern* informing the thought of 'postmodern' philosophers, from Foucault to Žižek.[9] Besides the risk of essentialist representation, Almond warns here also against the tendency of what he calls 'post-modernism' to deconstruct 'modernity' by instrumentally drawing upon the case of Islam, so reproducing once again a distorted depiction of the 'other'. On the other hand, however, anti-orientalist criticism has mostly chosen to disregard debates about the ontological foundation of Islam in favour of a study of its articulation into the plurality of contexts within which it is invoked. We can read here the quasi-slogan: no Islam but *Islams*.[10] Islam is thus disseminated into its constitutive parts, articulated in local events that allow the dismantling of a unitary substance. Naturally, the same applies to Islamism, which assumes 'Islam' as the corner stone of its political project. From this perspective there would not be such a thing as a single Islamism, for every Islamist 'experience' in a given social, historical or political setting would be irreducible to others.

---

[7] Bobby S. Sayyid, *A Fundamental Fear: Eurocentrism and the Emergence of Islamism* (London: Zed Books: 1997), p. 35.
[8] See, for instance, Bernard Lewis, *What Went Wrong?: The Clash between Islam and Modernity in the Middle East* (London: Weidenfeld & Nicolson, 2002); Daniel Pipes, *The Hidden Hand: Middle East Fears of Conspiracy* (Basingstoke: Macmillan, 1996); Patricia Crone, *God's Rule: Government and Islam* (New York: Columbia University Press, 2004).
[9] Ian Almond, *The New Orientalists: Postmodern Representations of Islam from Foucault to Baudrillard* (London: I.B. Tauris, 2007).
[10] Cf. Larbi Sadiki, *The Search for Arab Democracy* (London: C. Hurst, 2004); Mohammed Arkoun, *Islam: To Reform or to Subvert?* (London: Saqi Essentials, 2006); Ziauddin Sardar, *Postmodernism and the Other: The New Imperialism of Western Culture* (London; Chicago, IL: Pluto Press, 1997).

A Discourse Theory Approach

We mentioned that a widespread tendency in the literature of Islamism had drawn quite a stringent divide between ideas and organisation, and that a discourse theory perspective can help to overcome such a tension. The theoretical foundations of such an approach are not new. Indeed, the notion of discourse developed by Michel Foucault has but increased in influence over the last 40 years, providing 'compelling alternatives to the Marxist paradigm of ideology critique as well as to psychoanalytic accounts of subjectivation'.[11] A major reason for the increasing adoption of a discursive perspective has been the speculative attempt to reject the modern distinction between a plane of truth and a plane of representation, or between a level of immateriality and another of pure materiality, upon which the notion of ideology had rested for long time after its appearance.

In the wage of a long-standing elaboration, Ernesto Laclau defines a discourse as a 'structured totality articulating both linguistic and non-linguistic elements', i.e., ideas as well as organisations, documents, etc., therein offering a useful analytical tool able to account for the inherent complexity of Islamism.[12] According to Laclau, 'the basic hypothesis of a discursive approach is that the very possibility of perception, thought and action depends on the structuration of a certain meaningful field which pre-exists any factual immediacy.'[13] This requires pointing to the inscription of a transcendental plane determining the very condition of possibility of experience. Unlike Kantian philosophy, where the 'a priori' constitutes the basic structure of reasoning which transcends historical change, contemporary theories of discourse, however, acknowledge that the transcendental dimension of discursive fields is subjected to historical variations, contingency and change, so that 'the line separating the "empirical" and the "transcendental" becomes an impure one, submitted to continuous displacements'.[14]

It should be emphasised that the discursive constitution of objects has nothing to do with the admission that there is a material world external to thought. As Laclau and Mouffe put it in their 1985 seminal work on hegemony: 'An earthquake or the falling of a brick is an event that certainly exists, in the

---

[11] Fabio Vighi and Heiko Feldner, 'Ideology Critique or Discourse Analysis? Žižek against Foucault', *European Journal of Political Theory*, 6/2 (2007): 41.

[12] Ernesto Laclau, *On Populist Reason* (London: Verso, 2006), p. 13.

[13] Ernesto Laclau, 'Discourse', in Robert A. Goodin, and Philip Pettit (eds), *A Companion to Contemporary Political Philosophy* (Oxford: Blackwell, 1995), p. 431.

[14] Ibid.

sense that it occurs here and now, independently of my will. But whether their specificity as objects is constructed in terms of "natural phenomena" or "expressions of the wrath of God", depends upon the structuring of a discursive field'.[15] From this standpoint, a 'discourse' cuts across the divisions between structure and superstructure, mental and material, thought and action, linguistic and behavioural practices, all constituting the very condition of emergence of social phenomena, including institutions, rituals, techniques, and so on. In order to fully grasp the philosophical and linguistic premises informing the theory of discourse a central reference needs to be established, for the purposes of this book, to a post-structuralist reading of language and, particularly, to the idea of an endless circulation and movement of meanings.

In classic structuralism a linguistic system is thought of as the ensemble of its linguistic signs which are related through a network of differential relations. In Ferdinand de Saussure's foundational conceptualisation of structuralism, the idea of a linguistic 'structure' or 'system' is that of a closed structured totality composed of identifiable units and dominated by a logic of self-regulation. More specifically, the wholeness of language as a self-contained structure means that it is not only *structured* but also *structuring*. The laws of transformation of the system are internal to the system itself as that which perpetuates its self-referentiality and inner logic.[16] The analysis of language elaborated by Saussure was employed and extended to a variety of fields under the new name of *semiotics*.

However, this analysis was increasingly performed in the name of a critique posed against some of the basic assumptions of the Saussurean model. For instance, Saussure had maintained a strict isomorphism between the *signifier* (the acoustic image of a linguistic sign: i.e., the sound of a word) and the *signified* (the meaning referring to the acoustic image). This entailed preserving the linguistic and logical unity of the *sign* (which integrates both the signifier and the signified). Moreover, Saussure theorised the 'closure' of the system, considering changes merely to be internal to it, rather than external and contingent. Such a closure allowed the possibility of stable representations of the system itself. A so-called post-structuralist approach began instead to challenge the basic assumptions of classic structuralism. Given the particular relevance of Laclau's discourse theory in this book as well as the influence that Jacques Lacan's theory of the signifier have exerted in our analysis of Islamism, it is important to briefly outline the linguistic positions of these two theorists.

---

[15] Ernesto Laclau and Chantal Mouffe, *Hegemony and Socialist Strategy* (London and New York: Verso, 1985), p. 107.

[16] Cf. Ferdinand de Saussure, *Cours de linguistique générale*, trans. Wade Baskin as *Course in General Linguistics* (London: Fontana, 1974), pp. 73–4.

French psychoanalyst Jacques Lacan elaborated a subversive conceptualisation of the structuralist notion of the sign. While Saussurean linguistics had ended up stressing the structural unity between signifier and the signified, Lacan maintained the separation and causative dependence of the latter on the former, denying the very possibility of an independent meaning out of the chain of signifiers as well as the possibility to guarantee enduring representations. According to Lacan, the linguistic order was characterised by the 'the incessant sliding of the signified under the signifier' enacting the continuous fluctuation and movement of meanings, which entailed their over-abundance within speech, the impossibility to avoid a certain ambivalence, profusion and excess of meaning.[17] For Lacan, however, this impasse can be temporarily solved through the '*point de capiton*', translated as 'quilting point', 'anchoring point' or in Laclau's terms the 'nodal point'. Despite the continuous circulation of meanings in a certain discursive field, particular points emerge at which the signifiers and signified happen to be ultimately 'tied' together (another translation for the *points de capiton* can be 'button ties'), allowing the 'sliding of the signified under the signifier' to be temporarily stopped, and therefore de-limiting the boundaries and meanings of a certain discourse. In any particular field, thus, meanings converge around a specific element of a discourse, the *point de capiton*, which 'retroactively and prospectively' organises them by offering the temporary illusion of a referent, and making a process of signification possible.[18] It thus unifies that universe of fluctuating elements into a fictional totality.

By developing Lacan's conceptualisation of the *point de capiton*, Laclau assumes the nodal point as the particular element in the linguistic space around which a process of signification is enacted, and the provisional closure of a discursive totality enabled. This entails for every discourse the possibility to stand as a closed totality precisely because a certain element is absolving the universal function of nodal point allowing all the other signifiers of the discourse to converge around it. It is important to highlight that the concept of nodal point remains fundamentally linked to the idea of a constitutive instability of representations. A discourse stands as a temporary representation, the simple and contingent illusion of a stable reference. Laclau, in fact, accepts the basic tenets of the Saussurean analysis, which sees a structure as grounded in a signifying space where identities are given as merely differential. According to Laclau, however, social and linguistic systems are characterised by a strict analogy. In

---

[17] J. Lacan, 'The Instance of the Letter in the Unconscious', Écrits: The First Complete Edition in English (1st edn, 1957; New York: W.W. Norton & Company, 2006), p. 419.

[18] Jacques Lacan, *The Psychoses: 1955–1956*, ed. Jacques-Alain Miller, trans. Grigg, Russell (New York: W.W. Norton, 1993), pp. 267–8.

both systems *elements* or *identities* are linked by differential relations and can be articulated – that is related – so as to become *moments* of a new structured totality. This entails that the very process of articulation will modify the identity of the elements. In order to have this passage, from the floating elements of the linguistic space to a structured totality of collected and articulated moments, a central step is needed, aimed at drawing a line of demarcation or delimitation.

Drawing on Foucault's notion of 'regularity in dispersion', Laclau sees a discursive formation as an ensemble of differential positions; that is, as 'a configuration, which in certain contexts of exteriority can be *signified* as a totality'.[19] From this perspective, classical structuralism required the linguistic system to be thought of as a closed totality. This condition was essential to preservation of the differential model, as an open system would have entailed an infinite dispersion of elements. As a consequence, the specificity of each identity resulting from its differential relation with other identities would be impossible to grasp.

Despite his acceptance of the differential model, however, Laclau challenged the structuralist assumption of an essential closure of the structure. To have a closed totality, we need to draw the limits of this totality, which entails the construction of a 'beyond' against which such limits can be seen and drawn. This beyond will be one more difference against which the internal components of the closed totality can establish their unity. But since the system, in structural terms, is considered as the system of all differences, it could not be a true beyond and its position will remain 'undecidable' between that which is internal and external to it. Laclau overcomes this tension through the notion of 'antagonism'. The difference of the beyond needs to be of another order from that of the differential components of the totality. In other words, it needs to be thought of as an exclusion: 'not one more element but one in an antagonistic relation to an "inside" which is only constituted through the latter. In political terms, an enemy which makes possible the unity of all the forces opposed to it.'[20]

This approach entails the overcoming of the basic assumptions of the structuralist model. We have said that in order to have a meaningful totality we need to think about its internal components as 'different' from one another. When we conceive these internal components vis-à-vis the antagonistic *beyond* which fixes the boundaries of this totality, we see that they are 'equivalent' in

---

[19] Ernesto Laclau and Chantal Mouffe, *Hegemony and Socialist Strategy* (London and New York: Verso, 1985), p. 106.
[20] Ernesto Laclau, *Philosophical Roots of Discourse Theory*, p. 5; available at: http://www.essex.ac.uk/centres/TheoStud/papers/Laclau%20-%20philosophical%20roots%20of%20discourse%20theory.pdf, lastaccessed 1 May 2010.

opposing such an excluded, antagonistic beyond. Difference and equivalence come then to coexist and to determine the emergence of a paradoxical tension. The constitution of an outside is necessary to the creation of an inside, for it stands as a context of exteriority allowing a certain configuration of differential identities to be signified as a totality. At the same time, the outside is also what makes the inside impossible since it confers a paradoxical condition of equivalence on the differential positions of the inside – something that should not be present in a closed totality whose only condition of meaning relies on difference. Here we see that, in deconstructive terms conditions of *possibility* are said to imply also conditions of *impossibility*. 'Antagonism is therefore not a simple excess but also a "constitutive outside", providing the condition of possibility and impossibility for any discursive system, by both empowering and disrupting its claim to totality.'[21]

Laclau considers impossibility and necessity as two fundamental conditions in understanding the very nature of the *articulatory practice*, that is to say the process of 'articulating' different elements within a certain discursive formation.[22] In fact, it is the irresolvable tension between *difference* and *equivalence* around which all identities gravitate that makes a direct representation of a totality 'impossible'. The representation of a totality remains essentially unreachable and characterised by the oscillation between possibility and impossibility. However, if the antagonistic relation allows an inside to be thought of by virtue of its 'constitutive outside', this also entails that some form of representation of the totality is given. Such a representation will reflect the tension between possibility and impossibility, equivalence and difference and will be, for such a reason, a distorted and temporary representation; that is, not related to any possible object.

It is here that Laclau introduces his notion of *hegemony* as the 'decision taken in an undecidable terrain' by which a certain 'difference' maintains its specific and differential character, yet 'equally' representing the impossible totality of all the elements.[23] This is what happens for instance when a certain signifier in the linguistic order (e.g., Islam, communism, nation, etc.) is assumed as a 'nodal

---

[21] Nathan Widder, 'What's Lacking in the Lack: A Comment on the Virtual', *Angelaki: Journal of the Theoretical Humanities*, 5/3 (2000): 120.

[22] It should be noticed, however, that expressions such as 'articulatory practice', 'discourse', 'discursive totality', 'articulation', 'discursive practice' will be used throughout this research interchangeably to entail either the process of relating elements within a discourse or the discourse itself; that is, the end product.

[23] Ernesto Laclau, 'Discourse', in Robert A. Goodin and Philip Pettit (eds), *A Companion to Contemporary Political Philosophy* (Oxford: Blackwell, 1995), p. 435.

point' around which a discourse is constituted. Here, floating elements become fixed and signification given as possible so that a discursive totality is represented by virtue of its metonymic function. In this regard, it is interesting to notice that the nodal point is by Laclau defined as an 'empty signifier', a reminder of the split occurring when a particular differential element is partially emptied in order to receive the representation of all others. When considering a certain social and discursive articulation it (e.g., Islamism, socialism, nationalism, etc.), its hegemonic force will then rely on its ability to partially 'suture' a social field, temporarily representing the totality of the social until new discursive and articulatory practices will challenge its 'universal' position.

It should now be emphasised that although elements converge around a certain nodal point, enacting the temporary closure of a discourse and its ability to hegemonise social space, it is nonetheless true that the system remains an unstable and open one, dominated by decision, undecidability and contingency. All discourses are hence exposed to a potential dislocation, and so risk losing the ability to hegemonise social space, thereby releasing the elements that previously converged around their nodal point to the open space of the social. It is here that Laclau introduces another fundamental concept, *desedimentation*.

While Edmund Husserl had deployed the notion of 'sedimentation' to mean the fixation and accretion of meaning, Laclau defines the social as the space of 'sedimented' discursive practices whose 'contingent' institution is forgotten by their very routinisation.[24] Such a closure, however, is always exposed to crisis, dislocation or *desedimentation* through which the *naturalisation* of discursive practices is contested, social relations unsettled, the unity of a certain field of discursivity disarticulated and meanings de-fixed. A contingent historical event in a specific socio-political context, in fact, might engender the temporary dislocation of discourses in that setting, promoting the emergence of new articulations. In the next chapters, for instance, we shall see how the irruption of colonialism in the Middle East or the dislocating effects of globalisation both entailed fundamental moments of *desedimentation* of social and linguistic space, allowing for the emergence of distinct Islamist discourses, which challenged the role of dominant narratives in contexts respectively organised around the symbolic function of tradition and modernity. It is in fact in these moments of symbolic dislocations that a new *hegemonic* competition between discursive practices is again possible. This implies the *reactivation* (another Husserlian

---

[24] Edmund Husserl, The Crisis of European Sciences and Transcendental Phenomenology: An Introduction to Phenomenological Philosophy (Evanston, IL: Northwestern University Press, 1970); Ernesto Laclau, *New Reflections on the Revolution of Our Time* (London: Verso, 1990).

term) of contingency and decision; in other words, of the 'political' against the sedimented space of the 'social'.

We see then that, as was the case for the linguistic structure, the closure of the social structure is given as unstable. There will always be a constitutive outside that will both empower and disrupt any claim to totality of a particular discourse. As Laclau puts it: 'The centrality of hegemonic relations in discourse theory comes from the fact that the desire for fullness is always present, but fullness, as such, is unachievable and can only exist circulating among particularities which assume temporarily the role of incarnating it.'[25] The inescapable presence of a *discursive exterior* will always entail a 'surplus of meaning' in any signifying space (discursive and social), which no discourse can finally exhaust. In the end, no articulation will be able to avoid the ultimate contingency of signification.

An Analytical Frame: Islamism between Uniqueness and Discursive Complexity

The delineation of a discourse requires then first of all an examination of the structuring of the discursive field from which a range of social phenomena receive their particular meaning and through which their very condition of possibility is conferred. In this sense, no discursive field concerning Islamism can be addressed without assuming as its point of departure the necessary reference to 'Islam'. What does it mean, for instance, that Islamism may be considered as the discourse that primarily poses 'Islam' as the foundation stone of a political and social order? To answer this question Bobby Sayyid assigned to 'Islam' the discursive function of a 'master signifier'; that is, the nodal point around which a process of signification is enacted.[26]

As it was pointed out earlier, a classic orientalist tendency has been to consider Islam and Islamism on the basis of an essentialist reading, pointing to the 'cluster of essential attributes' that constitute these objects of inquiry. At the same time, anti-orientalist readings have rejected the idea of Islam and Islamism as single and monolithic entities composed of essential attributes. The tendency here has been to celebrate the irreducibility of each experience within its own context, and so produce a dissemination of Islams and Islamisms. In the light of the tension between these two approaches, discourse theory provides a way of preserving the uniqueness of Islamism together with its internal differentiations.

---

[25] Laclau, *Philosophical Roots of Discourse Theory*, p. 6.
[26] Sayyid, *A Fundamental Fear*.

In the attempt to highlight the discursive complexity of Islamism, Bobby Sayyid points out that Islam functions as a central element in a plurality of discourses, i.e., *fiqh* (jurisprudence of Islamic law), Islamic theology, etc.[27] As the central element of a discourse, Islam assumes the universal function of the *nodal point* or *quilting point*, offering the illusion of a referent, temporarily freezing the fluctuation of signifiers and making a process of signification possible within a certain articulation. A nodal point might thus aspire to assume the universal position of a whole social and discursive system, conferring a fictional and provisional sense of closure to that system by way of a *unique signifying gesture*. This means suturing temporarily a definite social space, *representing* its discursive totality. The universal position that a nodal point covers here can best be grasped through the Lacanian notion of *master signifier*, which highlights the ability of the nodal point to 'order' a chain of signifiers, giving meaning to all the elements that compose it. This expression is particular useful when considering the attempt of a nodal point to assert its hegemonic appeal in a context of social and discursive desedimentation, representing the whole society. In the words of Žižek:

> Let us imagine a confused situation of social disintegration, in which the cohesive power of ideology loses its efficiency: in such a situation, the Master is the one who invents a new signifier, the famous 'quilting point,' which stabilizes the situation again and makes it readable … The Master adds no new positive content – he merely adds a signifier which, all of a sudden, turn disorder into order, into 'new harmony,' as Rimbaud would have put it.[28]

In achieving this stabilisation, the master signifier provides all identities circulating in that space with both a common discursive horizon and the *signifying image* upon which their self-representation is constructed. When considering the idea of *Nation*, the master signifier figures as the sound that holds the community together, 'the Thing', which ontologically constitutes a community – such as a nation – because subjects 'believe' in 'it':

> Members of a community who partake in a given 'way of life' *believe in their Thing*, where this belief has a reflexive structure proper to the intersubjective space: 'I believe in the (national) Thing' is equal to 'I believe that others (members of a

---

[27] ibid., p. 47.
[28] Slavoj Žižek, *The Parallax View* (Cambridge, MA: MIT Press, 2006), p. 37.

community) believe in the Thing.' ... The national thing exists as long as members of the community believe in it; it is literally an effect of this belief in itself.[29]

From this perspective, Islam, as a master signifier, figures as that which holds the community of Muslims together, regardless of its semantic void and discursive articulations. Islam becomes the name invoked by the community, the sound around which the community gathers so that its discursive universe gets significance and ontological consistency. This is nonetheless made possible only by virtue of the fictional arbitration through which the master signifier is assumed and the sliding of the chain of signifiers becomes frozen. Ultimately, it will endure as long as the members of the community 'invoke' that name and preserve the 'reflexive structure of their intersubjective space' as expressed by their common belief in that community and in that name.

From what has been said so far, Islamism figures as an articulatory practice whose characterisation lies in its ability to hegemonise the whole discursive horizon by turning 'Islam' into the master signifier of the Muslim communities. The efficacy of the Islamist project therefore may be seen in the capacity to operationalise the ways through which Islam works as a nodal point in a variety of fields. This approach permits us to overcome the divide between orientalist and anti-orientalist perspectives. By considering Islamism as the attempt to assume Islam as the master signifier of the political order it is possible to safeguard the fictional and representational *uniqueness* of Islam. As a master signifier Islam is taken to represent a whole discursive and social universe, so providing the very base of the community. At the same time, this founding is achieved by maintaining reference to the various articulations that define Islam according to the linguistic and social context within which they are performed; that is, Islamism keeps figuring as a *multiplicity* of discourses, each one condensing a different set of 'signifiers' or 'demands', i.e., a *chain of equivalence*, in its own setting.

Bobby Sayyid's approach to Islamism has been of great inspiration in this book, reflecting one of the early attempts to deploy discourse theory in the study of Islamic phenomena. But the main goal of his work, *A Fundamental Fear: Eurocentrism and the Emergence of Islamism*, is to account for the emergence of Islamism as a discourse dislocating the Western monopoly over modernity (modernity as a synonymous of Westernisation).[30] The force of Islamism lies in

---

[29] Slavoj Žižek, 'Eastern Europe's Republics of Gilead', *New Left Review*, 1/183 (1990): 53.
[30] Sayyid, *A Fundamental Fear*.

its ability to express a counter-hegemonic potential in a 'postmodern context', which is marked by both an increasing decentralisation of cultural models and the enduring Eurocentric attempt to re-establish the West as the centre (well represented, according to Sayyid, by Western analyses of both Islamic societies and Islamism). A major objective in Sayyid's work is thus to focus upon the competition and interaction among major discursive formations such as Islamism and Kemalism, a discursive variant of Western nationalism. Although Sayyid acknowledges that Islamist articulations might differ in the way that they articulate three main discursive fields, *din* (faith), *dunya* (complete way of life) and *dawla* (a state or political order), his main concern is to highlight the relation of Islamism vis-à-vis competing discourses.[31]

In contrast, our study aims to underscore the 'plurality' of discursive manifestations characterising Islamism alone; that is, when different 'elements' come to be articulated as 'moments' around the master signifier 'Islam'. Focus here will be upon the way that subjective and spatial constructions have variously been devised and formulated *within* the Islamist discursive universe, which entails confronting competing 'vocabularies' such as modernity, tradition and transmodernity. Sayyid's discursive approach tends to highlight the force that a nodal point retains vis-à-vis alternative nodal points (e.g., 'Islam' against 'the Kemalist nation' or 'the socialist society') so as to aspire to the hegemonic role of master signifier in a certain linguistic space. In the next chapters, instead, attention will be given to the different *chains of equivalence* that Islamist discourses articulate around the *point de capiton* 'Islam'.

While the structuring of a certain discursive formation requires the *condensation* (to be thought of as a 'convergence') of several elements around the nodal point, the 'connotation' that the same discourse acquires depends on the particular range of elements that come to be represented 'retroactively and prospectively' by the *point de capiton*. Different chains of equivalence entail different discursive formations.

This book will hence account for this *multiplicity* of actualisations through an examination of three discourses in Chapters 4 (Hasan al-Banna), Chapters 5 (Sayyid Qutb) and Chapters 6 (Osama bin Laden). Such an approach requires, however, a consideration of the imaginary and symbolic 'context' in which 'elements' fluctuate before their articulation into 'moments' of a discourse takes place.

---

[31] Sayyid, *A Fundamental Fear*, p. 45.

The Symbolic Function of Tradition, Modernity and Transmodernity

In delineating the structural organisation of a discourse, the term *condensation* was used, a term that should here be spotlighted, for it highlights the ability of a discursive agglomeration to slow down the circulation of meaning and signifiers, freezing them within the borders of its discursive realm, and creating a sense of temporary closure. A 'discourse' has been defined in this book as a fictional totality articulating, in accordance with Laclau's understanding of it, both linguistic and non-linguistic elements. With this definition in mind, broader agglomerations of signifiers than a discourse can be imagined, which allow us to consider linguistic space as marked by the imaginary existence of major poles of attraction drawing discourses and signifiers to them, and therein creating constellations around which *condensed* totalities of signifiers (discourses) gravitate in apparent *proximity* to one another. These poles of attraction function as discursive *meta-structures*, or *vocabularies*, from which discourses draw. Hence, signifiers temporarily condense within discourses, while discourses temporarily gather, gravitate and condense around symbolic poles of attraction. It is by referring to such meta-structures that this book tackles major analytical categories such as tradition, modernity and transmodernity.

From a general perspective, the inclusion of discourses within these broader vocabularies very much reflects the way people themselves tend to qualify a certain narrative, defining it either as 'modern', 'traditional' or 'postmodern' (to be thought of at this first stage in the sense of 'transmodern'). We shall see in Chapter 4, for instance, that the subjective allocation of discourses to wider agglomerations is something that is manifest in the harsh cultural debates between *self-defining* 'modernists' and 'traditionalists' in Egypt in the 1920s. But, as we mentioned already, such an allocation is also explained on the ground of the linguistic proximity that discourses express in converging within a certain meta-structure, reflecting some kind of discursive *resonance* in the way the social is organised and accounted for. In other words, the proximity of discourses around broader constellations reveals the repetition of definite signifiers resonating within each meta-structure, and gravitating around certain paradigms.[32] This means that although a certain degree of fluidity is always present in delineating the discursive boundaries of tradition, modernity and transmodernity, their capacity *to appear* as fixed and stable vocabularies presupposes, in fact, their

---

[32] A paradigm stands, here, as the inner *logic* informing the construction of a certain discourse: whether, for instance, its spatial representations and subjectivity formations privilege a principle of exclusivity and closure towards externality and alterity (*dualism*) rather than inclusiveness and openness (*inclusivity*).

ability to organise the meta-structural proximity and discursive resonance of given discourses and signifiers, sustaining the imaginary potential of a complex self-enclosed totality. This meta-structural capacity of regulation, which we define as *symbolic function*, supports therefore the imaginary representation and appeal of tradition, modernity and transmodernity, allowing each of them to appear as a self-contained discursive horizon, as a 'history of argument and debate over certain fundamental doctrines in shared languages and styles of discourse'.[33] Although discourses within each pole of attraction might express differing views over specific issues, it is in fact the symbolic function regulating their proximity in terms of shared language and styles of discourse that supports the *imaginary appeal* that tradition, modernity and transmodernity exert as apparently coherent histories or discursive attitudes, and which, in turn, sustains the subjective allocation of discourses within these broader constellations.

In the light of such a perspective, tradition, modernity and transmodernity figure as *symbolic scenarios* from which discursive articulations draw in order to construct their respective representations. They work as *convenient indicators* or *indexes* in the organisation of discourses, standing as *fictional horizons* of the linguistic space, horizons to look upon in order to identify a series of more or less coherent discourses. As broader constellations, tradition, modernity and transmodernity can also be seen as *imaginative containers* or *reservoirs*: self-enclosed vocabularies delineating a plurality of discourses and embodying for that very reason the range of signifiers that each discourse articulates. Discursive articulations, however, are both enabling and constrained by their reference to these horizons.

The contingent origin of these reservoirs, in fact, becomes particularly evident when a process of social disintegration occurs. Neither discourses nor symbolic scenarios are fixed, closed and stable totalities. The very fact that discursive agglomerations, whether discourses or reservoirs, remain temporary and fictional condensations of signifiers, overcoming at any one moment the inner fluidity of language, means that their temporary sense of closure remains exposed, as we shall see in the next chapters, to contingent dislocation and desedimentation. As we mentioned already, it is by accounting for the desedimenting effects of colonialism, for instance, that we can trace the genealogical discursive context of Islamism, examining, in Chapter 4, the symbolic function of modernity and tradition in early twentieth-century Egypt, and detecting the discursive appeal of two dominant narratives at that time: the

---

[33] Muhammad Qasim Zaman, *The Ulama in Contemporary Islam: Custodians of Change* (Princeton, NJ: Princeton University Press, 2002), p. 4.

traditional discourse of Islamic universalism (i.e., pan-Islamism) and the modern discourse of the nation (both in its European or pan-Arab variant). Again, the 'traditional' character of universalism does not deny the ever-changing nature of that discourse, its intellectual transformations. Rather, it simply reflects the perception of universalism as 'belonging' to a specific body of knowledge, to a 'history' or 'language' different from modernity; that is, from that language that 'modernists' celebrated at that time when disseminating discourses on the nation state (we will see, for instance, that al-Banna himself associated the discourse of the nation with modernity while ascribing a universalistic conception of the world to a 'perceived' Islamic legacy).

In the light of this theoretical conceptualisation, tradition, modernity and transmodernity assume a central role in this investigation, figuring as key analytical parameters in the examination of Islamist discourses. They stand as distinct linguistic and social vocabularies offering different sets of 'signifiers' to the discursive formations here examined, and therefore conditioning the organisation of their respective *chain of equivalence*.

Chapter 2
Modernity and Tradition: Discursive Genealogies

> You taught me language; and my profit on't
> Is, I know how to curse. The red plague rid you
> For learning me your language![1]

An enduring approach to the conceptualisation of 'modernity' and 'tradition' over the years has been to rely on fixed categories and historicist explanations, ultimately denoting a fundamental core of properties through which both 'modernity' and 'tradition' are said to perform their 'condition' as distinct historical epochs or sociological settings. A classic example of this is the kind of conceptualisation that so-called 'modernist' theories have promoted since the 1950s in regard to these fundamental terms.[2] While a common approach here has been to reduce tradition to the simple and *unaltered* transmission of customs and beliefs from one generation to another, and the maintenance of a primitive, roughly articulated social structure devoted to the preservation of cultural and religious heritage, modernity has mostly been elevated to the historical time of the affirmation of rational thought, secularisation, industrialisation and the ultimate 'emancipation' from the yoke of the past.

A basic aspiration of modernist theories was to provide a theoretical explanation for the imbalance existing between what they defined as 'traditional' and 'modern' societies, though this endeavour very often ended up providing a simple cultural justification of that asymmetry. By using cultural, sociological and economic perspectives, a determinist and evolutionary conception of

---

[1] William Shakespeare, *The Tempest*, I. ii. 362–4.
[2] Although disagreements characterise the debate about what constitutes modernisation theory, besides the forerunner work of thinkers such as Weber, Spencer, and Durkheim, a background literature on the modernist perspective elucidated in this chapter includes David Apter, *The Politics of Modernization* (Chicago, IL, and London: University of Chicago Press, 1965); Talcott Parsons and Neil Joseph Smelser, *Economy and Society: A Study in the Integration of Economic and Social Theory* (London: Routledge, 1956); and Gabriel A. Almond, *Political Development: Essays in Heuristic Theory* (Boston, MA: Little, Brown, 1970).

development was eventually set in motion. Social change was seen as progressive, irreversible and inclining towards increasing structural complexity. In economic terms a number of stages were posed in the evolutionary process from 'traditional' to modern, 'mature' societies, with emphasis put on the process of industrialisation as being productive of socio-economic transformations (such as an increasing institutional differentiation) and distinct cultural paradigms (scientific rationality, democratisation, the belief in progress). Political modernity was also defined according to the level of differentiation and functional specialisation of political structures. Accordingly, while traditional societies were often depicted as agriculture-based, characterised by a clan structure, a patron-client based polity, fatalistic attitudes and poor or absent technological development, modern societies were said to have corrected most of these traditional features, presenting a highly sophisticated infrastructural, institutional and ideological complex. This also entailed a cultural transformation, with fatalistic attitudes removed from modern societies and traditional socio-religious establishment eroded in favour of rational, materialist and pragmatic approaches based on the authoritative structures of modern administration and efficient bureaucracy.

This understanding of modernity has been inextricably intertwined with the secularisation thesis, which linked the development of modernity to the structural differentiation of a number of social spaces (economy, law, science, politics, religion), ultimately arguing for the 'inclusion' of religion within its own sphere and the public erosion of religious feelings and institutions.[3] The implication of such discourses was that in a world dominated by science, rationality and progress there was little room for religion. Later debates on an assumed 'deprivatisation of religion' remained also trapped within the evolutionary logic at the core of modernist theories of secularism. These debates found original expression in the last four decades as an effect of the persistent and renewed visibility of religions throughout the world, which challenged modernist and secularist assumptions in the 1950s and 1960s regarding the progressive confinement of religion to a private sphere. The perdurance of religion in so-called 'mature' societies was thus explained as the result of a deprivatisation of religion in the modern world. In other words, religions would refuse 'to accept the marginal and privatized role that theories of modernity as well as theories of secularization

---

[3] Cf. Peter Berger, *The Social Reality of Religion* (London: Faber, 1969); David Martin, *A General Theory of Secularization* (New York: Harper & Row, 1979); Marcel Gauchet, *The Disenchantment of the World: A Political History of Religion* (Princeton, NJ: Princeton University Press, 1985/1999).

had reserved for them'.[4] This, however, did not entail a negation of modernist premises. According to theorists of deprivatisation, the modernist thesis of an incompatibility between religion and modernity remained partially true. The chance for a particular religion to be ascribed 'modern' attributes was in fact conditional upon its acceptance and adoption of the rules of public debate.

Despite common assumptions among so-called modernists, other approaches have maintained a more nuanced and open interpretation of both modernity and tradition. Alternative studies have valorised, for instance, the role that tradition and accumulation have played in the development of local economies from a structural perspective. To take an example from non-European settings, 'entrepreneurial familism' and nepotism have been said to have largely contributed to Hong Kong's economic development.[5] According to Dale Eickelman and James Piscatori, what was alien to early modernist theorists was the idea that 'accumulation, tradition and historical continuity' can fulfil an essential function in the process of modernisation and that religion and tradition interact and coexist with economic growth.[6]

More generally, it has been noticed that categories such as modernity and tradition have faced important semantic changes across the centuries, assuming either a positive or negative value in different historical times and cultural contexts.[7] The 'devaluation' of tradition that modernist theorists promoted has been explained by their post-enlightenment rationalist character, which entailed unconditional faith in the idea of progress.[8] A major consequence of this was the tendency to equate 'modernisation' with 'improvement', producing a kind of *historical discontinuity*:

> As a necessary historical law, the idea of progress entails the axiological identity between *melius* [better] and *novum* [new], that is to say the idea that what is modern, actual is intrinsically better than what is over. The radicalisation of this temporal perception ... ends consequently with a stress on the moment of rupture

---

[4] Cf. José Casanova, *Public Religions in the Modern World* (Chicago, IL: University of Chicago Press, 1994).

[5] Cf. Siu-Lun Wong, *Emigrant Entrepreneurs: Shanghai Industrialists in Hong Kong* (Hong Kong: Oxford University Press, 1988).

[6] See Dale F. Eickelman and James Piscatori, *Muslim Politics* (London: Princeton University Press, 2nd edn, 2004), p. 24.

[7] See, for instance, Hans Robert Jauss, *Toward an Aesthetic of Reception* (Minneapolis, MN: University of Minnesota Press, 1982); and Jürgen Habermas, 'Modernity versus Postmodernity', *New German Critique*, Special Issue on Modernism, 22 (1981): 3–14.

[8] Cf. Theodor W. Adorno and Max Horkheimer, *Dialectic of Enlightenment* (1st edn, 1947; London: Verso, 1997).

and discontinuity: *novum* becomes a value which needs to be pursued in itself, and even to be anticipated beyond every possible accumulation, tradition and historical continuity.[9]

This heterogeneous range of approaches towards modernity and tradition and the wide debate concerning the axiological dimension that they embody has been widely reflected in the literature relating to the political sociology of Islamist movements.

In Chapter 1, we mentioned that a long-standing tendency in the study of Islamism has been to consider this phenomenon as a social and political movement, rather than a discursive universe. In the light of this standpoint, Islamist organisations have been examined through a modernist lens, and often depicted as the ultimate advocates for, and defenders of 'tradition' against the process of rationalisation and secularisation.[10] In line with a modernist approach, tradition was conceived of as a set of fixed values centred upon a religious and anti-technological ethos. According to modernist theorists, this position was enriched by the Islamist perception of being overwhelmed by an unrestrained process of acculturation to the West, which produced a strong obscurantist and anti-imperialist stance. The result was the undeniable anti-western and reactionary character of Islamism.

In contrast, alternative perspectives have criticised modernist theorists for misinterpreting those very signals that could help us to recognise the 'modern' qualities of Islamism. The structure of a number of Islamist organisations has been deeply scrutinised to show the presence of modern social movements able to ground a wide set of heterogonous social and political activities – from educational programmes and non-state provision of social services to forms of private enterprise.[11] The ability of Islamists to transform their organisations into institutional forces capable of penetrating civil society has also given an indication of their capacity to interact with the modern socio-political system.[12]

---

[9] Gaetano Chiurazzi, *Il postmoderno* (Milan: Bruno Mondatori, 2002), p. 6.

[10] Cf. Seyyed Hossein Nasr, *Traditional Islam in the Modern World* (London: Kegan Paul International, 1987); William Montgomery Watt, *Islamic Fundamentalism and Modernity* (London: Routledge, 1988).

[11] Cf. Said Amir Arjomand, 'Social Change and Movements of Revitalization in Contemporary Islam', in James A. Beckford (ed.), *New Religious Movements and Rapid Social Change* (London: SAGE; Paris: UNESCO, 1986); Salwa Ismail, *Rethinking Islamist Politics: Culture, the State and Islamism* (London: I. B. Tauris, 2006).

[12] See John Esposito, 'Islam and Civil Society', in John L. Esposito and Francois Burgat (eds), *Modernizing Islam: Religion in the Public Sphere in Europe and the Middle East* (London: Hurst and Company, 2003), pp. 75–9.

In fact, by assuming control over specific areas of civil society, Islamist movements have been able to exert forms of political activity bypassing the limits imposed on political participation by domestic regimes, thus demonstrating a significant political awareness. A case in point has been the Muslim Brotherhood's growing influence on Egyptian professional syndicates over the last two decades.[13] Against the general backdrop outlined here, the following pages propose a discourse-centred reading of both tradition and modernity, highlighting the role that they fulfil as 'symbolic scenarios' of Islamism.

A Discursive Reading of Tradition and Modernity

When describing tradition, modernity and transmodernity as symbolic scenarios of Islamism in Chapter 1, we pointed out the ability of these reservoirs to work as fictional 'imaginary markers' of the linguistic space. In doing so, the inner *fluidity* of these categories was stressed; the fact that, despite their ability to condense a number of discourses and signifiers within their symbolic space, the temporary closure they achieve remains subjected to linguistic fluctuation, allowing for – in the same way as discourses do – the circulation and transition of signifiers from one reservoir to another in contexts of discursive desedimentation.

Tradition

In the face of modernist assumptions about tradition, which valorise a structural reading of it as a stable depository of fixed values and properties, a discourse-centred reading of tradition stresses its 'fluid' and 'contingent' character. From this perspective, customs and beliefs at the heart of a given cultural legacy are never transmitted without some alteration occurring consciously or unconsciously. This means, first and foremost, that despite a certain modernist emphasis on the coherent, rational and evolutionary quality of progress and change, social and economic transformations undergo *unconscious* alterations, which modify the meaning and the relevance embodied by ideas and customs. Cultural references might thus remain intact despite transformations occurring in the realm of traditional values. When considering Islamic tradition, for instance, the result of this approach has been the *modernisation of Islam* (e.g., the modernisation

---

[13] Cf. Salwa Ismail, 'State-Society Relations in Egypt: Restructuring the Political', *Arab Studies Quarterly*, 17/3 (1995): 44–7; and Moheb Zaki, *Civil Society and Democratisation in Egypt* (Cairo: Konrad Adenauer Stiftung – Ibn Khaldoun Center, 1995).

of religious and doctrinal practices) through which a series of minimal and unperceived changes occurred under the pressure of contingent historical events and the exposure to modern discourses. On the other hand, it is also true that, besides being unconsciously transformed, traditions are 'invented'. *Conscious* changes are undertaken in the face of current challenges, and legitimised, or more genuinely operationalised, by resorting to and reinterpreting a given cultural legacy. An example is the reinvention of the caliphate, a discourse that is here defined as constitutive of a 'traditional' symbolic reservoir. The Ottomans reinvented the tradition of the caliphate in order to legitimise their declining power during the eighteenth century, thus reviving an institution that had remained merely nominal following the decline of Arabs after the Abbasid age (750–1258).[14]

When advocating the authenticity of the past, the aim is often to face the present, reformulating tradition in a language consonant with such aspirations. Sometimes, tradition can simply be used, with more flexible interpretations, to appropriate modernity. It is by following this process that, for instance, an *Islamisation of modernity* took place as an effect of colonisation, revealing a counter-hegemonic and assertive use of tradition. The point to be emphasised here is that the symbolic function of tradition was not displaced by modernity *tout court*; it was rather constantly re-operationalised alongside it. Political and economic changes have accordingly been legitimised and realised through the creative re-elaboration of the past and the dynamic re-interpretation of tradition.[15] As Eickelman and Piscatori observe:

> because the line between occurred and perceived pasts depends upon construction, dissemination, and acceptance of authoritative historical narratives, the past of

---

[14] Halil Inalcık, in particular, pointed to 'a legend apparently fabricated in the eighteen century' by the Ottomans, which promoted the myth of a formal passage of the caliphate in the sixteenth century from the last descendant of the Abbasids to the Ottomans. Halil Inalcık, 'Introduction: Empire and Population', in Halil Inalcık and Donald Quataert (eds), *An Economic and Social History of the Ottoman Empire, 1300–1916* (Cambridge and New York: Cambridge University Press, 1994), p. 20; see also Halil Inalcık, 'The Rise of the Ottoman Empire', in P.M. Holt, Ann K.S. Lambton and Bernard Lewis (eds), *The Cambridge History of Islam* (Cambridge: Cambridge University Press, 1970), vol. 1A, pp. 295–323; and Kemal H. Karpat, *The Politicization of Islam: Reconstructing Identity, State, Faith, and Community in the Late Ottoman State* (New York and Oxford: Oxford University Press, 2001), pp. 241–4.

[15] Cf. Etienne Bruno, *L'islamisme radical* (Paris: Hachette, 1987).

occurred events exists mostly as a pool of resources which can be drawn upon in traditional and modern settings to sanction present practice.[16]

Thus, while maintaining its symbolic role through which the 'authoritative' function of 'historical narratives' is established, tradition is always subjected to forms of re-elaboration and alteration. Interestingly, this feature is revealed by its very etymology (Latin *tradere* 'deliver, hand over', from *trans-* 'over' + *dare* 'to give') where *tradition* is a doublet of *treason*; in the very handing over of beliefs and customs something gets lost, altered or *betrayed*. It is by carrying with itself the trace of its own contingency that the symbolic function of tradition is thus performed, allowing customs, beliefs and 'the past' to exist as a 'pool of resources' to be used in the face of present challenges. According to Samira Haj, this entails valorising a particular approach to tradition, one that assumes it more as a 'framework of inquiry rather than a set of unchanging doctrines or culturally specific mandates'.[17] Haj points here to Talal Asad's conceptualisation of tradition as the ensemble of those 'discourses that seek to instruct practitioners regarding the correct form and purpose of a given practice that, precisely because it is established, has a history'.[18]

This reference to the contingent and variable character of tradition allows for new formulations of the Islamic cultural heritage more consonant with current political and social aspirations. Mohammed Abed al-Jabri, for instance, agrees that Islamic tradition or legacy, *turāth*, plays a strategic symbolic function in the interpretation and legitimisation of political changes.[19] He notices, however, a tension occurring between rigid and fluid conceptions of tradition in Islamic settings, which parallels the difference between modernist and anti-modernist approaches. 'Orthodox fundamentalists', for instance, would express a religious tendency that is intimately attached to a rigid notion of tradition, and strategically opposed to political and social changes. Cultural heritage is taken here as an immutable set of values that can be grasped and transmitted through a literalist reading of religious texts. By thinking of tradition as a fixed set of values, therefore, orthodox fundamentalists deploy the same rigid approach that modernist theorists use.

---

[16] Eickelman and Piscatori, *Muslim Politics*, p. 29.

[17] Samira Haj, *Reconfiguring Islamic Tradition: Reform, Rationality, and Modernity* (Stanford, CA: Stanford University Press, 2009), p. 4.

[18] Talal Asad, 'The Idea of an Anthropology of Islam', *Qui Parle*, 17/2 (2009): 1–30.

[19] Mohammed Abed Al-Jabri, *Arab-Islamic Philosophy: A Contemporary Critique* (Austin, TX: University of Texas Press, 1999).

In contrast, al-Jabri identifies an approach to Islamic tradition which is more sensitive to the inner fluidity and the epistemological changes that have informed, consciously or unconsciously, the so-called Islamic legacy, arguing in favour of an open interpretation of it. This approach can be seen, for instance, in the 'reformist' movement of the late nineteenth and early twentieth centuries. Thinkers like Jamal ad-Din al-Afghani (1838–1897), Muhammad 'Abduh (1849–1905) and Muhammad Rashid Rida (1865–1935) encouraged a flexible use of tradition as a way to filter political change in the face of specific historical conditions. Inspired by an apologetic stance, they aimed to resist the increasing cultural and political influence of European powers by advocating a critical return to the *salafi* (the pious ancestors).[20] This return to the past, however, was functional to existing political challenges, and required for them the need of independent reasoning vis-à-vis orthodox and literalist approaches to tradition. By calling for the re-opening of *ijtihad* – the effort of interpretation, conceived of as the philological and hermeneutic analysis of holy sources (Qur'an and Sunna) – against imitative conformism, *taqlîd*, they played a major modernising role, encouraging renewal, *tajdid*, and paving the way for subsequent 'debates over the meanings of formative texts (even over which texts *are* formative) and over the need for radical reform of the tradition.'[21]

In this sense, however, later and more contemporary approaches to tradition should stress, for al-Jabri, the presence of the father in the son, opposing the historical tendency to link *turāth* to a linear and non-cumulative notion of 'inheritance' as the substitution of the son in the place of the father. 'To seek our modernity by rethinking our tradition' means for al-Jabri the valorisation of tradition as a permanent, cumulative process animated by a reformist attitude.[22] This notion of Islamic legacy 'simultaneously encompasses the cognitive and the ideological, so that the term *turāth* now carries the meaning of a cultural, intellectual, religious, literary, and artistic legacy enveloped in some sort of an ideological empathy'.[23]

Although al-Jabri does not clearly differentiate between 'fundamentalist' and 'Islamist' positions, Islamism is taken in our study to fully participate in this process of rethinking tradition in the face of present challenges. We will

---

[20] This is why this reformist movement if often described as 'salafi', though current uses of this term emphasise a far more conservative and orthodox connotation.

[21] Talal Asad, *Formations of the Secular: Christianity, Islam, Modernity* (Stanford, CA: Stanford University Press, 2003), p. 195.

[22] Al-Jabri, *Arab-Islamic Philosophy*, *passim*.

[23] Nelly Lahoud, *Political Thought in Islam: A Study in Intellectual Boundaries* (Abingdon: Routledge, 2005), p. 40.

see in Chapter 4, for instance, that unlike 'orthodox fundamentalists', Hasan al-Banna's discourse pursues assertively the opportunity for 'Islamising' modernity, reconstructing discourses on science, nationhood and democracy now disembodied from European cultural and political foundations through a creative reference to the Islamic tradition. At this point it is important to stress that, from a discourse-centred perspective, to say that tradition functions as a discursive meta-structure means that the beliefs and customs informing a certain idea of cultural legacy are articulated and organised through a number of discourses, which substantiate its symbolic realm. Distinct cultural heritages and traditions, therefore, allow for the condensation of different ranges of discourses in specific social and geographical contexts.

When considering the Islamic tradition, *turāth*, this cultural heritage works as a vocabulary embodying a plurality of discourses – such as *shari'ah* (Islamic law), *fiqh* (jurisprudence of Islamic law), personal status; *jihad* (spiritual and military effort on behalf of Islam); Sufi tradition; *dar al-Islam*, (Islamic territoriality); *waqf* (religious endowment); 'caliphate'; pan-Islamism, and so forth – and the collection of signifiers that these discourses have articulated. Most of these discourses have played a central role in Muslim settings through the centuries, providing subjects with meaning and a sense of horizon over time, and assuming a hegemonic role in the discursive organisation of the social. We will examine some of these discourses in the following chapters, showing, for instance, the influence that the discourse of the caliphate as well as normative discourses on *shari'ah* have exerted in the delineation of the different strands of Islamism addressed in this book. As mentioned, the discourse of pan-Islamism or Islamic universalism will, furthermore, be deeply scrutinised, as a detailed examination of its discursive structure will help detect a central *inclusive* paradigm behind Islamist representations of space and subjectivity, marking the genealogical background of Islamism. What is important to anticipate here, however, is that a process of desedimentation as a consequence firstly of colonisation, then of globalisation, eroded the hegemonic role that traditional discourses had hitherto played in Arab settings. We shall see soon the way in which the emergence of new signifiers and discourses began to challenge the authoritative role of tradition, allowing for a coexistence and competition with other symbolic scenarios, i.e., modernity and transmodernity.

Modernity

In his 1983 lesson on the Enlightenment, Michel Foucault defined modernity as an attitude rather than an historical time:

> Thinking back on Kant's text, I wonder whether we may not envisage modernity rather as an attitude than as a period of history. And by 'attitude,' I mean a mode of relating to contemporary reality; a voluntary choice made by certain people; in the end, a way of thinking and feeling; a way, too, of acting and behaving that at one and the same time marks a relation of belonging and presents itself as a task. A bit, no doubt, like what the Greeks called an ethos.[24]

The value of this passage is that it avoids fixed categories and historicist explanations while maintaining the relevance of modernity as a 'scenario' against which certain historical or social manifestations can be measured and understood. In the attempt to transpose the Foucauldian notion of 'attitude' upon a discursive plane it could perhaps be added that as 'a way of thinking and feeling', 'of acting and behaving', an 'attitude' is also a way of engaging with reality through language. From this perspective, modernity can be thought of as the symbolic context within which certain 'attitudes' have moulded a more or less consistent vocabulary around distinct cultural and political paradigms.

A crucial reference has to be established in this respect with *modernisation*, to be assumed here as the desedimenting process of increasing technological and economic development (industrialisation and mechanisation) and growing social articulation, which disrupted the symbolic coordinates of *tradition*. It is in the light of this framework that *modernity* emerged as a new and *alternative* symbolic horizon accompanying this desedimenting event with new interpretative paradigms through which reality could be made readable. This symbolic reservoir condensed a range of new discourses that challenged the role of traditional European narratives (e.g., pre-modern and medieval universalism, geocentrism, theism, etc.), determining thenceforth the coexistence of and competition between European tradition and modernity itself. Similarly, the increasing interference of colonial powers in non-Western settings and the structural transformations produced under the pressure of industrialisation, modernisation and the integration of colonial modes of production engendered new desedimenting effects in colonised areas – those spaces where distinct typologies of tradition were in place (Islamic, Hindu, Japanese, etc.).

It is useful at this point to clarify briefly the manner in which the semiotic structure of modernity can be accounted for in this study, elucidating its discursive morphology. Three main sources can be highlighted here, which have contributed to connoting specific aspects of modernity, consolidating its

---

[24] Michel Foucault, 'What is Enlightenment?' ('Qu'est-ce que les Lumières?'), in Paul Rabinow (ed.), *The Foucault Reader* (New York: Pantheon Books, 1984), p. 39.

symbolic boundaries through the articulation of different sets of discourses. First, a *structural* connotation of modernity, as expressed by modernist theories, has supplied a number of socio-economic categories, which have been central to its discursive development: for example, discourses on industrialisation conducive to social and institutional differentiation; scientific rationality; the belief in progress; secularisation; the thesis of deprivatisation of religiosity; and so on. Second, an *ideological* connotation in which modernity has been understood by critics as an ideological construct based on the elaboration of specific political paradigms: for instance, the deployment of a binary logic in the elaboration of dominant discourses on nationalism; colonialism; liberalism; and so forth. Third, since the nineteenth century, modernity has been claimed to have produced a series of 'discontents' that could also be figured in terms of the posing of a number of moral dilemmas for Europe, thus enriching the symbolic structure of modernity with a *moral* connotation. A number of crucial transformations in 'modern' societies began to be observed in this respect, with discourses on 'individualism'; 'atomism'; 'relativism'; 'materialism'; the dominant role of 'instrumental rationality' by modern bureaucratic systems as well exemplified by the Weberian image of the 'iron cage';[25] the general condition of 'alienation' and 'uncertainty' produced by a context where the production of short-lived goods no longer guarantees the fundamental condition of stability, that of being surrounded, as Hannah Arendt argued, by things whose 'life span' is longer than the time required for their production;[26] and so on.

Modernity, then, emerges as a language in which most of these discursive elements have played a central role: from the nation state to the idea of progress, from secularisation to individualism, and so forth. On a broad perspective, *dualism* provided a dominant logic presiding over modern subjectivity formations and space representations. Although its political workings will be examined in detail with reference to the constitution of the nation state discourse in the following pages, its relevance at the core of the symbolic structure of modernity can also be seen across a number of other discourses, which contributed, in different degrees, to provoke the type of Islamist reflections examined in this book. When considering, for example, the role that secularisation has fulfilled as a central hermeneutical category of modernity, many have pointed to the enactment of a dualistic modus operandi in this discourse, which marginalised

---

[25] Max Weber, *The Protestant Ethic and the Spirit of Capitalism* (New York: Charles Scribner's Sons, 1958), p. 181.
[26] Hannah Arendt, *The Human Condition* (New York: Doubleday, 1959), p. 83.

more inclusive conceptions of political space in other traditions as well as in premodern Europe. According to Talal Asad:

> the complex medieval Christian universe, with its interlinked times (eternity and its moving image ...) and hierarchy of spaces (the heavens, the earth, purgatory, hell) is broken down by the modern doctrine of secularism into a duality: a world of self-authenticating things in which we *really* live as social beings, and a religious world that exist only in our imagination.[27]

Asad contends that the secular, with its endorsement of a binary space, is a relatively recent construction. It was the modern creation of the 'social' as an 'all-inclusive secular space' in the nineteenth century that allowed the possibility of a distinction between the religious and the political. More precisely, it was 'the emergence of society as an organizable secular space that made it possible for the state to oversee and facilitate an original task by redefining religion's competence', allowing the religious to be retrospectively 'constructed, reformed and plotted'.[28]

This perspective sheds light on the all-encompassing dimension characterising the 'secular', and its intrinsic relation with 'society' and the 'nation state'; the nation state here being thought of as the political construction organising and regulating all social spaces deriving from the creation of the secular. We shall see in the coming chapters how the debate about secularisation has echoed in the discussion on so-called 'Islamic state' or 'Islamic order' among the articulations examined in this book. At the moment, however, it is useful to add a brief insight into the moral connotation of modernity, exposing also the dualistic logic at the core of the discourse of individualism. This will help highlight not only the kind of answer that such a debate has engendered across different Islamist discourses but also to the particular challenge that transmodernity posited to modern subjectivity formations.

As pointed out earlier, the reliance on a dichotomous organisation of social space – for instance the celebration of secularity and rationality against religion – was central to the discursive development of modernity. Max Weber's well-known description of the modern world as a 'disenchanted world' accounted for the secular erosion of the holistic and transcendental horizons that had followed the humanist revolution. Crucial emphasis in the narration of this process was put on the gradual enfranchisement from a higher, holy order

---

[27] Talal Asad, *Formations of the Secular*, p. 194.
[28] Ibid., p. 191.

to a re-centring on mankind.[29] In this context, liberals celebrated the emergence, expression and centrality of individuality vis-à-vis society.[30]

Most modern constructions of subjectivity in fact defined the individual in a dual relation with his/her social and cultural outside. In an etymological sense, the *individual* came to figure as the ultimate and *indivisible* constituent of society, whose ontological essence (rationality, egoism, altruism, etc.) was to be singled out and preserved against the context of an *outside* social. In Benjamin Constant's famous discourse of 1819, for instance, 'the liberty of the Moderns' coincides with individual liberty. According to Constant, it differed from the 'liberty of the Ancients' precisely because the latter extolled the political autonomy of the community assimilating the 'peaceful enjoyment of individual independence' to its needs.[31] The problem for modern discourses was precisely how to articulate such a relation. Whether to preserve, for instance, a radical focus on individual rights and private enjoyment vis-à-vis the cultural constraints of society and the administrative regimentation of the state, or to redefine the *social* in terms of the free and organic expression of individuals.[32] There is, nonetheless, a further meaning to be conveyed by the expression 'disenchantment of the world', one that points to the *modern* sense of meaninglessness in the absence of those horizons that had *traditionally* given sense to every aspect of individual and social existence. A common moral concern for liberal philosophers was, in fact, the degeneration of *individuality* to forms of *individualism* or *social atomism*. This fading, firstly of the transcendent and then of the social horizon, brought about a condition of *atomisation*, which can be characterised as a critical loss of sociability. The impression here was that the modern focus upon individuals entailed a narrowing of perspective, with the threat of losing the wider view for the social in the face of an almost exclusive focus on individual life. The effects of this condition upon a democratic industrial society were widely discussed throughout the nineteenth and twentieth centuries. In a modern context, where material interest and conformity seemed to dominate, 'not only does democracy

---

[29] Max Weber, 'Science as a Vocation', in H. Gerth and C. Wright Mills (eds), *From Max Weber: Essays in sociology* (New York: Oxford University Press, 1946), pp. 129–56.

[30] An interesting stance in classical liberal thought, for its celebration of individuality against forms of 'paternalism', is Wilhelm von Humboldt; see *The Limits of State Action* (London: Cambridge University Press, 1969).

[31] H.-B. Constant, 'The Liberty of the Ancients Compared with That of the Moderns', in B. Fontana (ed.), *Political Writings* (Cambridge, UK: Cambridge University Press, 1988), pp. 307–28.

[32] On this point see Charles Taylor, *The Malaise of Modernity* (Toronto, ON: Anansi, 1991) and *Sources of the Self: Making of the Modern Identity* (Cambridge: Cambridge University Press, 1989).

make every man forget his ancestors, but it hides his descendants and separates his contemporaries from him; it throws him back forever upon himself alone, and threatens in the end to confine him entirely within the solitude of his own heart'.[33]

Individualism meant that individuals, as the ultimate constituents of society, no longer perceived their original relation to the whole (hence the notion of the *atom* as an isolated unit which literally 'cannot be cut' or, again, *in-dividual* as an ultimate 'in-divisible' being). By over-emphasising their own *raison d'être* in regard to society itself, individuals ended up experiencing the crisis of a lost sociability where society was now to be maintained merely in the shadows. The modern sense of a loss of sociability therefore implied a fading of the social-outside as a consequence of the over-emphasis upon the individual-inside. The great impact of modern discourses about man and society lay in their potential to *dull* social atomism by promising a new sense of *belonging* (to a nation, a religious community or a social class), and thus filling the void left by a weakened sociability. Hence, the modern symbolic appeal of signifiers such as 'corporatism', 'comradeship', 'fellowship' and lay or religious 'brotherhood' after the French Revolution, and their radicalisation under the experience of totalitarianism in the twentieth century.

In the following pages, we shall examine the way in which such signifiers, and the *dualistic* logic here described came to be evaluated in the modern articulation of the nation state. We will then inquire into the traditional discourse of Islamic universalism showing the organising role of a different paradigm in the construction of space and subjectivity, one that could be described in terms of *inclusivity*. Both the discourse of the nation and the discourse of Islamic universalism have performed a crucial function in the organisation of and hegemonic battle between modern and traditional imaginaries, marking the genealogical background of Islamism. These discourses, however, have also provided a range and a place of particular linguistic signifiers such as 'territory', 'dar al-Islam', 'the people', 'the *ummah*', etc., which we will see articulated, through creative processes of re-activation and association, in the discursive practices examined in this study.

---

[33] Alexis de Tocqueville, *Democracy in America* (1st edn 1835; Stilwell, KS: Digireads. com Publishing, 2007), p. 370.

The Discourse of the Nation

We have seen that the variety of theoretical perspectives on 'tradition' and 'modernity' confer on such concepts a certain degree of indeterminacy and polysemy. We mentioned, for instance, that besides the structural and the moral connotation of modernity, critical analyses have highlighted an *ideological* connotation, stressing its role in the delineation of distinct political projects. So-called 'post-colonial' perspectives, for example, have amply scrutinised the political workings of modern sovereignty and modern subjectivity, exposing an increasing distortion of the *emancipatory* narrative of the Enlightenment on behalf of economic production and political dominance.[34] From a different angle, modernity has been seen as a complex historical and political reality characterised by an intrinsic condition of crisis as the result of an inner tension between creative and libertarian forces on the one hand and its boosts to control and supremacy on the other. Michael Hardt and Antonio Negri, in this respect, have underscored the existence of two different philosophical and political traditions: a 'plane of immanence', which allowed humanity to stand as the real producer of history, and a 'plane of transcendence'. Arising out of the humanist revolution, the latter was reactive to the former and consisted merely in the attempt to 'transplant the new image of humanity to a transcendent plane, relativize the capacities of science to transform the world, and above all oppose the reappropriation of power on the part of multitude ... order against desire'.[35] From a critical perspective, this second aspect of modernity is said to have prevailed over the first and engendered new forms of subjection, determining the creation of modern sovereignty and modern subjectivity as the corollary of this reaction. In fact, 'without a subject there could not be a practice of subjection (there could only be a mere and savage enslavement) and sovereignty would not be able to reshape itself using new authoritarian relations which tend to assume subjectivity as their historical representation'.[36]

---

[34] With such perspectives, we refer here to those authors who in different degree have questioned modernity and its related forms of power and knowledge, contesting modern essentialist and binary representations. See, for instance, Homi Bhabha, *The Location of Culture* (London: Routledge, 1994); and Gayatri Chakravorty Spivak, *A Critique of Postcolonial Reason: Toward a History of the Vanishing Present* (Cambridge, MA: Harvard University Press, 1999).

[35] Michael Hardt and Antonio Negri, *Empire* (London: Harvard University Press, 2000), p. 74.

[36] Salvo Vaccaro, 'Prefazione', in Todd May, *Anarchismo e post-strutturalismo* (Milan: Eleuthera, 1998), p. 11.

Within this framework, a central role has been ascribed to the deployment of a binary logic in the *modern* articulation of social and political relations, which resulted in the introduction of ideal and material borders. The separation between inside and outside and, in domestic political terms, between private and public, as well as the formation of identities rigidly distinguishing between Self and Other has indeed come to constitute a new mode of conceiving what it is to be a political community.[37] The world of modern sovereignty turned out to be a Manichean world, marked by a long series of dichotomies defining the friend and the enemy, the civilised and the uncivilised, and so forth. Such a conception is particularly telling when referring to colonialism insofar as it represents a phenomenon indicative of modernity's modus operandi in the construction of subjectivity, identity and otherness. In such a context colonised populations were to be perceived as 'Other' and defined in terms not simply of *difference*, but of *radical opposition*. In the light of this 'absolute negation', alterity was used in the production of Self through a reversal of its 'essences'. In other words, European identity was the outcome of a dialectical movement whereby colonial subjects were reduced to a few essences and 'subsumed (cancelled and raised up) within a higher unity'.[38] This is central, as the logic of exclusion enacted by modern narratives of citizenship does not simply entail the irreconcilable opposition between privilege and marginalisation. As Engin Isin rightly put it: 'the closure theories that define citizenship as a space of privilege for the few that excludes others neglect a subtle but important aspect of citizenship: that it requires the constitution of these others to become possible'.[39] When subsumed within this dialectical framework, the logic of exclusion implies a necessary and consubstantial definition of the self: 'the focus on otherness as a condition of citizenship and its alterity always emerged simultaneously in a dialogical manner and constituted each other'.[40]

As we discussed in Chapter 1, such a mind-set is best represented by the discourse of *orientalism*, which, besides initially reproducing binary strategies, exemplifies the Foucauldian link between systems of power and knowledge.[41] It

---

[37] Claudia Moscovici, *Double Dialectics: Between Universalism and Relativism in Enlightenment and Postmodern Thought* (Lanham, MD: Rowman & Littlefield, 2002), p. 141.
[38] Hardt and Negri, *Empire*, p. 128.
[39] Engin F. Isin, *Being Political: Genealogies of Citizenship* (Minneapolis, MN: University of Minnesota Press, 2002), p. 4.
[40] Ibid.
[41] See Michel Foucault, *Surveiller et punir: Naissance de la prison* (Paris: Gallimard, 1975), p. 32.

emblematises the way in which, in modern discourses, new and greater forms of control came to require new, deeper and systematic forms of knowledge: 'to know is to subordinate'.[42] This discussion is particularly useful to introduce the speculative terrain of the discourse of the nation, contributing to define modernity as a symbolic reservoir.

In attempting to offer a discourse-centred reading of the nation state, a first task consists in identifying recurrent features at the core of this discourse, in finding a common pattern in the various accounts of the nation, which give coherence to it, informing its *style of discourse*, so to speak. Despite the different ways of organising the European idea of the nation state, its internal consistency as a discursive universe would hardly be thinkable without the mobilisation, in different degrees, of three main signifiers articulated around the master signifier 'nation': sovereignty, territory and the people. The aim of this section is to suggest that the particular connotation that these signifiers have assumed within the discourse of the nation has been marked by a dichotomous logic. Although emphasis is given here to the particular configuration that the nation state discourse has assumed in Europe, a reference to a discursive variant of nationalism, i.e., pan-Arabism, will also be offered at the end of this section, so as to highlight the discursive complexity of nationalism. This will be useful to understand the articulatory process and the background context informing a territorial trajectory of Islamism.

In most classical treatises addressing the concept and history of the nation state in Europe, attention is given to the juridical and legal structure sustaining this political formation, which is seen as a later development of early modern absolutist and pre-modern patrimonial models of power. Central to this point here is the constitutional transformation of the modern state, which entailed the evolution of modern sovereignty in search of a new source of legitimation.[43] Sovereignty was conceptualised as the 'supreme power' (*summa potestas*) giving 'force' and 'authority' to a political order by way of its 'absolute and perpetual' (Bodin), 'exclusive and indivisible' (Hobbes) essence.[44] As supreme power

---

[42] Bryan Turner, 'Orientalism and the Problem of Civil Society', in Asaf Hussaini, Robert Oslon and Jamil Qureichi (eds), *Orientalism, Islam and Islamicists* (Brattleboro, VT: Amana Books, 1984), p. 24.

[43] For a general survey of the transition towards the nation state and an examination of previous patrimonial and absolutist models, see Gianfranco Poggi, *The Development of the Modern State: A Sociological Introduction* (London: Hutchinson, 1978); Perry Anderson, *Lineages of the Absolutist State* (London: N.L.B, 1974).

[44] Jean Bodin, *On Sovereignty: Four Chapters from the Six Books of the Commonwealth* (Cambridge: Cambridge University Press, 1992); Thomas Hobbes, *Leviathan* (Oxford: Oxford University Press, 1998).

of a political order, sovereignty was thought of, therefore, as the original, unrestricted and unique source of legitimacy of state control, which does not recognise any superior principle of power *outside* itself. Despite dissimilarities among theorists and practical implementations of the authority of the state, with differences always involving geographical and historical contexts, these features defined the main classical doctrines of modern sovereignty. Within this theoretical framework, there were major shifts regarding the *locus* of authority; that is, the *subject* embodying this supreme power of political order, from the transcendental power of God (medieval theories) to the immanent power of the state (modern doctrines), and, in immanent terms, from the absolute power of the *prince* (Machiavelli, Bodin, Hobbes), to the impersonal power of the law (Kant's juridical principle of practical reason) and so on. Central to my discussion here is that in the history of theories of sovereignty the locus of power ended up coinciding with the *nation state*, embodying *the people* of the state and its *territory*.

The appearance and institutional consolidation of the nation state has often been described as the product of the emerging productive forces of capitalism.[45] It reflected the need to impose a new source of legitimacy of state authority to reflect the growing economic influence of a rising bourgeoisie. In the struggle against the 'old powers', the focus shifted to the community of individuals, born in the same land and now sharing a new sense of belonging: the *nation* (from Latin *nasci*, 'to be born' into a certain land or community).[46] We have seen that secularisation became accepted in this framework as a central hermeneutical category, accompanying the destiny of modern doctrines of state and sovereignty. It was, in fact, within this space that national sovereignty emerged as the final step of a discursive movement re-qualifying the fundamental juridical traits of power along a dichotomous secular model, celebrating the priority of state immanence over a divine transcendent, and the ultimate primacy of the political over the religious.

This final anchoring of state power to the imaginary figure of the nation required modelling the *signifying image* of the subject upon which the self-representation of the nation could be projected: in other words, the articulation

---

[45] A number of approaches have illustrated this point: from Marxist positions, see Horace B. Davis, *Toward a Marxist Theory of Nationalism* (New York and London: Monthly Review Press, 1978); towards more recent world system analyses, e.g., Immanuel Wallerstein, *The Modern World System* (New York: Academic Press, 1974); to more heterogeneous and specialist prospects as the one assumed by Bassam Tibi, *Arab Nationalism: Between Islam and the Nation-State* (London: Macmillan, 1997).

[46] Georges Burdeau, *L'État* (Paris: Éditions du Seuil, 1980).

of *the people* of the nation as its historical manifestation. In articulating this central second signifier, the flexibility of tradition and the adaptability of the past as a pool of resources to be mobilised, whether with primordialist and romanticised narratives or more scientific tropes, proved to be crucial. National identity has been described as a creative energy, a product of the 'collective imagination' marking the shift from a passive to an active role for the population (with the final transition from the feudal 'subject' to the modern 'citizen').[47] It was constructed out of pre-existing ethnic and cultural identifications that came to be re-articulated around the new national artefact.[48] This is not to say that such pre-existing ties were original in an absolute sense. They should also, in fact, be viewed as the result of cultural and historical constructions 'that took place in earlier centuries and went through a successful process of sedimentation and/or re-activation'.[49] At the basis of this imagined order, local populations were depicted as communities with a *worldly past*, grounded upon the idea of a biological continuity of blood relation, history and language. This was a common framework among early thinkers in the eighteenth and nineteenth century, including Rousseau, Schlegel, or pre-Romantic writers such as Alfieri, Foscolo, etc. There were differences across time, however, some stressing the 'spiritual' origin of the nation based on race and language (e.g., von Herder and Fichte), while others stressed the 'voluntary choice of individuals' in constructing the nation (Mazzini) and defining its 'soul' (Renan).[50]

In this context, the ultimate logic organising the discursive articulation of 'the people' rested upon the mobilisation of a rigid binary dividing the new national citizen and its outside other. This separation was structurally associated with a principle of integrity and unity regarding this emerging national self. As discussed above, the constitution of national identities in Europe rested upon

---

[47] See Benedict Anderson, *Imagined Communities: Reflection on the Origin of the Spread of Nationalism* (London: Verso, 1983).

[48] Cf. Anthony Smith, *The Ethnic Origins of Nations* (Oxford: Blackwell, 1986); Patrick J. Geary, *The Myths of Nations: The Medieval Origins of Europe* (Princeton, NJ, and Oxford: Princeton University Press, 2002).

[49] Yannis Stavrakakis, with Nikos Chrysoloras, '(I Can't Get No) Enjoyment: Lacanian Theory and the Analysis of Nationalism', *Psychoanalysis, Culture and Society*, 11 (2006): p. 147.

[50] Johann Gottfried von Herder, in *Reflections on the Philosophy of the History of Mankind* (Chicago, IL, and London: University of Chicago Press, 1968); Gottlieb Fichte, *Addresses to the German Nation* (New York and Evanston, IL: Harper and Row, 1968): G. Mazzini, *Scritti Editi e Inediti* (Imola 1906, vol. 83), p. 885; Ernest Renan, 'What Is a Nation?', in Geoff Eley and Ronald Grigor Suny (eds), *Becoming National: A Reader* (New York and Oxford: Oxford University Press, 1996), pp. 41–55.

the internal abstract convergence of *blood, language* and *land*. This unitary and abstract convergence was achieved by over-emphasising similarities while, at the same time, subsuming differences within the *unitary* spiritual and henceforth transcendental dimension of the people.[51] Standardisation of national languages, homogenising representations of the race of the people and the institutional and legal qualification of the nation, with citizenship legally anchored to the two principles of *jus soli* ('right of the territory', citizenship based on birth in the territory of the nation state) and above all, in continental Europe, *jus sanguinis* ('right of blood', citizenship based on the line of descent) – all marked common features in the emergence and subsequent elaboration of the people. Thanks to this general *reductio ad unum* (reduction to one only), national identity was taken to constitute an indivisible *sacred* Self, which was put in radical *antagonism* with its outside. This principle of *exclusionary* negation of difference and creation of pure unity mark not only the pathological character that this discourse assumed in extreme forms of nationalism, but also its constitutive and foundational asset. Its role in the construction of European nations has been amply acknowledged.[52] In emphasising the quest for unity characterising the construction of the people of the nation, Hardt and Negri note that a central requirement for the transition to the new national order was the transformation of a multitude into a people:

> The multitude is a multiplicity, a plane of singularities, an open set of relations, which is not homogeneous or identical with itself and bears an indistinct, inclusive relation to those outside of it. The people, in contrast, tends toward identity and homogeneity internally while posing its difference from and excluding what remains outside of it. Whereas the multitude is an inconclusive constituent relation, the people is a constituted synthesis that is prepared for sovereignty.[53]

This distinction had already been discerned by Hobbes, who praised the unitary character of the people against the multitude: 'the people is somewhat that is one, having one will, and to whom one action may be attributed; none of these

---

[51] See Etienne Balibar and Immanuel Wallerstein, *Race, Nation and Class* (London: Verso, 1991); and Robert Young, *Colonial Desire: Hybridity in Theory, Culture and Race* (London: Routledge, 1995).

[52] Cf. Gerard Delanty, *Inventing Europe: Idea, Identity, Reality* (Basingstoke: Macmillan, 1995); Thomas Christiansen, Knud Erik Jorgensen and Antje Wiener (eds), *The Social Construction of Europe* (London and Thousand Oaks, CA: SAGE, 2001); David Campbell, *National Deconstruction* (Minneapolis, MN: University of Minnesota Press, 1998); Iver B. Neumann, *Uses of the Other: 'The East' in European Identity Formation* (Manchester: Manchester University Press, 1999).

[53] Hardt and Negri, *Empire*, p. 103.

can be properly said of the multitude'.[54] According to Hardt and Negri, although the link between the nation and the people emerged with all its revolutionary and popular capacity during the French Revolution, its democratic significance, as paradigmatically advocated by Sieyès, was quickly subsumed by the emergent forces of the bourgeois capitalist drive and 'consigned to all the Thermidors'.[55] Two points here need to be stressed.

First, the tension between a progressive and a reactionary understanding of the nation, though won in Europe by the mobilising repressive forces of capitalism in the aftermath of the French Revolution, has remained in principle. We will see in the next pages that such tension reappeared during the fight for independence of colonised populations, with nationalism playing an important democratic and counter-hegemonic function. Secondly, the difference between the unitary character of the people and the dispersive nature of the multitude offers an interesting point from which to consider the relation between the traditional pan-Islamic ideal of the *ummah*, the community of all Muslims (to be discussed in the next section), and the modern national concept of the people. This tension between the 'nation' and the '*ummah* (which could be associated to the inclusive idea of 'multitude') is central to grasp Islamist subjective representations in the next chapters.

The constitutive effects of a dualistic paradigm are also detectable in another central signifier for this discourse: the territory. Alongside nationalist representations of community, a new spatial formation, the national *territory*, was also devised in modern doctrines of state, which substantially adopted the same binary mechanism of inclusion/exclusion. The consolidation of the modern state, particularly in the later development of the nation state, required first and foremost the delineation of clear-cut national borders. This entailed the absorption of those portions of landscape that had previously separated the land of different lords, and that were not recognised by any state. In his 1977–1978 lectures at Collège de France, Foucault observed that, while territory and population had remained quite vague and non-formalised notions until the emergence of modern states, an increasing process of rationalisation of land and population was enacted under the modern notion of sovereignty.[56]

---

[54] Thomas Hobbes, *De Cive* (Whitefish, MT: Kessinger Publishing Co, 2004), p. 102.

[55] Hardt and Negri, *Empire*, p. 101. Emmanuel Joseph Sieyès (1748–1836) was one of the key figures of the French Revolution, and the author of the 1789 pamphlet: *What is the Third Estate?* (London: Pall Mall Press, 1963).

[56] Cf. Michel Foucault, *Security, Territory, Population: Lectures at the Collège de France, 1977–1978* (Basingstoke: Palgrave Macmillan, 2007).

It is with the modern absolutist state and the nation state in particular that territory became fully rationalised, with borders across European states being marked by territorial contact. In this sense, it should be stressed that a common word for 'border' among some European languages is 'confine' (con-fine), which implicates the idea of a sharing of the same limit (from Latin *com-* 'with, sharing' +*finis* 'end, limit').[57] Conversely, it is the very idea of limit that requires, from this perspective, some sort of necessary sharing. Like the binary construction of the people, the national concept of 'territory' entailed a *necessary* and *exclusionary* model of space, as the end of 'my' territory *necessarily* coincides with the beginning of 'yours' – hence the spatial hypertrophy of the national territorial model epitomised by the theatrical construction of walls demarcating a clear-cut, *shared*, and *necessary* distinction between 'us' and 'them'. The antagonistic character of this model lies not so much in the existence of a relationship with an outside, but in the nature of this relationship. As for the notion of the people, the territorial outside is not treated as a difference, but is assumed as a 'necessary' absolute negation, where 'exclusion' *needs* to be maintained for the basic functioning of the inside as a whole, as an *Us*.[58]

By reflecting the form, *par excellence*, of identification based on the 'us' and 'them' paradigm, the nation state, with its binary construction of space and subjectivity, was able to exert significant control within its borders while competing with other nation states for political and economic dominion outside its boundaries.[59] Given the competitive and aggressive relation between European nations as a result of this exclusionary model, and as a consequence of the expanding forces of capitalism, the tragic events of the two world wars, and the systematisation of colonialism were among the effects of this process. Relating identity to territory, the doctrine of the new nation state exerted a massive capacity of control under the banner of imperialism, ensuring high level of mobilisation well beyond Europe. Although differences have characterised the articulation of the national discourse in definite settings (for instance, signifiers such as 'religion' or 'race' have played different roles in connoting the signifier 'people' in distinct environments), the dualistic structure of this model remained substantially intact in colonial contexts, where the mobilising power of national sovereignty had to be played from a subaltern position. As Euan

---

[57] Cf. Giacomo Marramao, *The Passage West: Philosophy after the Age of the Nation State* (London: Verso, 2012).

[58] See Figure 2.2 for a representation of this exclusionary model of space.

[59] Cf. Aletta Norval, 'Trajectories of Future Researches in Discourse Theory', in David Howarth, Aletta Norval and Yannis Stavrakakis (eds), *Discourse Theories and Political Analysis* (Manchester: Manchester University Press, 2000).

Hague observes, 'the limited sovereignty and territory of the colony was already imagined for the colonized by the colonizers'.[60]

Nationalism in Colonial Settings: The Pan-Arab Variant

We mentioned that the idea of the nation has been an important tool in the fight for the political emancipation of the colonised world. According to Ernest Gellner, while the emergence of nationalism in Europe was heavily dependent on material and socio-economic processes sustained by industrialisation, ideological motivations have played a primary function in the nationalist version of the colonial world.[61] This has led to distinguish between a first and a second wave of nationalism in Gellner's schema: 'First wave nationalism was, in part, spurred by the outgrowth of industrialization: imperialism. Second wave nationalism is a rebellious impulse against first wave nationalism. This second wave assumes the ideological rhetoric of industrialization without the material reality of industrialization in the country itself.'[62]

As previously emphasised, since the French Revolution the discourse of the nation has expressed a twofold tendency: a democratic progressive impulse on the one hand, and a reactionary tendency on the other. A notorious argument in this sense could be found in the dispute between Luxemburg and Lenin on the 'national question'.[63] Whilst Lenin defended the progressive character of nationalism when assumed by subordinated populations, Rosa Luxemburg stood against the 'right of self-determination' of Poland, censuring nationalism for its unavoidable tendency to expropriate democratic claims on behalf of capitalist production. Despite critical positions, however, it has been widely observed that 'whereas the concept of nation promotes stasis and restoration in the hands of the dominant, it is a weapon for change and revolution in the hand of subordinated'.[64]

In colonial settings, the constitution of independent nations was quickly assumed to be a viable alternative to foreign rule. The language of colonial

---

[60] Euan Hague, 'Benedict Anderson', in P. Hubbard, R. Kitchin and G. Valentine (eds), *Key Thinkers on Space and Place* (London and New York: SAGE, 2004), pp. 18–25.

[61] Ernest Gellner, *Nations and Nationalism* (1st edn, 1983; Malden, MA: Blackwell, 2006).

[62] Aliya Haider, 'The Rhetoric of Resistance: Islamism, Modernity, and Globalization', *Harvard BlackLetter Law Journal*, 18 (2002): 100.

[63] Horace B. Davis, *National Question: Selected Writings by Rosa Luxembourg* (New York: Monthly Review Press, 1981); Vladimir Ilyich Lenin, 'The Right of Nations to Self-Determination', *Collected Works*, vol. 20 (Moscow: Progress Publishers, 1972), pp. 393–454.

[64] Hardt and Negri, *Empire*, p. 106.

powers was thus accepted and integrated; yet it was used against Europe as a tool of political emancipation.[65] Nationalist discourses were elaborated in new forms that progressed substantially beyond the particularistic dimension of European single states. A brief discussion of Arab nationalism is useful in this respect, evidencing a counter-hegemonic appropriation of nationalism in colonial contexts.

Arab nationalism emerged as a discourse promoted by Arab intellectuals, both Christians and Muslims, in order to gain independence from Ottoman rule through the unification of Arab people and provinces: hence its other name 'pan-Arabism'. The discursive features of this discourse, however, drew on the same binary representation of space and subjectivity that European nationalism articulated, celebrating the common linguistic, ethnic and cultural (but not religious) heritage of Arab populations and the need to create an Arab independent 'territory'. That is, subsuming linguistic and cultural differences within the ideal of a unified Arab nation.

In the aftermath of the First World War, however, once European powers had replaced the Ottomans in the Middle East, the concept of nation was deployed by European forces to legitimise de facto partition and control within the boundaries of the imagined pan-Arab land. With the introduction of new nation states in the region as a consequence of the mandate system, pan-Arabism had to face a new context.[66] It had to oppose the consolidation of the new 'nations' as they had been arbitrarily defined by European powers. At the same time, the concept of nation had to be retained and mobilised against Europe within a territorial pan-Arab framework; that is, the idea of a great and unified Arab 'nation' absorbing single Arab states needed to be maintained and used in an anti-imperialist perspective.[67] In the following decades, the diffusion of

---

[65] In the Algerian movement for independence, for instance, French legislation on civil associations was adopted by Algerian nationalists to bypass legal and political restrictions in Algeria; see Chafika Kahina Bouagache, 'The Algerian Law on Associations within Its Historical Context', *The International Journal of Not-for-Profit Law*, 9/2 (2007).

[66] See Bahgat Korany, 'Alien and Besieged Yet Here to Stay: The Contradictions of the Arab Territorial State', in Ghassan Salamé (ed.), *The Foundation of the Arab State* (London: Croom Helm, 1987); and As'ad AbuKhalil, 'A New Arab Ideology? The Rejuvenation of Arab Nationalism', *Middle East Journal*, 46/1 (1992): 27. The Mandate system refers to a set of agreements enabling the victors of the First World War to administer former territories of the Ottoman and German empires as 'mandates' from League of Nations. In the Middle East, responsibility to govern former Ottoman provinces was given to France (over the current states of Syria and Lebanon) and Britain (over the current states of Iraq, Egypt, Palestine and Jordan).

[67] cf. Tibi *Arab Nationalism*, p. 202.

broadcasting media, the increasing movement of workers from one Arab state to another, and the interconnected process of economic modernisation in the region, helped Arabism to transcend the boundaries of single Arab countries and delineate the imaginary borders of the whole Arab nation.[68] This is best exemplified by the massive appeal that Nasser's pan-Arabism was able to exert upon neighbouring populations, especially during the short-lived alliance of the United Arab Republic (UAR) between 1958 and 1961. It is only in the aftermath of the 1967 Arab–Israeli War that pan-Arabism began its decline.[69] Temporarily or otherwise, national and particularistic identities started to gain ground as demonstrated, for instance, by the increasing consolidation and appeal of a Palestinian 'national' identity.

The Discourse of Islamic Universalism

In attempting to account for the discourse of Islamic universalism, a terminological and conceptual link has to be established with 'pan-Islamism', as the latter will be used interchangeably with the former in this study. The term 'pan-Islamism' was 'probably adopted in imitation of Pan-Slavism, which had become current in the 1870s'.[70] With this term, English scholar Dwight E. Lee identified two distinct visions. On the one hand, there was the traditional concept of *Islamic universalism*. This expressed the classic Islamic ideal of Muslim unity, aimed at establishing Islamic society on a global scale. This ideal was said to be 'inherent in Islam', and based on both religious texts and the tradition of Islam.[71] On the other hand, pan-Islamism came to indicate a political movement in the nineteenth century that was promoted by Sultan Abdul Hamid II, Emperor of the Ottomans, and inspired by the writings of Persian philosopher and Islamic reformer Jamal ad-Din al-Afghani (1838–1897). This movement called for the unification of all Muslims in order to resist the growing political and military influence of emerging colonial powers from Europe, re-articulating the tradition of Islamic unity, and revitalising its symbolic appeal for anti-imperialist purposes.

---

[68] See Roger Owen, *State, Power and Politics in the Making of the Modern Middle East* (London: Routledge, 1992).
[69] See Fouad Ajami, 'The End of Pan-Arabism', *Foreign Affairs*, 57/2 (1978/9).
[70] C.H. Becker, 'Panislamismus', *Islamstudien*, vol. 2 (Leipzig, 1932), p. 242, quoted in Dwight E. Lee, 'The Origins of Pan-Islamism', *The American Historical Review*, 47/2 (1942): 279.
[71] Ibid.

British control of India, Russian aggression in Central Asia (1877–1878) and increasing European military and financial penetration in the Arab provinces of the enfeebled Sublime Porte left al-Afghani convinced of the need to build a more independent and reformed society across Muslim countries, reviving traditional and religious sentiments and combining them with activism, rationality, and political and military strength. Although 'a late convert to pan-Islam, not a lifetime devotee', al-Afghani strongly criticised the very concept of nation (*jansiyya*) which he reduces to mere tribalism – a matter of race and ethnic belonging when confronted with the universality of religious ties.[72] In this context, al-Afghani celebrated the traditional unity of Islam, advocating the need 'to respond' to (and somehow to spurn) the Ottoman pan-Islamic and anti-imperialist appeal, eliciting anti-foreigner sentiments across Muslim populations in the 'Islamic community' (*millat-i islāmiyyeh*).[73] In a letter to Sultan Abdül Hamid, al-Afghani acknowledges that 'the perpetuation of religion depends on the perpetuation of this [Ottoman] government', which requires the contribution of all Muslims to the achievement of a full unity of Islam (*ittihād-i tāmm-i islāmiyyeh*). Such a contribution is the result of a cultural, political and religious effort, 'a religious struggle and a national endeavour' (*muhārabeh-yi dīniyyeh wa mujāhaddeh-yi milliyyeh*).[74]

Despite the tendency to consider pan-Islamism as a movement epitomising the intellectual position of al-Afghani and other reformists in the pre-colonial and colonial era, this section focuses on pan-Islamism as the discourse of 'Islamic universalism', a discourse that most contributed to define tradition as a symbolic scenario, and also inspired al-Afghani's vision. It is not possible here to account for all the different doctrines and intellectual positions characterising the discourse of Islamic universalism throughout the centuries, from classical views in Islamic thought (e.g., Abu al-Hasan al-Mawardi, Muhammad Shaybani, Ibn Taymiyya, etc.) to more recent elaborations among Islamist scholars (e.g., Taqiuddin al-Nabhani, Ali Shari'ati, etc.). The attempt will be rather to enucleate key historical features in the complex development of this discourse, outlining the general model of spatial representation and subjectivity formation that a universalistic framework enacts, with its instantiation of an *inclusive* paradigm.

---

[72] Nikki R. Keddie, *An Islamic Response to Imperialism: Political and Religious Writings of Sayyid Jamāl ad-Dīn 'al-Afghānī'* (Berkeley, CA: University of California Press, 1983), p. 59.
[73] Jamal ad-Din al-Afghani, 'Persian Appeal' (presumably dated *c.*1878), translated in Nikki R. Keddie, *Sayyid Jamāl ad-Dīn'al-Afghānī': A Political Biography* (Berkeley, CA, and London: University of California Press, 1972), p. 136.
[74] Ibid.

In broad terms, the discourse of Islamic universalism promoted the 'realization of the Islamic ideal, the unity of the world in Islam, the central direction under a leader (Imam) of the world community'.[75] While the ideal of 'Islam as a universality' functioned as the master signifier of such a discourse, it found historical representation in the signifier *caliphate*; that is, the power embodying and guaranteeing Islamic universality. Around this ideal, two main signifiers substantiated the discursive structure of Islamic universalism: *dar al-Islam* (the 'domain of Islam'; also referred to as 'abode of belief') and the *ummah* (Muslim community). It is the relation between these two signifiers that the following historical and discursive examination will take into account so as to highlight the paradigmatic difference between pan-Islamism and nationalism in respect to spatial and subjectivity constructions and better clarify the genealogical context of Islamism.

Dar al-Islam

In a remarkable article written in the early 1980s, Manoucher Parvin and Maurie Sommer tracked the line of theoretical and historical development of what they saw as the 'dynamic, accommodating processual notion of dar al-Islam'.[76] In this essay, the authors consider Islamic territoriality to be based on 'interaction patterns – human, environmental, systemic' so that, because of 'context- and time-dependence', its integrity relies on a sort of 'spatial response' and not 'spatial immutability'.[77] *Dar al-Islam* is a legal and religious construct literally meaning the abode or house where Islam prevails. Although not explicitly mentioned in the Qur'an, it has played a vital role both in the theoretical elaboration of religious and legal schools and the dynamic development of Muslim space over time. Naturally, conceptual differences have marked juridical understandings of *dar al-Islam* in classical times regarding the extension and prerogatives of this domain. In his insightful exploration of the classical and more contemporary legal approaches to *dar al-Islam*, Shahrul Hussain, for instance, notices that an illustrious definition of it by prominent Hanafi jurist Muhammad ibn Ahmad ibn Abi Sahl Abu Bakr al-Sarakhsi (d. *c*.483/1090) was: 'a place which is under the authority or ownership of Muslims and the proof of this is that Muslims

---

[75] Lee, 'The Origins of Pan-Islamism', p. 280.
[76] Manoucher Parvin and Maurie Sommer, 'Dar al-Islam: The Evolution of Muslim Territoriality and Its Implications for Conflict Resolution in the Middle East', *International Journal of Middle East Studies*, 11/1 (1980): 18.
[77] Ibid., p. 2.

are safe therein'.[78] Others from different juridical perspectives – for example al-Kasani (Hanafi School), al-Dasuki (Maliki School) or Ibn Muflih (Hambali School) – linked *dar al-Islam* to the manifestation of Islamic law and Islamic rule, though the specific features defining the latter remained largely vague or undefined. In the Shafi'i juridical tradition, al-Bujayrimi privileged residency over al-Sarakhsi's emphasis on ownership, extending the notion of *dar al-Islam* almost universally so as to include also those lands where Muslims reside, even if they have come to be ruled by non-Muslims, or even lands that have been once inhabited by Muslims but no longer have Muslim residents. From an overall perspective, however, classical scholars mostly agree on the ability of *dar al-Islam* to guarantee the inviolability and sanctity of life and property ('*ismah*), while also allowing Muslims to openly profess Islam and implement Islamic law and authority.

In the early days of Islamic expansion, while acknowledging the universality of *dar al-Islam* in principle, legal doctrines had to recognise the existence of lands ruled by non-Muslims. They constituted the *dar al-harb* (abode of war or chaos) under which the designation of any land *outside* Muslim jurisdiction fell, and where the outside figured as an enclave of the assumed universality of Islam. Within this legal framework, the relation between Islamic and non-Islamic lands was a dynamic one. It was marked, over the centuries, by restriction and expansion by way of *jihad* and *hijra* (migration). *Jihad*, the 'effort' in the path of Islam, while signifying in legal doctrine a plurality of approaches to religion (from more spiritual to material), also implied a military interpretation – either defensive, as a collective duty in cases of aggression, or expansive, as a way to Islamise new lands, as an alternative or in association to *da'wa*, the Islamic call (missionary persuasion). It can be said, therefore, that, though not reducible to military action, the relation between *dar a-Islam* and *dar al-harb* was characterised, among other things, by an expansionist attitude by which the universalistic claim of Islam could potentially be played against non-Islamic lands.[79] As Hussain puts it, the objective and duty of Muslims was 'to spread the message of Islam to people. As Islam grew in population, strength and popularity, nations were forced to recognize the Islamic State and consequently they had to either enter into a treaty ('ahd) with Muslims or risk being ostracized and

---

[78] Shahrul Hussain, *Dar al-Islam and Dar al Harb* (Tripoli: Al Hikma Publishing, 2012), p. 133.
[79] Cf. Michael David Bonner, *Jihad in Islamic History: Doctrines and Practice* (Princeton, NJ: Princeton University Press, 2006); Rudolph Peters, *Jihad in Classical and Modern Islam: A Reader* (Princeton, NJ: Markus Wiener Publishers, 2005).

put their lives and property in danger.'[80] Although war played a central role in sustaining the universalistic ethos of the early times and promoting the classical differentiation between *dar al-Islam* and *dar al-harb*, the specific dynamism between these two domains could also result from forms of persuasion and convenience and relocation, and could include contractions of *dar al-Islam* as result of voluntary migration of Muslims or external aggressions.[81]

However, in the face of the permanence and increasing visibility of non-Muslim lands, the dynamic yet expansionist movement that had characterised the golden age of Islam since its founding in the seventh century up to the decline of the Abbasid era in the thirteenth century brought about important changes in the doctrine of *dar al-Islam*. A principle of pragmatism on behalf of the Islamic interest, *maslaha*, led to the assumption of new legal approaches, especially within the Shafi'is and Hanbali legal schools. A new middle-ground level, the *dar al-'ahd* (land of truce; also referred to as *dar al-sulh*, abode of peace), was thus acknowledged as a practical device to ensure peace and stability with non-Muslim lands and to reduce the cost of a permanent *jihad*. It consisted of those lands with which a formal agreement was stipulated, guaranteeing the protection of Muslims under foreign rule or the protection of non-Muslim regions behind tributary taxation or, extensively, any area in which open warfare was absent.[82] This legal construct moderated the potential polarity between *dar al-Islam* and *dar al-harb*, freezing or virtualising the inherent universalism of Islam so that its practical realisation was postponed *sine die*, whilst still fulfilling a dynamic, mobilising function as an ideal or a promise to be delivered. As Majid Khadduri has argued:

> Nor did the peaceful relations between dar al-Islam and dar al-Harb, which were often constructed on the basis of mutual respect and interest, carry with it the implied idea of equality between the two dars, since dar al-harb could not possibly attain a normal or permanent status unless its inhabitants either adopted Islam or accepted the status of the tolerated religions. In practice, however, the

---

[80] S. Hussain, *Dar al-Islam and Dar al Harb*, p. 131.
[81] Cf. Sami A. Aldeeb Abu-Sahlieh, 'The Islamic Conception of Migration', *International Migration Review, Special Issue: Ethics, Migration, and Global Stewardship*, 30/1 (1996): 37–57.
[82] Cf. Robert Ignatius Burns and Paul E. Chevedden, *Negotiating Cultures: Bilingual Surrender Treaties in Muslim-Crusader Spain* (Leiden: Brill, 1999); and Bernard Lewis, *The Political Language of Islam* (Chicago, IL, and London: University of Chicago Press, 1988).

more habituated the Muslim became to a dormant jihad the more reconciled they tended to be to the permanency of a law of Peace.[83]

As the expansionist drive of the early Islamic age became gradually reduced, and the permanence and increasing visibility of non-Muslim lands ended up clashing with the universalistic ideal, this third legal and spatial category, *dar al-'ahd*, became more and more important, playing a significant role in the modulation of antagonistic relations within the universalistic model. The temporary division between *dar al-Islam* and *dar al-'ahd*, in fact, remained subject to perpetual renewal, as the limits between them were never formalised. We see here that a principle of mediation intervened in the legal doctrine of *dar al-Islam* mitigating Islamic potential for radical polarity against any domain outside of Islam. *Dar al-Islam* remained first and foremost a legal concept throughout this process marked by a fluid territorial characterisation that legal doctrines managed to mobilise. This meant for *dar al-Islam* the possibility to keep thinking of Islamic territoriality as a universality, a full plenitude with no outside, notwithstanding the contingent presence of non-Muslim lands, whose inclusion and absorption in Islam would be realised at some indefinite time in the future. This discussion is useful, for in qualifying the historical and doctrinarian development of *dar al-Islam* it highlights how an inclusive logic was gradually constructed, deployed and re-elaborated within the discourse of pan-Islamism, facing different geopolitical circumstances.

The porosity of Islamic territoriality as developed by legal schools was, in part, the result of the historical predicament characterising the life of Arab populations even before the Islamic era. Parvin and Sommer argue that a 'tribal' dimension composed of two main streams, nomadism and the Arab quality of urban settlement, contributed to the consolidation of the dynamic nature of Islamic territoriality. On the one hand, nomadic tribes in the Arab peninsula and in large portions of the Middle East expressed a non-sedentary culture. The need to move continuously around the desert and inhospitable lands of the region, and to compete for the use of exploitable lands and the control of main routes of commerce by way of looting and razzia (*ghaziyya*), led these populations to become accustomed to a permanent form of 'relocation'.[84] 'Territory was thus a function of time more than space; as a tribe moved, its territorial bounds were, in a sense, picked up, carried about, and set down quite unconsciously, rather

---

[83] Majid Khadduri, *War and Peace in the Law of Islam* (Clark, NJ: The Lawbook Exchange, 2006), p. 145.

[84] See Martha Mundy and Basim Musallam (eds), *The Transformation of Nomadic Society in the Arab East* (Cambridge: Cambridge University Press, 2000).

like material possession.'[85] For Islamic doctrine, this entailed a partial adaptation to such nomadic features, to the extent that early Islamic expansion by way of military jihad has been seen as a form of 'sacralization of the Beduin razzia' or a rationalisation of it.[86]

On the other hand, the nomadic availability to continuous forms of relocation was reinforced by the environmental predicament characterising urban settlements in large parts of the Arab peninsula. Being relatively isolated, surrounded by massive portions of deserts, and by seas, Arab cities also had to be available to forms of mobility. To a certain extent, they also had to assume an itinerant attitude aimed at gaining access to and control of commercial routes in competition with other tribal urban settlements and with the incursions of Bedouins. Again, this helped to develop a notion of territoriality based more on occupancy and mobility than formal ownership and permanency, as was the case in Europe. The flexibility of Arab conceptions of space contributed, then, to consolidating the inclusive ethos of Islamic universalism, facilitating the expansionist movement of Islam, and sustaining the idea of an Islamic universality, which could be claimed to be virtually *sine finibus* (without limits).

This inclusive character of Islamic universalism, aimed at the *virtual* absorption of non-Muslim lands and the realisation of a realm of full plenitude in a way that was not too dissimilar to imperial conceptions of space in the Roman Empire and the *Res publica christiana*, reveals therefore an important difference from the European binary construction of national space. Although the presence of *dar al-harb* was acknowledged as an historical manifestation and agreements were ultimately taken to postpone the inclusion of non-Muslim lands and avoid the costs of a permanent *jihad*, the existence of *dar al-Islam* did not require *in principle* fixed or presumed borders to be shared with the outside states, or the presence of an outside against which its specificity could be played, as was the case with the modern construction of the national *territory*. *Dar al-Islam* was in fact imagined as an immediate presence whose nature is necessary and self-asserting, as Nietzsche might say, as a 'triumphant yes-sayer' to itself.[87] It is true that an outside, *dar al-harb*, is also represented here, but it emerges by

---

[85] Parvin and Sommer, 'Dar al-Islam', p. 7.

[86] Bat Yeor, Miriam Kochan and David Littman, *Islam and Dhimmitude: Where Civilizations Collide* (Madison, NJ: Fairleigh Dickinson University Press, 2002), p. 42.

[87] This schema aligns to Nietzsche's distinction between 'Good and Evil' and 'Good and Bad'; that is, between the dialectical logic of slave morality with *ressentiment* requiring a first, '*necessary* direction toward the outside' and the values of a pre-Christian aristocracy focusing of self-affirmation. Friedrich Wilhelm Nietzsche, *On the Genealogy of Morals* (New York: Vintage Books, 1989), p. 19.

way of a secondary movement that is not assumed to be a necessary condition for the presence of Islam itself. We have seen that the national territory's binary structure instead entails a primary definition of the domain of the outside, against which, in the guise of an absolute opposition, it is possible to think of the inside as a closed totality. While the national territory assumes its respective outside as a constitutive and irreducible exteriority, the *dar al-harb* remains a contingent and transient manifestation within history to be integrated, at some point in time, by Islam.

In attempting to offer a heuristic and illustrative representation of these two models, the following figures can perhaps account for the internal spatial dynamics that inclusivity and dualism set in motion within competing forms of territoriality. In Figure 2.1, an illustration of Islamic 'territoriality' is provided, depicting the delineation of a non-binary *structuring*; that is, a continuous and self-rearticulating territorial surface. In Figure 2.2, the spatial model of the national 'territory' is instead depicted, highlighting the constitution of a binary *structure*; that is, a closed surface modelling a dualistic representation of space. The former is obtained by resorting to the topology of the Möbius strip. It is well known that the Möbius is a three-dimensional figure that, like other topological figures, subverts Euclidean ways of representing space. Unlike simple shapes of Euclidean geometry where all points are set in a plane and neat distinctions can be drawn between the internal and the external, this figure problematises all referents of interiority and exteriority. Although it seems to embody a two-sided dimension, its open and non-orientable surface has only one side and only one boundary component. By running along the surface of the strip, in fact, it is possible to move from the foreground to the background, yet remain on the same and only side.

Because of their properties, Euclidian figures can instead conveniently be used to illustrate the spatial dimension of those political formations whose discursive organisation relies on a binary logic. As Diane Coole argued, dichotomous constructions have mainly relied on two figurative models. 'In one, a line divides space in two; in the other, a circle is drawn, its circumference marking a boundary between inner and outer. But the separation and identification of these areas make no sense unless they are internally as well as hierarchically related: each is defined by not being its other.'[88] Since these models are interpreted in the sense of higher and lower or inclusion and exclusion, the space of nation can be best represented through the delineation of a circle, emphasising the exclusionary

---

[88] Diana Coole in 'Cartographic Convulsions: Public and Private Reconsidered', *Political Theory*, 28/3 (2000): 337–54.

logic of the nation, rather than possible hierarchical implications. With its circumference epitomising the national border and therein allowing for a neat (though paradoxical on a substantial level) separation between the inside the nation and its respective outside, a circle best exemplifies the construction of a closed totality, the national *Us*, against which an outside alterity can be played. The stronger the demarcation of the circumference is imagined, the more hypertrophic and rigid the distinction between the national inside and its outside (e.g., radical forms of nationalisms).

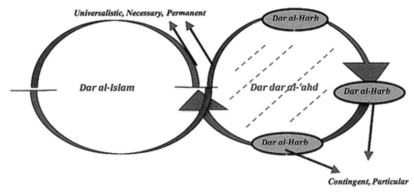

Figure 2.1   An inclusive model: Territoriality

Within this framework, *dar al-Islam* coincides in Figure 2.1 with the all-encompassing surface of the Möbius strip, expressing an inclusive spatial model, which I define in terms of *territoriality*. Non-Muslim lands in the figure can only be conceived of as internal differences or temporary manifestations of an outside to be integrated into the structuring of the universal surface. That is, *dar al-harb* maintains a contingent, particular character whose territorial specificity is subsumed by the universalistic, permanent and necessary dimension of *dar al-Islam*. For a long time, Islamic territoriality and the related notion of *ummah*, remained inclusive and accommodating, regulated by difference and integration, with an outside, *dar al-harb* and, in some respect, *dar al-'ahd*, treated as a temporary differential space to be subsumed under the banner of Islamic universalism. As Majid Khadduri observes, in fact, 'dar al-Islam, in theory, was in a state of war with the dar al-harb, because the ultimate objective of Islam was the whole world'.[89] This meant that no real and permanent outside could be thought of in the all-encompassing space of Islamic universality, for non-Muslim lands were destined to be either integrated as internal differences (in the form of tolerated communities) or Islamised and henceforth assumed as internal Muslim constituencies. In a reference to *Kitab al-Mabsut* (The Book of Expatiation), a key legal text by al- Sarakhsi, Khadduri notes that 'if the dar al-harb were reduced by Islam, the public order of *Pax Islamica* would supersede all others, and non-Muslim communities would either become part of the Islamic community or submit to its sovereignty as a tolerated religious community or as an autonomous entity possessing treaty relations with it'.[90]

The complexity of this figure will be examined in more detail when inquiring into the discourse of Sayyid Qutb in Chapter 5, thereby showing the particular re-elaboration of the traditional concept of *dar al-Islam* that this thinker instantiated. At this point, it suffices to stress the non-necessary quality that Islamic universalism traditionally ascribed to the notion of 'outside' when compared with the national model. The outside mostly retained over the centuries a vague, virtual and indistinct character, leaving hazy margins in comparison with the unambiguous, necessary and clear-cut form that it assumed in respect to the modern national border.

Figure 2.2   An exclusionary model: Territory

---

[89]   Majid Khadduri, *The Islamic Law of Nations: Shaybani's Siyar* (Baltimore, MD: Johns Hopkins Press, 1966), p. 13.
[90]   Ibid.

In Figure 2.2, the space of nation expresses an *exclusionary model*, which I define in terms of *territory*. This territory is obtained by opposing two circles so as to create an inside and an outside divided by a common boundary. The nation realises a unified sacred Self whose lines of demarcation are shared by its respective outside so that, as pointed earlier, the end of 'my' territory *necessarily* coincides with the beginning of 'yours'. We will see shortly that this same modality affects the distinction between the traditional conception of *ummah* and the modern idea of the people. Again, the difference lies not so much in the existence of an outside. It is the nature of the opposition that counts, as the opposition that a constitutive outside enacts in a binary mode remains an exclusionary and necessary one.

The spatial model provided in Figure 2.1 fits particularly well with the early expansive movement of Islam, expressing the ability of its strong universalistic ethos to absorb non-Muslim lands in this phase. The theoretical development of *dar al-Islam*, however, underwent significant changes over the centuries as a supplementary effect of internal factors. That is, as a consequence of the growing economic and customary diversification which had resulted from the territorial expansion of Islam. The massive extension of Islamic territoriality in the early centuries of the Islamic age entailed the 'inclusion' of a variety of new cultural and environmental realities under the new faith. The need to harmonise such a variety within the political Islamic order, and to relate faith and authority, was not an easy task. As the geographical expansion of Islam increased, new forms of particularism (political, ethnic, dynastic, doctrinal) arose, thereby challenging the universalistic ethos of *dar al-Islam*. Islam had to face a context which required diversity and flux to be domesticated and somehow assumed within its political, religious and doctrinal spirit; that is, harmonised under the flag of an intrinsic universalism. This produced some important shifts in the conception of *dar al-Islam* and in the legal doctrine embodying it.

Whilst 'Monists', as a more conservative stream of Islamic jurisprudence, retained the ideal of *dar al-Islam* as an unbounded kingdom with no possibility for territorial and political divisions, a more pragmatic approach acknowledged that changes were in fact occurring.[91] Since the tenth century, Muslim traders had begun to track and report geographical and cultural transformations of *dar al-Islam*. The period following the decline of the classic 'golden age' of Islamic history (758–1258) marked the beginning of a sort of medieval epoch in Islam, where cultural and political fragmentation challenged the unitary notion of Islamic universalism that the caliphate represented. After the death of

---

[91] Parvin and Sommer, 'Dar al-Islam', p. 11.

Muhammad, the office of caliph, *khalīfah*, had embodied the universalistic ideal of Islam, standing as the supreme political leader of the Muslim community, *imam*, and the holder of its power (sovereignty). With the decline of the Abbasid dynasty, however, this office faced increasing challenges. New political realities emerged with dynastic families such as the Ayyubids, Seljuks, Almoravids, claiming political autonomy.

Although the caliph maintained its nominal and symbolic role over the centuries as the guarantor of Islamic unity, the increasing number of ethnic and political divisions affected the Islamic administration of political power (not to mention the major split between Sunni and Shi'i, which occurred in the aftermath of the Prophet's death over the question of the leadership and resulted in the creation of two alternative political domains that soon developed theological differences as well). 'The battle lines inevitably became drawn across tribal, clan, and regional lines. New identities began to compete: Iraqis and Egyptians versus Syrians, Yemenis (southern Arabs) versus Mudaris (northern Arabs), Kufa against Basra, and Arabs vs. non-Arabs, and so on.'[92] New administrative, political and territorial dominions began to undermine the universalistic nature of Islamic sovereignty, fostering the consolidation of autonomous ethnic and communitarian identities, even though, for a long time, frontiers remained vague and indistinct. In fact, although Muslim geographers stressed the natural separation between regions (by mountains, rivers, and so on), Islamic and non-Islamic countries remained separated by large sections of landscape, which did not belong to any ruler.

In sum, for a long time, a tension remained at the core of the Islamic concept of *dar al-Islam*, with a sense of fluidity still pervading Islamic territoriality yet countered by the growing attention placed on frontiers by local rulers in response to the increasing visibility of political enemies. The Crusades contributed to exacerbating this tension. Non-Muslim lands were now assumed to be a fact with which the universalistic notion of *dar al-Islam* had to coexist. This in turn led to the indefinite inclusion of *dar al-harb* within the realm of *dar al-'ahd*. As European powers evolved in the form of nation states, European ideas became inescapable constructs to be faced and confronted, affecting Islamic notions of territoriality.

The insights of Parvin and Sommer are particular telling here: 'Individual allegiances were shifting from religious to territorial affiliations as Islamic law, formerly synonymous, to the Muslims, with international law, became divorced

---

[92] Abdelwahab El-Affendi, *Who Needs an Islamic State?* (London: Grey Seal, 1991), p. 171.

from affairs of state. Political segregation necessitated the adoption of territorial sovereignty and territorial law.'[93] Parvin and Sommer take these events to be a primary consequence of the Crusades, while downplaying the role of the nation state system and colonialism. It seems, however, that the encounter with modern sovereignty and modern subjectivity in the following centuries introduced a more radical rupture, infusing the Islamic conception of territoriality with a binary trait. The increasing confrontation with European colonial powers engendered the tension between the universalistic ethos of pan-Islamism and the Arab forms of nationalism that was described in the previous section, a tension that defined the genealogical background of Islamism and that Islamist discourses attempted to solve. An insight into the pan-Islamic signifier '*ummah*' will better evidence the paradigmatic difference at stake in this tension.

The Ummah

The term *ummah* is mentioned a number of times in the Qur'an, although its origin predates its Islamic utilisation, stemming, as it does, from the Arab root *umm*, 'mother, source'. In the Qur'an, we first encounter this term to signify an ensemble of single living beings, *umam*, sharing certain features. Then, mankind figures as that particular species that, departing from its 'single original *ummah*', *ummatun wahidatan*, ended up by producing more than one ensemble as a result of the plurality of ideas articulating human groups.[94] In the course of the Revelation, the *ummah* is also taken to designate the members of a wider community who constitute a 'committed' closely knit group, as well as the set of ideas of a grouping and the lifespan or civilisation of a specific historical community. In this sense, the Muslim *ummah*, *Ummatul Muslimīn*, differentiates itself from other groupings, expressing the worldwide ensemble of believers, the set of values and teachings and the new historical age that stem from and knot around the guidance of God as expressed in Islam. The *ummah* of Muslims is historically rooted in the establishment of the first Muslim community in the city of Medina, just after the Prophet Muhammad and the small group of adherents to his teachings migrated from the hostile major urban settlement of Mecca (with the so-called *hijra*, migration, that marks the beginning of the Islamic period).

The constitution of the Muslim *ummah* entailed a major shift in the way the individual's loyalty to his/her group was perceived. In social terms, for instance,

---

[93] Parvin and Sommer, 'Dar al-Islam', p. 14.
[94] Qur'an: 10:19; 11:117–19; 16:93; 42:8.

Arab tribalism in its nomadic and sedentary variants was characterised first and foremost by kinship (*silat ar-rahim*) as the most elementary form of social bond. This was not only the motif of an intense solidarity within the same tribe or with allied tribes, but also a reason for sectarianism and difference that the universalistic spirit of Islam condemned.[95] While assimilating the strong sense of brotherhood and equality of pre-Islamic Arab tribes, Islam overcame tribal particularism (often expressed in wars among tribes) subsuming it within its universalistic call. This process of assimilation engendered the re-articulation of the role of the tribe, which lost its traditional independent power to become a source of only secondary importance within Islamic universality.[96]

This transition is well reflected in the intellectual work of Arab polymath Ibn Khaldun (1332–1406). In his *Introduction to History*, he saw in tribal solidarity, *al-asabiyyah* – based on consanguinity (*nasab*) but also, as a secondary level of solidarity, on social and political affiliation (*wali*) – the primary force behind the development of human aggregations and the formation of political entities.[97] In his view, Islam was a harmonising force, which maintained and composed within its *oecumene* the 'multiplicity' of its particularisms as expressed by *al-asabiyyah*.[98] Tribal solidarity then strongly influenced – and still affects – Muslim forms of identification within the realm of Islamic territoriality, *dar al-Islam*. It can be said that the relation between Islam and tribal particularism inspired the construction of the *ummah* on a larger scale. The inclusive complexity and universality of the Muslim community stands for its ability to include differences. This is a point to be stressed when comparing the traditional notion of Muslim community with the unitary conception of nationhood. Like the notion of multitude examined in the last section, the *ummah* maintains and reflects within its universal frame a principle of difference; that is, it remains 'an inconclusive constituent relation'.[99] Its *oecumene* does not dissolve its internal

---

[95] In the Sunna, for instance, Muhammad declared: 'One who calls towards 'asabiyyah (tribal solidarity) is not from us, one who fights for 'asabiyyah is not from us and the one who dies on 'asabiyyah is not from us' (Mizan al-Hikmah, hadith # 130359); see also Qur'an: 'And hold fast all of you together to the rope of Allah, and be not disunited' Al-Imran (House of Imran), chapter 3: verse 103.

[96] Cf. Abdullah al-Ahsan, *Ummah or Nation: Identity Crisis in Contemporary Muslim Society* (Leicester: Islamic Foundation, 1992).

[97] Ibn Khaldun, *The Muqaddimah: An Introduction to History*, ed. Bruce Lawrence, trans. Franz Rosenthal (Princeton, NJ: Princeton University Press, 2005).

[98] Cf. Francesco Gabrieli, 'Il concetto di 'asabiyya nel pensiero storico di Ibn Khaldun', in *L'Islam nella storia. Saggi di storia e storiografia musulmana* (Bari: Dedalo spa, 1966).

[99] Hardt and Negri, *Empire*, p. 103; See also Paolo Virno, 'Virtuosity and Revolution: The Political Theory of Exodus', in Paolo Virno and Michael Hardt (eds), *Radical Thought in*

distinctive dynamics. It rather articulates them as a multiplicity of singularities expressing their historical and cultural manifestations.

As with the case of *dar al-Islam*, a religious and normative character of the *ummah* informed this universality. Talal Asad, for instance, claims that, in classical theological views, the Islamic *ummah* is 'not an imagined community on a par with the Arab nation waiting to be politically unified but a theologically defined space enabling Muslims to practice the disciplines of *din* in the world'.[100] Although Asad acknowledges the communitarian nature of the *ummah*, he claims that members of every community imagined the *ummah* to be based on a specific character and related to each other on the basis of that feature. 'The crucial point therefore is not that it is imagined but that what is imagined predicates distinctive modes of being and acting. The Islamic *ummah* presupposes individuals who are self-governing but not autonomous.'[101] This means that while functioning as a universal abstract principle, the shared ethical form of life that the *ummah* expresses, in conjunction with its spatial transposal in the *dar al-Islam*, is based on a 'multiplicity' of representations, each one defining a 'particular' (cultural, historical), 'mode of being' of that universality. The complexity implied by the theological space of the *ummah* is solved politically in the immediacy of its historical and social articulations. The *ummah* figures as the abstract universe, whose distinctive manifestations at the same time enact and are the expression of its inclusive and complex multiplicity.

As discussed earlier, the expansion of *dar al-Islam* entailed the emergence of new factors (e.g., inclusion of rural regions, intra-Islamic divisions and differences), which challenged the fluid conceptualisation of Islamic territoriality across the centuries. Against this backdrop, the caliphate provided a powerful symbol – a major *nodal point* – against which the complexity and universality of the *ummah* could be maintained. In fact, neither such changes or the progressive secularisation and politicisation of the institution of the caliphate, nor its increasing enfeeblement across time or the emergence of new political enemies outside the domain of Islam succeeded in winning its universalistic ethos once and for all. This is best demonstrated by the importance that the symbolic recognition or sanctioning from the caliph had for local Muslim rulers over the centuries – not to speak of the legitimising power played by the myth of a direct transferral of the caliphate from the Abbasids to the following rulers since the thirteenth century. Although changes have certainly produced some

---

Italy (Minneapolis, MN: University of Minnesota Press, 1996), pp. 189–210.
[100] Asad, *Formations of the Secular*, p. 197.
[101] Ibid.

desedimenting effects, engendering a first oscillation between universalistic and particular conceptions of the Muslim community, for a long time the universalistic ethos of Islam prevailed against centrifugal forces. One peculiarity of the *ummah* remained its open character, the manner by which it was marked by a notion of integration rather than opposition and closure towards the outside, as is the case with the concept of the nation. This inclusive stance is best demonstrated by the variety of ethnic groups that, at different times, took pre-eminence over the *ummah*, assuming the historical role of its diffusion and expansion (i.e. in the dominion of Arabs, Mongols, Turks, and so forth).[102]

Another important example in this direction is the traditional notion of *dawla*, the political entity that, following the increasing political fragmentation of Islam after the decline of the Abbasids in the thirteenth century, begun to appear as administrative units of *dar al-Islam*. Although the *dawla* is often associated with the concept of nation state, the two constructs reveal significant conceptual differences. Unlike the nation state, the *dawla* figured as a substantially open entity, expressing a complex sense of loyalty which blurred the distinction between inside and outside. The ruler of the *dawla* was not only accountable internally towards its domestic constituencies (the 'subjects' of the *dawla*). An outward accountability was also established externally with the caliph, which epitomised the whole Muslim community on a global scale.[103] The focus can be here placed upon the global dimension of both *dar al-Islam* and the *ummah*, revealing the pre-eminence of a universalistic paradigm.

In this regard, it was European military and cultural penetration across Islamic lands since the eighteenth century that first posed a radical challenge to the universalistic doctrine of the community. The colonial dissemination of modern paradigms opened up a *radical* breach in the discursive universe of Islam, engendering the traumatic irruption of dislocation and desedimentation. Within this passage, a crucial moment came with the decision of Kemal Atatürk to abolish the caliphate in 1924. Mustafa Kemal Atatürk (1881–1938) was an army officer, and leading figure of the Young Turk Revolution which had seized power from the declining regime of Sultan Abdül Hamid II in 1908, thereby promoting important constitutional reforms.[104] After the defeat of the Ottoman

---

[102] Cf. Stefano Allievi, *Musulmani d'Occidente: Tendenze dell'Islam Europeo* (Rome: Carocci, 2002), pp. 21–5.

[103] Tamim Barghuthi, *The Umma and the Dawla: The Nation State and the Arab Middle East* (London and Ann Arbor, MI: Pluto Press, 2008).

[104] The Young Turks were an alliance of different groups of Turkish nationalists, willing to promote constitutional reforms in the Ottoman Empire based on pluralism, and Western-oriented secularism.

Empire in the First World War, Kemal Atatürk led the Turkish national movement towards the foundation of the Republic of Turkey, becoming its first President. From this institutional position, he endorsed a rapid and radical transformation of the former Ottoman Empire into a modern, democratic, and secular nation state, contributing to the dissemination of a variant of the national discourse marked by a strong secular, authoritarian and militarist character, and known as Kemalism.[105] Within few years most traditional institutions at the core of the Ottoman Empire were also dismantled, challenging the role of tradition as a dominant symbolic scenario.

As previously mentioned, a certain fluid and creative use of tradition enabled the institution of the caliphate to play a central symbolic role over the centuries, functioning as the master signifier of the Muslim community. This role proved to be vital in resisting centrifugal forces within *dar al-Islam*, requiring local rulers, for instance, to demand official investiture to the caliph. It is therefore not surprising that a strong sense of anxiety spread in the Muslim world when the caliphate was abolished in 1924 following the replacement of the Ottoman Empire with the 'modern' Republic of Turkey. A number of unsuccessful international conferences in the following decades aimed at re-establishing this institution outside Turkey reflecting the sense of lost identity that the abolition of the caliphate enacted in Muslims settings, from India to Egypt.

In a highly destabilised context marked by colonialism, among the utmost factors of desedimentation of Muslim settings the defeat of the Ottoman Empire in the First World War, the dissemination of nationalist discourses in the form of local nationalisms, pan-Arabism and Kemalism, and the ultimate abolition of the caliphate did certainly play a crucial role. The ending of the caliphate denoted the traumatic penetration of modern dualistic discourses into the Islamic land, with the traditional ethos of Islamic universalism now irremediably challenged by binary representations of space and community so central to national discourses. It is this historical context that defines the genealogical background of Islamism, with the first Islamist discourse articulated in 1928 by Hasan al-Banna, the founder of the Muslim Brotherhood.

---

[105] Cf. Kemal H. Karpat, *The Politicization of Islam: Reconstructing Identity, State, Faith, and Community in the Late Ottoman State* (New York and Oxford: Oxford University Press, 2001); and B.S. Sayyid, *A Fundamental Fear: Eurocentrism and the Emergence of Islamism* (London: Zed Books, 1997).

Chapter 3
Globalisation and Transmodernity

Every story is a travel story – a spatial practice.[1]

In recent years, terms such as 'globalisation', 'virtuality', 'flexibility' have played a primary symbolic function, accounting for some of the major changes of our contemporary time and denoting the emergence of new discourses that challenge consolidated representations of the world. The resulting debates about the effects of globalisation and the current state of affairs of capitalism have been translated into distinctive symbolic structures that are used to organise respective views discursively. Discourses on difference, hybridity, virtual communities, empire, global citizenship, *liquid, post-,* or *hyper-* modernity, for instance, question the hegemonic position that widely accepted representations about reality have covered so far – e.g., in the form of *modern* discourses about the nation state, the liberal dichotomy between private and public spheres, the core-periphery circulation of capital, the rigid and hierarchical distinction among First, Second and Third World countries and the modern tension between organic communities and mechanic societies. In turn, we have seen that this latter set of discourses posed a similar challenge to the discursive universe preceding their emergence and organising the hitherto dominant vision of the world: *traditional* universalistic discourses about the *Caliphate* in Muslim settings or the *Res Publica* Christiana in Europe, the transcendent nature of sovereignty, geocentrism, and so forth. A challenge that did not entail the replacement of one set of discourses with another, but rather involved their coexistence and, henceforth, mutual competition in the ability to make the world *readable*. Hence a testimony to the ability of 'traditional' views about God to survive both the 'modern' *furor theologicus* of Enlightenment and *Zarathustra's* pronouncement about the death of God, and to coexist with modernist socio-economic categories about 'institutional differentiation', 'scientific rationality', the belief in 'progress', 'mature' societies, etc.

Similarly, we can now testify to the competition between views that preserve a 'modern' Westphalian representation of the world, maintaining the role of the

---

[1] Michel De Certeau, *The Practice of Everyday Life* (Berkeley, CA: University of California Press, 1984), p. 115.

nation state as the main actor in international affairs, and those views that point to the erosion of the nation state's legitimacy or to the concrete disappearance of national sovereignty from global politics. Here, the role of modern discourses has been challenged by new visions that seek to provide a renovated representation of reality accounting for a global and decentred context; a tension that is best exemplified by the linguistic competition between expressions such as *international relations* and *world politics* in most political science texts.

The following pages attempt an examination of the symbolic structure sustaining most of the discourses that have emerged in the last decades, and that inform what shall be named here *transmodernity*. It is useful to remark that the term transmodernity in this study is used to distinguish this concept from the common analytical category of postmodernity, so highlighting a symbolic and discursive dimension. As amply discussed in the previous chapters, we are proposing a *discourse-centred reading* of tradition, modernity and postmodernity, which transcends their qualification as definite historical epochs or sociological conditions (otherwise well exemplified by the prefix *post-* of postmodernity indicating a condition following modernity). In this respect, although an intimate link marks the relation between transmodernity and postmodernity, they remain distinct notions insofar as the latter provides the former with an 'internal' discursive component, one that, among others, contributes to the consolidation of its morphological structure. As we will see, transmodernity figures as a broader discursive scenario incorporating both sociological and historical discourses about *postmodernity* as well as so-called *postmodernist* political and philosophical theories. Transmodernity not only coincides with each of these specific domains, but also crosses them embodying different discursive connotations. Hence the prefix *trans-*, which aims to highlight the discursive complexity of transmodernity, its *traversing* the restricted historical, sociological or philosophical dimension of *postmodernity* and *postmodernism*. But the prefix *trans-* serves also the task of uncovering a specific modality of engagement with the modern scenario, reflecting the symbolic condition of a coextensive *over-development* of modernity.

On a broad perspective, to inquire into the symbolic function of transmodernity requires uncovering the role that globalisation has been playing in its consolidation. In the following section, three major desedimenting effects of globalisation will be examined, i.e., *spatial displacement*, *virtuality* and *fragmentation*, which help us detect the 'critical' dimension of globalisation as a traumatic process of dislocation of social space. A reference to this broader context of desedimentation will permit mapping out, in the last part of the chapter, an illustrative range of discourses, which we consider to be central to the structuring of the transmodern symbolic scenario.

The Global Context: Spatial Displacement, Virtuality and Fragmentation

As an integral part of our contemporary language, the term 'globalisation' has, over the last few decades, come to signify the process of increasing 'interconnectedness' occurring on a global scale in almost every sphere of life. We saw already that opinions differ about the extent of such a process as well as the vocabulary that can best account for it. In terms of global politics, for instance, self-called 'transformationalists' have taken the changes brought about by globalisation to be productive of a new scenario characterised by the erosion of the 'modern' divide between domestic and international affairs.[2] For some, this reflects a dwindling of the power of national discourses. Nation states are said to have lost massive portions of their sovereignty to military and political transnational organisations (e.g., UN agencies, NATO, NGOs, corporations, etc.), while even their ability to regulate their exchange rates autonomously has been enfeebled, subject as they are to the fluctuations of global finance.[3] Sceptics, on the other hand, maintain that despite an increasing global interconnection, the juridical notion of national sovereignty still plays an essential function, testifying to a heightened function of the nation state in the 'model of sectoral governance'.[4] Others have introduced a higher degree of complexity. According to Wendy Brown the often-celebrated demise of national sovereignty can hardly be conceived as the inaugural moment of a post-sovereign or post-state era. Countering what in her reading is Michael Hardt and Antonio Negri's claim that 'nation-state sovereignty is transformed into global Empire', and Giorgio Agamben's thesis that 'sovereignty has metamorphosed into the worldwide production and sacrifice of bare life (global civil war)', Brown maintains that

---

[2] Cf. Anthony McGrew, 'Globalization and Global Politics', in John Baylis and Steve Smith (eds), *The Globalization of World Politics: An Introduction to International Relations* (Oxford: Oxford University Press, 2005, 3rd edn), pp. 19–40.

[3] Cf. K. Ohmae, *The End of the Nation State* (New York: Free Press, 1995); J.A. Scholte, *Globalization: A Critical Introduction* (London: Macmillan, 2000); Michael Hardt and Antonio Negri, *Empire* (London: Harvard University Press, 2000).

[4] M. Mann, 'Has *Globalization* Ended the Rise of the *Nation-State*?', *Review of International Political Economy*, 4/3 (1997): 472–96; R. Gilpin, *Global Political Economy* (Princeton, NJ: Princeton University Press, 2001).

states endure as *non-sovereign* actors in a post-Westphalian world.[5] What the increasing erosion of national sovereignty signals is rather the separation of the Westphalian correlation between modern sovereignty and the state, and the gradual subsumption of the former to the yoke of political economy (capital) and religiously legitimated violence, two domains that the Westphalian order had attempted to regulate.

Despite differences about the *degree* and the *intensity* of global transformations, most of the changes occurred over the last 40 years have been, however, amply acknowledged and scrutinised, with widespread consensus emphasising the *novelty* that globalisation would embody. Transformations in different parts of the world have thus been detected in the realm of labour, exchange and production, which have led to the affirmation of new central categories in social and political analysis such as 'world market' and 'post-Fordist society'.[6] The re-shaping of the international arena after the end of the Cold War, a radical process of deterritorialisation and cultural deracination accompanied by massive movements of people across the world, and crucial innovations in the realm of technology – with informatisation affecting not only communication but also industrial production – have been taken to reflect the symptoms of an epochal transformation of political, economic and cultural paradigms. Although contact and substantial migrations of people have always occurred in history, and technology and trade have always entailed forms of exchange – with the very process of modernisation 'naturally' leading to a capitalist world-system – it is only with globalisation that the world is said to have finally become a *global network*.[7] Within this general framework, new factors embody the *desedimenting* power of globalisation, promoting the disarticulation of dominant hegemonic fields of discursivity and the emergence of new 'transmodern' representations of space and subjectivity. These desedimenting effects of globalisation parallels

---

[5] W. Brown, *Walled States, Waning Sovereignty* (Brooklyn, NY: Zone Books, 2010), p. 23.

[6] Roughly, with 'post-Fordism' we point here to the transition from a rigid organisation of labour and a homogenised form of economy based on national loyalties (so-called Fordism) to a transnational, flexible and diversified regime of production and exchange of capital. In terms of the organisation of labour, it involves the valorisation of difference, with the so-called feminisation of the work force, and increasing levels of flexibility and variety in the skills and knowledge of workers. The Fordist sociological targeting of social classes is furthermore abandoned in favour of a growing attention on 'consumers' (with a focus on taste, lifestyle, interests which problematises the modern notion of class). Cf. Ash Amin (ed.), *Post-Fordism: A Reader* (Oxford: Blackwell, 1994).

[7] Cf. Immanuel Maurice Wallerstein, *Utopistics: or Historical Choices of the Twenty-First Century* (New York: New Press, 1998).

the kind of discursive desedimentation that we discussed in Chapter 2 with reference to colonialism, and the related appearance of modern discourses that challenged traditional representations of the world.

Spatial Displacement and Virtuality

According to David Harvey, a basic feature of globalisation and one that is constitutive of a new human predicament – the so-called 'postmodern condition' – can be found in what he calls 'time-space compression'.[8] This expression refers to the general tendency of 'capitalist modernisation to be very much about speed-up and acceleration in the pace of economic processes and, hence, social life'.[9] A continuous acceleration of the time of production and circulation of exchange enabled capital – in a process of increasing mobility and internationalisation – to erode spatial barriers, melting differentiated places into a global indistinct space, and transforming local economies into a *global market*. Technology has played a central role in this context, bringing about dramatic transformations in the way in which space, time and communication are perceived. In accounting for these changes, the expression *spatial displacement* identifies in this study a sort of double movement produced by this process, involving both the *dislocation* and *re-shaping* of notions of *space* and related cognitions of *time*.

In the early days of so-called Computer-mediated Communication (CMC), the expression 'electronic highway' was used to highlight the sense of optimism that informatisation gave rise to by promising to bridge the gaps between remote geographical areas of the world.[10] The sensation that a 'second media age' had just started was thus immediately associated to a general idea of spatial discovery.[11] The novelty of this technological innovation was in fact located in its ability 'to do by way of electronic pathway what cement roads were unable to do, namely, connect us rather than atomise, put us at the controls of a "vehicle" and yet not detach us from the rest of the world'.[12] What soon became clear, however, was

---

[8] David Harvey, *The Condition of Postmodernity: An Enquiry into the Origins of Cultural Change* (Oxford: Blackwell, 1990).

[9] Ibid., p. 230.

[10] The expression 'Information Superhighway' was popularised in the early 1990s by USA Vice President Al Gore who encouraged the administration's plan (*Global Information Infrastructure*) to improve the structure and the scope of the Internet; see Al Gore, 'Forging a New Athenian Age of Democracy', *Intermedia*, 22/2 (1995): 4–6.

[11] Mark Poster, *The Second Media Age* (Cambridge: Polity Press, 1995).

[12] Steven G. Jones (ed.), *CyberSociety: Computer-Mediated Communication and Community* (Thousand Oaks, CA: London: SAGE, 1995), p. 11.

that the information highway was not only the simple *medium* of our travelling, but was itself also a *place*. In this place new ways of thinking, new discourses and narratives began quickly to emerge and circulate, denoting the emergence of a new social construction of reality that was not just constituted *by* the Internet, but *in* the Internet. In a pioneering work on electronic communication, Steve Jones quickly noticed that CMC 'not only structures social relations, it is the space within which the relations occur and the tool that individuals use to enter that space. It is more than the context within which social relations occur (although it is that, too), for it is commented on and imaginatively constructed by symbolic processes initiated and maintained by individuals and groups'.[13] Notions such as *cyberspace* – first used by William Gibson in his 1984 novel *Neuromancer* – and *virtual reality*, indicated not only the new technological structure of multimedia communication but also the emergence of a new way of *experiencing* space and reality. They expressed the double dimension involved in the process of spatial displacement as the dislocation of the way space and time were hitherto perceived, and the promotion, at the same time, of new formulations of reality. Cyberspace and virtual reality are important examples of the intimate link existing between the very process of spatial displacement and the recent phenomenon of *virtuality*.

Virtuality is to be thought of as a new way of perceiving reality based on the deployment and *inter*-action of technological and computerised artefacts. Its novelty lies in its ability to problematise *spatiality*, *temporality* and *institutionalised space* (public and private spheres). When considering *spatiality*, for example, virtuality blurs not only the phenomenological understanding of space, but also all that constitutes its inner referentials (e.g., presence and absence, closeness and remoteness, origin and destination). Media theorist Mark Nunes noted that social networking websites, chat rooms or simple emails encourage users to interact by using metaphors of proximity rather than distance.[14] This phenomenon also modifies a further phenomenological referent: *temporality*. The immediacy of chat rooms, emails and file-sharing software permit an *enduring* and *simultaneous* interconnection across users. Moreover, new developments in informatisation, such as Ubiquitous Computing or Augmented Reality, contribute to modifying our very cognition of material things. Objects become *sensible*, moving in relation to our movements; listening, speaking, satisfying and anticipating everyday needs in a continuous and imperceptible way. In

---

[13] Ibid., p. 16.
[14] Mark Nunes, 'Baudrillard in Cyberspace: Internet, Virtuality, and Postmodernity', *Style*, 29/2 (1995): 322.

this scenario, virtuality – in the form of cyberspace – questions the otherwise modern institutionalisation of social space and its organisation around a public/private divide.

In the previous chapter, emphasis has been put on the dualistic logic underpinning important modern constructions such as secular space, nationality, individuality, and so forth. Over the last decades, spatial displacement and virtuality have contributed to the desedimentation of these representations, engendering new spatial and social imaginaries that overcome the strict binary organisation of modern spaces. Emblematic of these transformations is the use of the term *forum*. Once referring to the wide and 'open court' of a Roman city in which the market was situated and administrative, religious, and juridical general affairs were undertaken, it embodied the realm of the outside where 'public' life was organised. Unlike its classical connotation, the term is now associated with a new gathering space in which the formation of public opinion has been relocated within its 'private' counterpart: the house. In the virtuality of the forum, subjects celebrate the contemporary figure of the indistinction between the public and the private, the spatial tension of speech that exceeds the dual field of the public and the private. Today, the Internet provides us with a new measure of *publicness*, whereby personal popularity is less and less dependent on public recognition outside in the street, and is increasingly reliant on the number of Google search-results pages in which one's name is listed, which takes place in the intimacy of one's home. This discussion highlights the way in which global and technological changes have been re-shaping important levels of experience. Another major sign of globalisation, however, which we define as *fragmentation*, has also undermined established representations of space and subjectivity.

Fragmentation

This trend towards an increased blurring of binaries, and the capacity of virtuality to overcome the modern organisation of institutionalised space should be considered alongside the process of *subjective decentring* that globalisation and informatisation have fostered in the last decades. This is a process that we call *fragmentation*. While spatial displacement and virtuality suggest some form of dislocation occurring on established representations of *space* and *time*, a focus on fragmentation requires an examination of the particular disarticulation that modern *subjectivity* constructions have undergone with the fading of modern binaries.

We pointed earlier to the intimate relation between globalisation and informatisation. We should now stress that this relation entails a *critical* transition: a movement from a period of mechanisation and industrialisation to that of a *quantitative* and *qualitative* domination of services and information in the domain of production. While the process of industrialisation remains, it has been transformed through the emergence of methods of production centring upon the utilisation and manipulation of information. Despite problems related to spatial displacement, this transition has led to a process of increasing *intensification* of the internal dynamics organising modern constructions of social space. This point can be better illustrated by referring briefly to the debate about individualism. In Chapter 2, we pointed to the binary logic organising the relation between the modern 'individual' and his/her social and cultural outside, emphasising the emergence of modern discourses about social atomism and individualism with which a general sense of lost sociability was grieved and described as a modern disquiet. Against this scenario, social and political analyses in the last 40 years have insisted on the increasing erosion that modern binary representations of social life would undergo as an effect of the recent overlap of communication and informatisation. This is particularly evident as far as the modern dualistic organisation of political and social space is concerned, with its strict division between the private and public. As Hardt and Negri observe: 'the liberal notion of the public, the place outside where we act in the presence of others, has been both universalized (because we are always now under the gaze of others, monitored by safety cameras) and sublimated or de-actualized in the virtual spaces of the spectacle. The end of the outside is the end of liberal politics'.[15] Baudrillard has similarly analysed the dissolution of modern paradigms, progressing beyond Guy Debord's 1967 anticipatory vision of the society of spectacle produced by communication as a virtual place, a non-place of politics that tends to nullify the distinction between inside and outside.[16] According to Baudrillard, 'obscenity' came soon to replace 'spectacle', bringing about a new condition of transparency, which further develops the process of nullification of modern categories:

---

[15] Michael Hardt and Antonio Negri, *Empire* (London: Harvard University Press, 2000), pp. 188–9. See also the interesting analysis of Diana Coole in 'Cartographic Convulsions: Public and Private Reconsidered', *Political Theory*, 28/3 (2000): 337–54. Coole questions the liberal public/private dichotomy, which according to her should be problematised pointing to a further differentiation between the 'domestic' realm of family, economy (work and production), and state.

[16] See Guy Debord, *La société du spectacle* (Paris: Buchet-Chastel, 1967).

Neither public is yet a spectacle, nor is private still a secret ... The consumer society was lived under the sign of alienation; it was a society of the spectacle, and the spectacle, even if alienated, is never obscene. Obscenity begins when there is no more spectacle, no more stage, no more theatre, no more illusion, when every-thing becomes immediately transparent, visible, exposed in the raw and inexorable light of information and communication. *We no longer partake of the drama of alienation, but are in the ecstasy of communication.*[17]

It is within this transformation that we locate the shift from the *alienated* subject of the modern world to the *fragmented* subject of transmodernity, pointing to a process of de-centring of subjectivity. Unlike atomism, *fragmentation* does not occur as a result of lost sociability or from the incapacity to refer any longer to a society (no longer perceptible even as a trace). Instead, it stands as the outcome of a *hyper-intensification* of the modern binaries which had opposed individuals to society. Baudrillard uses the notion of 'hypertelia' (from the Greek *hyper* 'over, beyond, above measure' and *thele* 'nipple' or *thelys theleia thelia* 'female') to refer to the movement of a system beyond its own ends, of a model that outdoes the state it aims at comprehending. The term is borrowed from biology and indicates a condition of over-development of an organ (e.g., supernumerary nipples or mammary glands), which compromises its functionality, expressing an 'excess of functional imperatives'.[18] Such a notion is particularly useful when considering the movement of over-development that we propose in relation to modern constructions, where the over-emphasis on the centre of the individual-inside against the social-outside was described as the result of a constant but increasing process of intensification of the dualistic logic underpinning it. Following this same process of intensification and over-development, largely strengthened by the constant acceleration of capitalist processes and the effects of globalisation and informatisation, we see that the growing *focus* on the individual centre has paved the way for its critical fragmentation or implosion.

While the modern emphasis on the opposition 'individual-society' *initially* produced atomism, its inner over-development has brought about the disappearance of this opposition and the corresponding emergence of fragmentation. When modern subjectivity becomes fractured as a result of the fading of the binaries that lie behind its construction, then fragmentation emerges as a *residual* entity. It could be said that where the modern *individual*-self experiences a loss of sociability, the fragmented *subject* produced by

---

[17] Jean Baudrillard, *The Ecstasy of Communication* (NY: Semiotext(e), 1988), pp. 21–2.
[18] J. Baudrillard, *The Transparency of Evil* (New York: Verso, 1993), p. 31.

globalisation and informatisation experiences the loss not only of the public but also of the private. Being also *deprived of the private*, the fragmented subject experiences the loss of the modern Self. Hence a discursive universe that would aspire to appeal to a fragmented subject should start by inventing a new form of selfhood. We noticed that modern discourses such as nationalism and communism reconstructed identities by promising to fill the void left by the lack of sociability, thereby providing a new sense of *belongingness*. Hence, the modern symbolic appeal of signifiers such as 'corporatism', 'comradeship', 'fellowship' and lay or religious 'brotherhood' after the French Revolution. In a time in which both public and private vanish, a *transmodern* discourse points to the reinvention of notions of selfhood and community beyond any binary opposition to a specific outside.

The Transmodern Symbolic Scenario

Before mapping out the range of discourses and signifiers that have most contributed to the emergence of transmodernity as a *symbolic scenario*, a point needs to be stressed. Although spatial displacement, virtuality and fragmentation are constitutive features of globalisation, it would be inappropriate to assert that they affect the entire world in the same manner and with the same intensity, producing similar problems of desedimentation everywhere. In some contexts, in coping with the challenge posed by modern discourses over their traditional equivalents, people might experience problems of excessive individualism, loss of sociability and social atomism. Other environments might be more sensitive to the desedimenting effects of globalisation, promoting new formulations of subjectivity beyond modern binaries (private vs. public, domestic vs. foreign, etc.). We are considering here a 'complex' linguistic matrix within which different symbolic scenarios operate simultaneously, overlapping and even opposing each other with varying degrees of intensity. This is a crucial point, as it is in reference to such a complex matrix that we can grasp the discursive specificity of the Islamist articulations examined in this study, differentiating between different modes of constructing space and subjectivity within these discourses. We also mentioned already that the complexity of such a matrix is reflected in the very term *trans*-modernity, which has been used here to highlight its internal discursive intricacy vis-à-vis common readings of *postmodernity* as the historical epoch or sociological condition replacing modernity. From this perspective, transmodernity has been described in the previous pages as the symbolic condition of a coextensive *over-development* of modernity, one that finds its condition of possibility in the hypertelic implosion of modern binaries under the pressure of globalisation.

An example of the discursive complexity described here is the recent debate in psychoanalysis about the radical change that is allegedly occurring in our contemporary era concerning the 'end of the paternal dogma'; that is, the erosion of the transcendental function of the father.[19] Here, the idea is that *hyper-* or *post-* modernity would be responsible for what has been called the 'decline of the Oedipus, where the paradigmatic mode of subjectivity is no longer the subject integrated into the paternal Law through symbolic castration'.[20] This entails the transition from a modern ideal of limitation and sacrifice to a self-referential logic of profit for profit's sake, which transforms social bonds into objectified and consumerist relations. In a system of unleashed consumerism, whose message is 'disguise the limit, *just do it*', social relations would face a sort of 'melting into air' of the experience of the limit (limits to one's own pleasure for instance) – a limit that was once embodied by the paternal function in psychoanalysis as a metaphorical stand-in for symbolic castration – asking subjects to produce and consume increasing quotes of pleasure.

The point to be emphasised here is that whether the decline of the Oedipus is acknowledged or not depends upon which reservoir we use to 'read' social reality and the type of discourse that we are considering. Do we tend, for instance, to rely in our life on a discourse celebrating the limiting function of the Law, thereby promoting austerity, prohibition and sacrifice of our desire, or to a discourse extolling the ideal of unlimited and dissipating enjoyment? Interestingly, Žižek points to the current coexistence between the modern discourse of democracy, which manifests a hysterical structure valorising the central function of desire, and the multicultural discourse of late capitalism, with its perverse injunction to enjoy.[21] What Žižek emphasises here is the contemporary overlapping of modernity and transmodernity, desire and perversion, politics and post-politics, conflict and illusion of perpetual peace within the general structure of the symbolic.

Having established that transmodernity stands as a symbolic scenario alongside tradition and modernity, and that this scenario finds its 'paradigmatic' point of consistency in the over-development of modernity, it is possible to define transmodernity as *the symbolic condition under which modernity experiences a sense of crisis as the result of a higher degree of sophistication*. Spatial

---

[19] Michel Tort, *La fin du dogme paternel* (Paris: Flammarion, 2007).
[20] Slavoj Žižek, *The Ticklish Subject: The Absent Centre of Political Ontology* (London: Verso, 2000), p. 248.
[21] Ibid., p. 248.

displacement, virtuality and fragmentation intensify an over-development of modern binaries to a critical point of disruption, where modern conceptions of space and subjectivity fade. It is at this critical point that new transmodern formulations of selfhood and space are enacted and articulated, displaying their counter-hegemonic action in the desedimented space of the social. But how can one account for transmodernity from a semiotic perspective? We argued that three main sources contribute to determining the modern scenario, each one condensing a more or less defined range of discourses (i.e., structural, moral and ideological). Naturally, the borders of such a categorisation are not clear-cut. They rather play a purely indicative function, distinguishing between different levels of the debate about modernity. It can be said, for instance, that discourses contributing to the ideological connotation of modernity, such as liberalism or socialism, partake also in the determination of a moral connotation of modernity focusing on individualism and alienation. Using this categorisation as a point of departure, we will now account for a range of discourses that have emerged as an effect of the process of desedimentation enacted by spatial displacement, fragmentation and virtuality. Again, the allocation of discourses to specific semiotic connotations of transmodernity is purely indicative insofar as each transmodern discourse might contribute to the definition of more than one connotation resonating on different levels.

Transmodernity: An Ideological Connotation

A point of departure in understanding the diversified range of problems that transmodern discourses have tackled is the well-known notion of 'postmodernity'. Over the last 40 years, this term has evoked a plurality of approaches animating a dynamic ongoing debate. At first glance, the set of discourses that constitute the concept of 'postmodernism' define what could be understood as an *ideological connotation* of transmodernity. Postmodernist perspectives, particularly when associated to post-colonial analyses, reflect the general attempt to question modernity and its related forms of power and knowledge. Whether through the analytical critique of rationality that emerged with the Enlightenment or through an evaluation of colonialism as a power practice intrinsically related to modernity, all these perspectives stand together in the contestation of essentialist and dichotomous modern paradigms and the common celebration of notions of difference and multiplicity. In the face of modern binaries hierarchically dividing the world between centre and periphery, civilised and uncivilised, colonial powers and colonised populations, postmodernist discourses focus on 'transnational citizenship' (Balibar, 2004), 'diaspora communities' (Bhabha,

1994), 'hybridity' (Brah and Coombes, 2000), 'liminality' (d'Haen and Bertens, 1994), 'mestiza' (Anzaldúa, 1999), 'cyber identity' (Haraway, 1991; Turkle, 1995), 'transgender' (Stone, 1991). They aim to deconstruct modern binaries, promoting the elaboration of anti-foundationalist and anti-dichotomous subjectivities (the mestizo/a, the transgender, the cyborg, the nomad, etc., all categories used to go beyond the opposition between the white and the black, the masculine and the feminine, the organic and the inorganic, the domestic and the foreign, and so forth).[22] Social theorist Krishan Kumar, for one, points out that despite old essentialist approaches that continue to reside even amongst multiculturalist theorists, 'the future appears as one of "hyphenation", "hybridity", "syncretisation", "creolisation", and the creative invention of "diaspora cultures"'.[23] These are all emblematic examples of the range of signifiers that postmodernist theories articulate, contributing to the symbolic definition of a *transmodern* discursive scenario.

Despite aspiring to promote political resistance, some 'critics' have described postmodernist tendencies as the 'ideological' superstructure of late capitalism (Jameson, 1991), which, for some, have followed the erosion of the left at the end of the Cold War (Anderson, 1998).[24] The constitutive features of

---

[22] A detailed examination of postmodernist theorists lies outside the scope of this book. The above-mentioned authors, however, are indicative of this trend: Etienne Balibar, *We, The People of Europe?: Reflections on Transnational Citizenship* (Princeton, NJ, and Oxford: Princeton University Press, 2004); Homi K. Bhabha, *The Location of Culture* (London: Routledge, 1994); Krishan Kumar, *From Post-Industrial to Post-Modern Society: New Theories of the Contemporary World* (New York: Wiley-Blackwell, 2004); Avtar Brah, *Cartographies of Diaspora: Contesting Identities* (London: Routledge, 1996); Avtar Brah and Annie E. Coombes (eds), *Hybridity and Its Discontents: Politics, Science, Culture* (London: Routledge, 2000); Theo d'Haen and Hans Bertens (eds), *Liminal Postmodernisms: The Postmodern, The (Post-)Colonial and the (Post-)Feminist* (Amsterdam: Rodopi B.V. Editions, 1994); Gloria E. Anzaldúa, *Borderlands/La Frontera: The New Mestiza* (San Francisco, CA: Aunt Lute Books, 1999); Vilém Flusser, 'Thinking about Nomadism', in A. Finger (ed.), *The Freedom of the Migrant: Objections to Nationalism* (Urbana, IL: University of Illinois Press, 2003); Michel Maffesoli, *Du nomadisme: Vagabondages initiatiques* (Paris: Librairie Générale Française, 2000).

[23] Krishan Kumar, 'The Nation-State, the European Union and the Transnational Identities', in Nezar N. AlSayyad and Manuel Castells (eds), *Muslim Europe or Euro-Islam: Politics, Culture, and Citizenship in the Age of Globalization* (Oxford: Lexington Books, 2002), p. 60.

[24] See Fredric Jameson, *Postmodernism: or, The Cultural Logic of Late Capitalism* (London: Verso, 1991); David Harvey, *The Condition of Postmodernity: An Enquiry into the Origins of Cultural Change* (Oxford: Blackwell, 1990); Perry Anderson, *The Origins of Postmodernity* (London: Verso, 1998).

postmodernism have been located in the aesthetics of citationism, or in a mode of textual practice underlying the widespread adoption of a 'soft relativism' (Taylor, 1991).[25] In a provocative and seminal essay, Habermas accused postmodernism of constituting a mere recurrence of a Counter-Enlightenment project.[26] Notions such as 'liminal' or 'hybrid' identity, 'internationalism of people in the diaspora', as well as the attention given to local and subcultures or to the relativistic nature of culture itself, have constituted, for some critics, the very core of postmodernist ideological approaches. A postmodernist anti-foundationalist perspective tends to use the play of difference and contingency against logocentric 'subjective' representations (gender, social, cultural, etc.) in the ultimate celebration of the pleasures of the 'local, the popular, and, above all, the body', thereby becoming a 'ludic postmodernism'.[27] Although able to deconstruct and disarticulate modern discourses and open up a new space for discursive articulations, postmodernism would represent the ultimate product of late capitalism and late patriarchy. Far from providing an effective remedy against forms of domination, postmodern discourses have been seen as the 'symptoms of the passage' towards new forms of global governance.[28] Hardt and Negri note that new economic and political powers have achieved a postmodernist mindset in recent years, thriving upon the very fluid subjectivities and micro-differences that postmodernism extols. New practices of marketing and consumption suggest the increasing valorisation of a postmodernist polity based on difference. 'Trade brings differences together and the more the merrier! Differences (of commodities, populations, cultures and so forth) seem to multiply infinitely in the world market, which attacks nothing more violently than fixed boundaries: it overwhelms any binary divisions with its infinite multiplicities'.[29] This position is supported by new developments in management and organisational theories which, in the last two decades, have increasingly drawn upon postmodern approaches, celebrating the mobility and flexibility of organisations and their ability to deal with difference.[30] A

---

[25] Charles Taylor, *The Malaise of Modernity* (Toronto, ON: Anansi, 1991).
[26] Cf. Jürgen Habermas, 'Modernity: An Incomplete Project', in P. Brooker (ed.), *Modernism/Postmodernism* (Harlow: Longman, 1996); Habermas, 'Modernity versus Postmodernity', *New German Critique*, 22 (1981): 3–14.
[27] Teresa Ebert, *Ludic Feminism and After: Postmodernism, Desire, and Labor in Late Capitalism* (Ann Arbor, MI: University of Michigan Press, 1996).
[28] 'Symptoms of Passage' is the title of a chapter in Michael Hardt and Antonio Negri's *Empire*; the authors consider here postmodernism as the sign of an emerging imperial power.
[29] Hardt and Negri, *Empire*, p. 150.
[30] Business courses about how to learn postmodernist management theory and achieve a postmodernist organisational attitude are mushrooming: '"Postmodernists reject unifying, totalising and universal schemes in favor of a new emphasis on difference, plurality,

multicultural and multiracial milieu is often celebrated by top managers of transnational corporations as the best strategy to maximise creativity, profit and consumption.

Transmodernity: A Structural Connotation

Apart from the ideological connotation of transmodernity in the form of particular variants of postmodernism, other scholars have tackled 'postmodernity' as both a socio-economic condition and a historical time. Unlike postmodernist theorists, their aim is not to devise political projects based on difference and multiplicity. They point rather to an analytical critique of our contemporary era. The result is that a new array of discourses and signifiers has been produced, which enriches transmodernity with an *historical* and *structural connotation*. By expressing a diversified range of qualitative investigations, and semantic and terminological innovations, new conceptualisations have taken the analysis of postmodernity beyond Lyotard's seminal definition of it as the condition of 'incredulity towards metanarratives'.[31] Hence, we find notions such as 'second modernity' or 'risk society' (Beck, 1992), 'network society' (Castells, 1996), 'late' or 'high' modernity (Giddens, 1991), 'liquid' modernity (Bauman, 2000), 'hypermodernity' (Lipovetsky and Charles, 2005), 'transmodernity' (Rodríguez Magda, 2005; Dussel, 1995), 'supermodernity' (Augé, 1995), etc.[32] In different terms and to different degrees, all these perspectives reflect the

---

fragmentation, and complexity ..." (Best and Kellner, 1997). Join us in learning how to apply this new thinking to organizations!'; http://web.nmsu.edu/~dboje/TDworkshop Boston.html. See also http://business.nmsu.edu/~dboje/postmoderntheory.html where it is stated: 'The value in looking at a postmodernist approach to chaos and complexity lies in getting beyond the reductionist thinking of "modernist" managers'.

[31] Jean-Francois Lyotard, *The Postmodern Condition: A Report on Knowledge* (Manchester: Manchester University Press, 1984), pp. xxiii.

[32] Cf. Ulrich Beck, *Risk Society: Towards a New Modernity* (London: SAGE, 1992); Manuel Castells, *The Information Age: Economy, Society and Culture. Vol. 1: The Rise of the Network Society* (Cambridge, MA: Blackwell Publishers, 1996); Anthony Giddens, *The Consequences of Modernity* (Cambridge: Polity Press, 1990); Giddens, *Modernity and Self Identity* (Cambridge: Polity Press, 1991); Zygmunt Bauman, *Liquid Modernity* (Cambridge: Polity Press, 2000); Gilles Lipovetsky and Sebastien Charles, *Hypermodern Times* (Cambridge: Polity, 2005); Marcus Novak, 'Transarchitectures and Hypersurfaces: Operations of Transmodernity', in Stephen Perrella (ed.), *Hypersurface Architecture* (New York: John Wiley and Sons, 1998); Paul Virilio and Sylvere Lotringer, *Pure War* (New York: Semiotext(e), 1983); Rosa María Rodríguez Magda, *Transmodernidad* (Barcelona: Anthropos, 2005); Enrique Dussel, *The Invention of the Americas: Eclipse of 'the Other' and the Myth of Modernity* (New York: Continuum, 1995).

emergence of new discourses assuming postmodernity to be a definite historical phase or sociological reality with features of its own which would somehow progress beyond the social, political and linguistic constituents of 'modern time'. As discussed already, our use of the term transmodernity encompasses the range of discourses that have emerged with globalisation and which define the ideological, historical and structural dimension of *postmodernity*. All these dimensions express, therefore, distinct and respective 'connotations' of the *transmodern* symbolic scenario: not only *postmodernist* anti-foundationalist discourses celebrating difference and hybridity, but also historical, economic and sociological analyses of *postmodernity* assessing the constitutive features of this new 'reality'.

Transmodernity: A Spatial Connotation

In addition, transmodernity includes a number of discourses, for which convenient general designators could be 'globalism', 'virtualism' and 'universalism', celebrating a new *global* or *deterritorialised* cognition of space, and defining a *spatial connotation* of transmodernity. As discussed above, a major effect of globalisation has been a process of *spatial displacement*, which has modified the way in which space is experienced, imagined and constructed. In addressing this predicament, new discourses have emerged which have reformulated the link between identity and space overcoming the modern binary relation between the individual and his/her outside social and cultural context. A new relation has been constructed between *a fragmented subject* on the one hand and an *indistinct externality* on the other: e.g., the globe, the depthless surface of the screen, cyberspace, various forms of potential communities or virtualities (communities to come, not yet realised, such as the perfect Islamic society, global citizenship) and various forms of already established multiplicities (the multitude, the global ummah, and so forth). Central to this movement is the increasing inability of people to firmly grasp external place. Notions such as 'universal placelessness' (Relph, 1976), 'release from gravity', 'megalopolis' (Olalquiaga, 1992), or 'geography of nowhere' (Kunstler, 1993) all illustrate a context in which spatial referentials have lost meaning, bringing about the discursive desedimentation of a whole signifying space and the formulation of new quests for personal and collective identities.[33] Celeste Olalquiaga's notion of 'psychasthenia', for instance,

---

[33] Celeste Olalquiaga, *Megalopolis: Contemporary Cultural Sensibilities* (Minneapolis, MN: University of Minnesota Press, 1992); James Howard Kunstler, *The Geography of Nowhere: The Rise and Decline of America's Man-Made Landscape* (New York: Simon & Schuster, 1993).

refers to the condition of disorientation and the identity loss that occurs when external boundaries fade and the subject ends up losing itself in the vagueness of the outside space:

> Incapable of demarcating the limits of its own body, lost in the immense area that circumscribes it, the psychasthenic organism proceeds to abandon its own identity to embrace the space beyond. It does so by camouflaging itself into the milieu ... Psychasthenia helps describe contemporary experience and account for its uneasiness. Urban culture resembles this mimetic condition when it enables a ubiquitous feeling of being in all places while not really being anywhere.[34]

Within this psychasthenic condition of spatial and subjective decentring, new images strive to return a sense of closure and coherence, valorising the role that new transnational actors play in this deterritorialised context, and the possibility for the latter to be still reconnected to some 'fluid' idea of unity and order. The term *globalism* can efficaciously been used to indicate those discursive perspectives that, while acknowledging the substantial mobility of spatial and subjective relations under globalisation, point to an imaginary of 'interconnectedness' and 'transnational networking', celebrating the image of a new world order in which to relocate the action of a fragmented subject. Space and subjects are thus re-composed in what Manuel Castells defines in terms of a 'network society', where a 'space of flows' (flows of people, goods, information) replaces the modern 'space of place' and creates a new 'interdependent' externality. We will see, in this direction, the relevance that signifiers such as 'global network', 'transnational actors', 'global order', 'globalisation' play in the articulation of the *transterritorial* Islamist trajectory examined in Chapter 6 (Osama bin Laden's discourse). A *globalist* perspective here re-elaborates traditional pan-Islamic imaginaries in line to current global challenges.

Universalism, in this respect, provides another trope from which to consider transmodern spatial and subjective configurations, celebrating the role that new collective actors play in a global space. A universalistic ethos is here recovered in the celebration of an inclusive dynamic which allows differences to be absorbed while preserving, at the same time, forms of political litigation. In the recently popularised notion of 'multitude', for instance, we saw in Chapter 2 that unlike the people, the multitude figures as a plane of singularities expressing an inclusive relation to those outside it. While preserving an idea of inclusivity, openness and integration of difference, it overcomes the essentialist and modern idea

---

[34] Olalquiaga, *Megalopolis*, p. 2.

of the 'individual', standing as 'multiplicity of singularities, already creolised, embodying immaterial and intellectual labour'.[35] Universalistic discourses can also draw upon eschatological representations, resonating with traditional religious discourses, as is the case with the revived ideal of a global *ummah* (Muslim community) among certain jihadist trajectories. As we will see in a moment, these discourses show that certain parallels can be established between transmodernity and tradition. The result is that the desedimenting process enacted by globalisation might allow traditional discourses to be revitalised in opposition to modernity and in conjunction with transmodernity.

Finally, the term *virtualism* offers another useful designator from which to consider transmodern discursive representations of reality, which emphasises the desedimenting effects of virtuality, its contribution to the fading of modern categories, and the corresponding impact on subjectivity formations and ideas of externality. An example of virtualist perspective is offered by Jean Baudrillard's analysis of technology and the related 'liquidation of all referentials'.[36] For Baudrillard, our contemporary epoch figures as a sort of virtual reality where art replaces life as an all-encompassing form of aesthetics producing a 'disneyfication of the world', within which the spectator is 'more and more stimulated, and yet held as an hostage'.[37] A complex global network of microchips and computer devices, the infinite reproduction of images and information, and the 'virtualisation' of everyday practices has led to a questioning of the very possibility of distance, engendering, in the words of Virilio, the 'perpetually repeated hijacking of the subject from any spatial-temporal context'.[38] In this scenario, Baudrillard elaborates and articulates an emblematic transmodern signifier: *hyperreality*. By radicalising Borges's allegory of simulation, which envisages a map of the empire so detailed as to cover the exact surface of its territory – thus not merely symbolising but literally substituting and merging with its object – Baudrillard perceives the age of media communication and informatisation through the emergence of a new order of reality in which a 'precession of simulacra' supplants physical and symbolic

---

[35] Antonio Negri and Danilo Zolo, 'L'Impero e la moltitudine: Un dialogo sul nuovo ordine della globalizzazione' (The Empire and the Multitude: A dialogue over the new order of globalisation), in *Jura Gentium: Rivista di filosofia del diritto internazionale e della politica globale*, 1/1 (2005).

[36] Jean Baudrillard, *Simulacra and Simulation* (Ann Arbor, MI: University of Michigan Press, 1994), p. 254.

[37] Jean Baudrillard, *The Conspiracy of Art: Manifestos, Interviews, Essays* (New York: Semiotext(e), 2005).

[38] Paul Virilio, *The Aesthetics of Disappearance* (New York: Semiotext(e), 1991), p. 101.

referentials. Although the Internet exemplifies this global trend, manifesting itself as a closed, self-contained networked totality that precludes the empirical interrelation with a beyond, this predicament encompasses 'an irradiating synthesis of combinatory models', a technological appropriation of the entire world by way of microchips, electric devices, satellites, etc.[39] In this ultimate stage of simulacra, a phenomenological representation of space is lost in favour of a ubiquitous narcissistic void in which *fractal* identities fluctuate restlessly. Once we are everywhere – it suffices to be online – there is no longer a place defining our location and no longer an original 'fragment' of ourselves to be maintained. Fractality and ubiquity – our infinite division into self-same parts and the unceasing reproduction of them in the seriality of the matrix – are the corollary of simulation. Hence the narcissistic stupor of virtual travelling, which absorbs users into the microworld of their dreams. Baudrillard describes this process in terms of a transition from *seductio*, the seduction by the other for the other, to *subductio*, the hypnotic obscene fascination of the self, eternally reproduced in the narcissistic abyss of the screen.[40] In a world characterised by the mobility of boundaries, the reformulation of identity parallels spatial de-centralisation, testifying to the fragmentation of subjectivity and the attempt to recover forms of spatial externality and collective identity beyond modern binaries.

In this direction, other more optimistic discourses playing on the chord of virtualism revolve around the notion of 'virtual community'.[41] Pointing to a valorisation of cyberspace, a seminal definition of virtual community has been that of 'social spaces in which people still meet face-to-face, but under new definitions of both "meet" and "face"'.[42] Virtual communities point to the erosion of modern representations, recovering the traditional ideal of intimate, close and unmediated relationships in contexts where the environment framing our 'meetings' and the 'face' through which we represent ourselves socially can be creatively re-programmed. In doing so, they are functional to a global context where new technological opportunities allow people to reinvent communitarian ties beyond any direct relation with a specific geographical or

---

[39] Baudrillard, *Simulacra and Simulation*, p. 254.
[40] Jean Baudrillard, *The Ecstasy of Communication* (New York: Semiotext(e), 1988), p. 43.
[41] For a seminal examination of the virtual community, see Howard Rheingold, *The Virtual Community: Homesteading on the Electronic Frontier* (Cambridge, MA, and London: MIT Press, 2000).
[42] Allucquére Rosanne Stone, 'Will The Real Body Please Stand Up: Boundary Stories about Virtual Cultures', in M. Benedikt (ed.), *Cyberspace* (Cambridge, MA: MIT Press, 1991), p. 85.

cultural outside, responding to the new predicament produced by fragmentation and spatial displacement. Virtual communities, in fact, offer the chance to reformulate collective bonds on the basis 'not of common location', but of 'common interest', with 'individuals' being reconstructed as 'members' of a new, deterritorialised space.[43]

Some Remarks

To conclude, a final remark is needed to address the link between transmodernity and tradition. We contended that the desedimenting effects of globalisation have, in many respects, jeopardised the hegemonic position that modern discourses have covered over the last century. A clear example is the enfeebling of the political role of the nation state or the increasing inadequacy of modern binaries to cope with the changes produced by technology and informatisation. This predicament has spawned a twofold movement. On the one hand, transmodernity has emerged as a new discursive scenario alongside tradition and modernity. On the other hand, a *re-activation* of the symbolic appeal of tradition has allowed traditional discourses to be revitalised and re-articulated in a creative way, working alongside transmodernity to challenge the language of modernity. Here, tradition provides alternative symbolic sources to redefine space and subjectivity in a globalised world. This can be seen in the re-activation of discourses that stress the tribal and subnational character of identities. One example is the rejuvenated Arab notion of *al-asabiyyah* (tribal solidarity) used by scholars to show how traditional forms of identification challenge the role of national narratives in Islamic settings.[44] When considered in association to those transmodern trajectories stressing the supranational dimension of identity, it is clear that both these strategies reflect viable answers to the complex effects of globalisation, particularly with regard to its *g-local* character. The erosion of modern conceptions of space might alternatively induce the revitalisation of *traditional* ideals of 'subnational' ties, promoting a renewed emphasis on subcultures and 'the local' vis-à-vis 'the global'.

Another example in this direction, but from an inverted perspective, concerns the re-activation of literalist approaches to tradition through which a homogeneous reading of texts is promoted as a way to deal with global challenges

---

[43] Cf. J.C.R. Licklider and R.W. Taylor, 'The Computer as a Communication Device', *Science and Technology*, 76 (1968): 21–31. See also Peter Ludlow, *High Noon on the Electronic Frontier: Conceptual Issues in Cyberspace* (Cambridge, MA: MIT Press, 1996).

[44] See, for instance, Larbi Sadiki, *The Search for Arab Democracy* (London: Hurst & Company, 2004).

without ceding to forms of localism. A fleeting reference in the Conclusion of this book will show that 'neo-fundamentalism' – a term used by French scholar Oliver Roy to refer to neo-orthodox groups such as *Tablighi*, the *Taliban*, and so forth – points precisely to this kind of pattern, describing a number of conservative tendencies, whose rigid and scriptural reading of the holy texts is functional to a globalised and mobile context.[45] These currents can produce a rejection of local cultures, where holy texts are reduced to a set of well-defined literal injunctions deprived of any cultural reference. The norms that are drawn from holy texts express a deculturised vision of religion, for they are taken to reflect the tenets of creed alone. They can consequently be used in any location, despite the cultural and social context of reference, so producing a standardisation of behavioural practices and values, and maintaining a universal validity that can be very useful in a globalised environment. Here homogeneity rather than heterogeneity is celebrated as the best way to confront globalisation, revealing both an affinity to transmodern attempts to cope with spatial displacement and fragmentation, and an alternative to those postmodernist discourses that might rather conceptualise global space in terms of hybridity and difference.

This intricacy well exemplifies the complexity of the global arena where processes of homogenisation and differentiation traverse the entire globe, affecting even the production and reproduction of urban spaces.[46] Hence, the need to account for such an overlapping of discursive, structural, imaginary registers and codes, where, to say with Harvey, 'spaces of very different worlds seem to collapse upon each other, much as the world's commodities are assembled in the supermarket and all manner of subcultures get juxtaposed in the contemporary city'.[47]

In this complex scenario, the counter-hegemonic challenge to modern discourses that tradition and transmodernity promote is furthermore characterised by some degree of resonance between the two reservoirs. Contemporary discourses on universalism, for instance, provide interesting examples of the kind of symbolic appeal that tradition elicits for transmodernity itself, particularly when considering theoretical alternatives to national configurations. The *rebirth* of concepts such as 'empire' or 'multitude' testifies to the transmodern attempt to rearticulate traditional signifiers in a manner adequate to the challenges posed within the new global context. In their seminal

---

[45] Olivier Roy, *Globalized Islam: Fundamentalism, Deterritorialization and the Search for a New Ummah* (London: Hurst & Company, 2004).

[46] Edward W. Soja, *Postmodern Geographies: The Reassertion of Space in Critical Social Theory* (London: Verso, 1989).

[47] Harvey, *The Condition of Postmodernity*, p. 302.

essay on advanced capitalism, Hardt and Negri point out that some traditional concepts such as empire, *bellum justum* (just war) and *jus ad bellum* (right to make war) 'have reappeared in our postmodern world'. Though 'far from merely repeating medieval notions', these concepts 'present some truly fundamental innovations'.[48] A further example is provided in this respect by Zielonka's analysis of the European Union, where a traditional conceptualisation of sovereignty is used to define the emergence of a 'neo-medieval' supranational entity: 'The [European] Union is on its way to becoming a kind of neo-medieval empire with a polycentric system of government, multiple and overlapping jurisdictions, striking cultural and economic heterogeneity, fuzzy borders, and divided sovereignty'.[49] As we can see, such a 'traditional' and 'medieval' dimension is put in contrast with the hierarchical world of modernity that we discussed in Chapter 2, where binary constructions, based on notions of exclusivity and necessity, leave no room for the fuzziness of frontiers.

The last decades have thus testified to an increasing revitalisation of tradition vis-à-vis modernity, with discourses paralleling, in many respects, transmodern discursive trajectories. In the next part of the book, we trace the transposal of such an intricacy in Islamic settings, examining, for instance, the way in which the traditional discourse of Islamic universalism has been recovered and re-articulated in the 'transitional' trajectory of Sayyid Qutb as a tool against modern discourses (Chapter 5), or inquiring into the relation between tradition and transmodernity in the 'transterritorial' discourse of Osama bin Laden (Chapter 6).

---

[48] Hardt and Negri, *Empire*, p. 12.
[49] Jan Zielonka, *Europe as Empire: The Nature of the Enlarged European Union* (Oxford: Oxford University Press, 2006), p. vii.

PART II

Chapter 4
The Discourse of Hasan Al-Banna: A Territorial Trajectory

> Awakening: Just as political aggression had its effect in arousing nationalist feelings, so has social aggression in reviving the Islamic ideology.[1]

In line with our discourse-centred reading of modernity, tradition and transmodernity in Part I, the following pages examine the symbolic function that tradition and modernity have played in the discursive trajectory of Hasan al-Banna (1906–1949), one of the most influential figures of Islamist thought. We shall see that al-Banna's vision presents evidence of a double engagement with the modern and the traditional symbolic scenarios, reflecting an increasing valorisation of modernity in the articulation of what we term a *territorial trajectory* of Islamism. Taking a broader perspective, the term 'territorial' is used to describe here the tendency to prioritise local and domestic reality in a way that reveals a 'counter-hegemonic' articulation of national signifiers. Their integration within al-Banna's discourse is in fact re-signified by their juxtaposition with the master signifier 'Islam', and the language of tradition.

The historical context framing the discourse of Hasan al-Banna was marked by harsh cultural and political tensions, very much the result of the increasing penetration of colonial powers into Muslim settings. In Chapter 2, we saw that, among the dramatic events preceding al-Banna's foundation of the Society of the Muslim Brotherhood (*Al-Ikhwān Al-Muslimūn*; from now on, the Brotherhood or the Society, which al-Banna founded in 1928, thereby giving birth to the first Islamist movement of the twentieth century), the abolition of the caliphate by the westernised Young Turks in 1924 had represented a traumatic turning point, contributing to the process of social and discursive desedimentation begun under the pressure of colonialism. In Egypt, the persistent and assertive presence of the British exacerbated political tensions in a social context already divided between a number of different factions: the 'modernists', who advocated a stronger secularism in Egypt (emblematised by the secularist position of

---

[1] Hasan al-Banna, *Between Yesterday & Today* (pamphlet, 1939); available from http://www.youngmuslims.ca/online_library/books/byat.

intellectuals such as Taha Husain and Ali Abd al-Razik), the Muslim orthodox, who assumed a conservative stance and opposed most political and cultural changes (epitomised by al-Azhar university), and the religious reformists who advocated an assertive defence of Islam from secularism, while, at the same time, demanding *ijthad*, that is, some form of interpretation and reform of religious doctrines (see for instance, the position of Muhammad Rashid Rida).[2] But divisions also arose between pro-Western lay nationalists on the one hand, who celebrated the Pharaonic and 'ethnic' origin of the nation, and on the other, those nationalists who wanted to preserve the Islamic quality of Egypt.[3]

After the declaration of a British Protectorate over Egypt during the First World War, British recognition of Egyptian 'independence' in 1922 remained a formal one, with the right for Britain to retain control over Egyptian foreign and internal policy in the name of British interests in the Suez Canal and Sudan.[4] Egypt remained a de facto colony dominated by the manoeuvrings of the Egyptian king and the British who aimed to discredit political opposition.[5] The exclusion from power and the obstacles faced by the popular nationalist party *Wafd*, despite its persistent political and electoral success, slowly succeeded in undermining the image of Egyptian 'liberal nationalism' epitomised by the *Wafd* itself. At the same time, however, this contributed to discrediting liberal politics in general, creating the context for alternative and more radical discourses to emerge – namely, Islamist, Arabist, and Socialist.[6]

It was in this context that the young Egyptian schoolmaster Hasan al-Banna (1906–1949) founded the Muslim Brotherhood in 1928, a movement articulating a new kind of political discourse, which will henceforth be known as 'Islamism'. The Brotherhood was thought of as an organisation that aimed to provide welfare services for the population, encouraging and defending morality, and 'Islamising' society. When discussing modernist theories in Chapter 2, we took historical and political analyses of the Brotherhood in the 1950s and the

---

[2] Marcel Colombe, *L'Évolution de l'Égypte: 1924–1950* (Paris: G.P. Maisonneuve et Cie, 1951).

[3] Irving Sedar and Harold J. Greenberg, *L'Egypte entre deux mondes* (Paris: Éditions aux carrefours du monde, 1956).

[4] Gabriel R. Warburg, *Egypt and the Sudan: Studies in History and Politics* (London: Frank Cass, 1985); William Yale, *The Near East: A Modern History* (Ann Arbor, MI: Michigan University Press, 1953).

[5] Gema Martín Muñoz, *Politica y Elecciones en el Egipto Contemporaneo: 1922–1990* (Madrid: M.A.E., 1992).

[6] Marius Deeb, 'Continuity in Modern Egyptian History: The Wafd and the Muslim Brothers', in AAVV, *Problems of the Modern Middle East in Historical Perspective: Essays in Honour of Albert Hourani* (London: Ithaca Press/Garnet Publishing, 1992).

1960s as an example of modernist approaches to modernity and tradition.[7] The Brotherhood was here reduced to the fundamentalist idea of a return to a mythical past, which was said to reflect a dismissal of modernity as such. Its emphasis on spirituality, religion and social integration was seen as proof of its essential incompatibility with 'modern' features such as social differentiation, rationality and so forth. In a theoretical framework defining tradition and modernity as fixed sociological categories, modernist historians emphasised not only the Brotherhood's opposition to acculturation and Westernisation, but also its uncritical observance of a tradition mostly connected to the symbolic role of the ulama of al-Azhar.[8] Although there were other analyses more inclined to acknowledge the modern quality of the Brotherhood, it is mostly in the last decades that its compatibility with modernist features has come to be fully appreciated.[9] Recent examinations, for instance, have emphasised the reformist attitude of the Brotherhood, highlighting, in some cases, a critical approach displayed by Society towards not only the more secularist intellectual trends at that time, but also the religious establishment of al-Azhar.[10] The latter was blamed for having failed to preserve religious feelings among the population, and for having rejected any possibility of mediation with modernity, so confining tradition to a sterile 'imitative conformism' (*taqlīd*). A quote by Muhammad

[7] Franz Rosenthal, 'The "Muslim Brethren" in Egypt', *Muslim World*, 38 (1947); James Heyworth-Dunne, *Religious and Political Trends in Modern Egypt* (Washington, DC: The author, 1950); Christina Phelps Harris, *Nationalism and Revolution in Egypt: The Role of the Muslim Brotherhood* (The Hague: Mouton & Co., 1964) and Robert Mitchell, *The Society of the Muslim Brothers* (London: Oxford University Press, 1969).

[8] Al-Azhar (literally, the most flourished) is one of the oldest institutions of high learning in the world. Linked to the Al-Azhar mosque, one of the most important religious schools of Islamic studies, the school has played a central role in the authoritative embodiment of tradition. Those graduated in Al-Azhar, in fact, were historically assigned the formal title of *shaikh*, thus becoming officially recognised religious scholars (ulama).

[9] Earlier attempts to stress the novelty and the modern traits of the Brotherhood include: Ishaq Musa al-Husayni, *The Moslem Brethren: The Greatest of Modern Islamic Movements* (Beirut: Khayat's College Book Cooperative, 1956); Francis Bertier, 'L'idéologie politique des frères musulmans', *Orient*, 8 (1958).

[10] Mohammed Zahid, *The Muslim Brotherhood and Egypt's Succession Crisis: The Politics of Liberalisation and Reform in the Middle East* (New York: I.B. Tauris, 2010); Brigitte Maréchal, *The Muslim Brothers in Europe: Roots and Discourse* (Leiden and Boston, MA: Brill, 2008); Mariz Tadros, *The Muslim Brotherhood in Contemporary Egypt: Democracy Redefined or Confined?* (London: Routledge, 2012); Carrie Rosefsky Wickham, *The Muslim Brotherhood: Evolution of an Islamist Movement* (Princeton, NJ: Princeton University Press, 2013); Emad El-Din Shahin, *Political Islam in Egypt*, CEPS Working Document No. 266, May 2007.

Ghazali, one of the former and outstanding members of the Brotherhood, is an example of this: 'I know men among the sheikhs of the Azhar who live on Islam, as do the germs of bilharzia and anchylostomiasis on the blood of the wretched peasants.'[11]

But besides the critical attitude towards orthodox Islam, the modern trait of the Brotherhood has also been located in their call for an *Islam of the effendia*.[12] The aim of this was to promote 'the creation of a new image which repudiated the ingrained images of reactionism and religious inertia which had been the hallmark of established Islam.'[13] The co-optation of lower and, more crucially, educated middle classes (*effendia*) into the higher ranks of the Society was thus another factor indicative of the *modernising* force expressed by the Brotherhood in the political context of twentieth-century Egypt:

> The Muslim Brothers represented a growing and self-conscious Muslim middle or lower middle class. By addressing the latter's demands for political participation, socio-economic reforms as well as religious renewal the Muslim Brothers became the spokesmen for disenchanted young men who had been alienated by the traditional political parties, which were controlled and manipulated by the ruling elite.[14]

Crucially, the most important rival organisation, the Wafd, while able to mobilise large sections of society, was still dominated by the upper landowning elite, as can be seen in the presence of numerous 'Pashas' among its leaders.[15] Moreover, the Wafd was still largely structured upon the patron-client relationship rather than

---

[11] Muhammad al-Ghazali, *al-Islam al-muftara 'alayh bayn al-shuyu'iyin wa'l-ra'smaliyin* (Cairo: published by the Society of the Muslim Brothers, 3rd edn, 1953).

[12] In pre-republican Egypt, the term *effendi* designated the urban middle-class whose members were provided with a Westernizing education. In this sense, they were usually distinguished from official *sheikh*s who earned their education in traditional religious schools; see Israel Gershoni and James P. Jankowski, *Redefining the Egyptian Nation, 1930–1945* (Cambridge: Cambridge University Press, 1995), p. 225.

[13] Branjar Lia, *The Society of the Muslim Brothers in Egypt: The Rise of an Islamic Mass Movement 1928–1942* (London: Ithaca Press/Garnet Publishing, 1998), p. 186.

[14] Ibid., p. 280.

[15] 'Pasha' is a term of Persian origin (*bādishā*) meaning 'lord'. It was deployed by Turks to denote the honorific title granted by the Ottoman regime to high-ranking civil servants, administrators and military officers. In Egypt, an Ottoman province from the time of the Ottoman-Mamluk War (922–3/1516–17), this title survived the downfall of the Sublime Porte. The king of Egypt bestowed it to the members of aristocracy. More in general, it was the title associated to the pre-revolutionary upper landowning elite.

upon a programmatic and ideological platform. Conversely, although honorific committees were created for those notables that supported the Brotherhood, they were in fact given little possibility to interfere in the elaboration of its strategies. Meritocracy and ideological commitment remained the rules regulating the promotion of members within the Society.[16]

Many of these innovative factors are essential features of the activities and the tendencies recently shown by Islamist movements. The social composition of Islamist organisations is still highly reflective of the ideological appeal exerted by moderate political Islam on the middle class. Moreover, the contestation of the religious establishment is in line with an erosion of social and religious authority in contemporary times, which produces very significant effects in terms of a re-elaboration of religious tradition. In contesting the monopoly over religious discourses held by traditional sheikhs, the emergence of new religious leaders, often with a professional degree such as that of engineer or doctor, echoes the kind of innovation that the Brotherhood first displayed.

In a notable essay on the early development of the Society, Branjar Lia describes the Muslim Brotherhood as the largest mass social movement of modern Egypt, accounting for a number of novelties such the combination of social and religious credentials, the deployment of a highly structured organisation, the use of new tools of recruitment and propaganda, and the already-mentioned ability to integrate emerging middle classes and new urban professionals (*effendia*).[17] Other studies have proceeded in a similar direction, emphasising the original traits of the Brotherhood's ideological vision and its anti-imperialist battle.[18] It has often been observed that there are important similarities between al-Banna and the great reformists of the nineteenth century, such as Jamal al-Din al-Afghani and Muhammad 'Abduh, showing a common aim to modernise the Islamic tradition.[19] Although the increasingly troubled

---

[16] See Bjorn Olav Utvik, 'The Modernizing Force of Islam', in John L. Esposito and Francois Burgat (eds), *Modernizing Islam: Religion in the Public Sphere in Europe and the Middle East* (London: Hurst & Company, 2003), p. 59.

[17] Cf. Lia, *The Society of the Muslim Brothers in Egypt*.

[18] Ibrahim M. Abu-Rabi, *Intellectual Origins of Islamic Resurgence in the Modern Arab World* (Albany, NY: State University of New York Press, 1996); Ahmad S. Moussalli, 'Hasan Al-Banna's Islamist Discourse on Constitutional Rule and Islamic State', *Journal of Islamic Studies*, 4/2 (1993): 161–74; Brigitte Maréchal, *The Muslim Brothers in Europe: Roots and Discourse* (Leiden and Boston, MA: Brill, 2008).

[19] On this topic, see also N. Lahoud and A.H. Johns (eds), *Islam in World Politics* (Abingdon: Routledge, 2005); Tariq Ramadan, *Aux sources du renouveau musulman: d'al-Afghani à Hasan al-Banna, un siècle de réformisme islamique* (Lyon: Tawhid, 2002); Anour Abdel-Malek, *La pensée politique arabe contemporaine* (Paris: Éditions du Seuil, 1970).

political context favoured the radicalisation of the Brotherhood's political philosophy and tactics – just like its 'secular' nationalist counterparts – the main focus of the Society remained for long time the adoption of a reformist attitude aimed at an Islamisation 'from below' and 'education for the masses'.[20]

Hasan al-Banna was killed in 1949, allegedly on the instructions of the government's secret police.[21] A few years later, a secret organisation within the Egyptian army, the Free Officers succeeded, in cooperation with the Brotherhood, in overthrowing the Egyptian King Farouk, replacing the monarchy with a Republic in what has been known as the Egyptian Revolution of 1952. Although initially supportive of the Free Officers, the Muslim Brothers very soon began to criticise the new regime as ideological differences emerged, with most of the Free Officers inclining towards the establishment of a secular regime rather than the Islamisation and moralisation of society. Finally, the attempted murder of the new leader of the Free Officers, Jamal Abdel Nasser, led to the dismantling of the Society in 1954 and the imprisonment of thousands of members together with other political opponents. The contribution of Hasan al-Banna is mainly linked to the Society's earlier period. Two decades of Islamist dormancy followed the abolition of the Brotherhood, with nationalist and pan-Arab narratives dominating the political arena in the Middle East and Muslim regimes repressing Islamist activities within their borders. It was only in the late 1960s that Islamism, as a general discursive universe, 'revived', challenging the hegemonic role of nationalism and pan-Arabism, and taking advantage of a changed political environment. A brief examination of this historical conjuncture will be pursued in the next chapter, when a 'transitional' trajectory of Islamism will be analysed (Sayyid Qutb's discourse).

As far as this first phase of Islamism is concerned, it should be noted that the complex historical context surrounding the early years of the Brotherhood played an essential role in forging al-Banna's strategic and theoretical agenda. An overall examination of his discourse in the next pages will trace major discursive shifts in his trajectory, denoting a gradual downplaying of the original pan-

---

[20] Nelly Lahoud, *Political Thought in Islam: A Study in Intellectual Boundaries* (Abingdon: Routledge, 2005), p. 17. See also Francois Burgat, *Face to Face with Political Islam* (London and New York: I.B. Tauris, 2003); Olivier Carré and Michel Seurat, *Les frères musulmans (1928–1982)* (Paris: L'Harmattan, 1983); Gilles Kepel, *Muslim Extremism in Egypt: The Prophet and Pharaoh* (Berkeley and Los Angeles, CA: University of California Press, 1985).

[21] Peter G. Mandaville, *Global Political Islam* (London: Routledge, 2007), p. 72; A.B. Soage and J.F. Fraganillo, 'The Muslim Brothers in Egypt', in B. Rubin (ed.), *The Muslim Brotherhood: The Organization and Policies of a Global Islamist Movement* (New York: Palgrave Macmillan, 2010), p. 41.

Islamic ideal – as expressed in his early writings at the beginning of the 1930s – in favour of an increasing prioritisation of Egypt and celebration of national signifiers. From a general perspective, this transition is reflected by the political activity of the Brotherhood in general. From the moment of its foundation, the Brotherhood has never stopped looking at the entire Islamic world, promoting its anti-imperialist agenda and its Islamic call well beyond Egyptian borders. A pan-Islamic ethos played a crucial role in the Brotherhood's pro-Palestinian campaign organised during the dramatic riots in Palestine in 1936–7, and again behind the Brotherhood's military and ideological contribution to the first Arab-Israeli War in 1948, eventually allowing the Society to gain a strong reputation among the Egyptian army and the population. However, the political focus rested primarily on the reformation of Egyptian politics, not on a universal Muslim community. The Brotherhood's vision remained focused on domestic politics.

The link between al-Banna's discursive trajectory, as expressed in his writings and speeches, and the political activity of the Brotherhood reflects the authority that al-Banna exerted on this movement, which remained in some respects a creature of its founder. Structured as a hierarchical organisation, the Brotherhood required members to swear absolute loyalty to the high ranks of the Society, at the top of which was Hasan al-Banna as the 'Supreme Guide' of the movement. Naturally, some ideological differences emerged among the leaders of the Society over time, with defections taking place on some occasions and leading to internal schisms when no compromise could be found. Thanks to al-Banna's charisma and authority, however, the Brotherhood remained a substantially coherent whole until his death, reflecting his aspirations and political agenda.

Hasan al-Banna's Articulatory Practice: A Discursive Inquiry

Although al-Banna never offered a specific theory of religion and politics, his general vision of Islam can be reconstructed from the various articles and pamphlets that he wrote. Beyond particular contributions in letters, speeches, articles for the journals of the Brotherhood, programmatic statements and conference reports, the most organic and general treatise, comprising of biographical detail and some ideological discussion, is al-Banna's *Memoirs of the*

Call and the Preacher.²² Most of the themes discussed in his memoirs, however, were already anticipated in his *rasal:* a kind of pamphlet which served as a major mode of communication for al-Banna throughout his political life.²³ A wide and comprehensive selection of the most important pamphlets by al-Banna will be examined here in chronological order.²⁴

Critics have often pointed out that the dispersed nature of al-Banna's writings, in addition to his pragmatic and flexible style – with tones and contents often changing in relation to the audience – have determined an inconsistent theoretical corpus which lacks systematisation.²⁵ Although we agree that al-Banna's careful appraisal of the political context and the limits implied by a definite audience helps explain contradictions in his writings, intellectual incoherencies and twists can hardly be reduced to a question of strategy or, even worse, to simple ineptitude. Unlike the evaluation of al-Banna as a skilful militant, the analysis of his discursive trajectory has often suffered from a certain lack of historical perspective. Variations in al-Banna's writings have rarely undergone a diachronic assessment capable of detecting the dynamics of his intellectual route in response to historical circumstances (for instance, his increasing openness towards the party system or the nation state in the 1940s). This is why a chronological order of analysis will be pursued in the next pages, so as to highlight major discursive changes in his discourse.

---

[22]   Hasan al-Banna, *Memoirs of the Call and the Preacher (Mudhakkirāt Al-Da'wah Wa-Al-Dā'īyah)* (Cairo: 1947), [first parts published in instalments in 1942].

[23]   Literally meaning 'letter', the term *rasal* indicated, traditionally, a religious treatise; hence the English translation 'tract' to emphasise its contents or 'pamphlet' to stress its format.

[24]   A vast collection of al-Banna's 'letters' was published in Arabic under the title, Hasan al-Banna, *Majmū'at Rasā'il Al-Imām Al-Shahīd 'asan Al-Bannā* (Bayrūt: al-Mu'assasah al-Islāmīyah lil-'ibā'ah wa-al-'I'āfah wa-al-Nashr, 1981). An English collection of five major rasals can be found in *Hasan al-Banna, Five Tracts of Hasan Al-Bannā (1906–1949): A Selection from the Majmū'at Rasā'il Al-Imām Al-Shahīd 'asan Al-Bannā*, trans. Charles Wendell (Berkeley, CA: University of California Press, 1978). In the next pages, we will mostly refer to a new English online translation comprising almost the entire production of al-Banna's rasals, *The Complete Works of Imam Hasan Al-Banna* (the name of the translator is unknown, though a preface is included with a reference to Dr A.M.A. Fahmy, International Islamic Forum). The translation was posted on June 2008 in the blog http://thequranblog.wordpress.com (available at http://thequranblog.wordpress.com/2008/06/07/english-translation-of-majmuaat-rasail-the-complete-works-imam-hasan-al-banna).

[25]   Paul Brykczynski, 'Radical Islam and the Nation: The Relationship between Religion and Nationalism in the Political Thought of Hassan Al-Banna and Sayyid Qutb', *History of Intellectual Culture*, 5/1 (2005).

The Early Writings (1928–1930s)[26]

Hasan al-Banna began his teachings in the coffee shops of Ismailia, a small town near the Suez Canal where the presence of British soldiers and settlers, besides marking a strong social inequality between Egyptians and Europeans, entailed the direct and visible influence of the West. In his first article after the foundation of the Society of the Muslim Brothers in 1928, al-Banna explicitly criticises the spiritual quiescence of official Islam and the Egyptian political establishment in general, together with their inability to counter Western secularisation and materialism:

> What catastrophe has befallen the souls of the reformers and the spirit of the leaders? What has carried away the ardour of the zealots? What calamity has made them prefer this life to the thereafter? What has made them ... consider the way of struggle [sabil al-jihad] too rough and difficult?[27]

From the very beginning, al-Banna focuses his attention on the 'way of struggle [*sabil al-jihad*]' for an Islamisation from *below*; that is, the assertive endeavour to awaken people's conscience by calling for the sovereignty of God in every section of society. Hence, a place of pleasure such as a coffee shop is transformed into a platform for the Islamic call (*da'wa*).

In one of the early pamphlets written in 1934, *To What Do We Invite Humanity?*, while inviting Muslims to 'rebuild' the community on the basis of Islamic tenets, al-Banna is adamant in considering this major task not as a consequence of a state initiative but as the ultimate result of individual spiritual efforts in the path of God:

> Muslims, this is a period of rebuilding: re-build yourselves, and your Umma will as a consequence be rebuilt![28]

---

[26] While Italics will be used in this section to emphasise specified terms or concepts, or, alternatively, when typing words in languages other than English, single quotation marks will be deployed to quote al-Banna's own words as found in the original text, and should be taken to express potential *signifiers* in the articulation of al-Banna's discourse.

[27] Hasan al-Banna, 'Da'wa ilā Allāh', *Majallat al-Fath*, no.100, 1346/1928, cited in Lia, The Society of the Muslim Brothers in Egypt, p. 33.

[28] Hasan al-Banna, *To What Do We Invite Humanity?* (Cairo, 1934); also appeared as a pamphlet in 1936; available at: http://thequranblog.files.wordpress.com/2008/06/_2_-to-what-do-we-invite-humanity.pdf.

This signals al-Banna's early attempt to assume a moderate and gradualist bottom-up approach to Islamisation (from the individual to the society). In this same pamphlet, moreover, the main objectives of the Brotherhood are defined in clear terms:

> To establish Allah's sovereignty over the world. To guide all of humanity to the precepts of Islam and its teachings. (without which mankind cannot attain happiness)[29]

A few caveats are needed, however, in consideration of this key statement. First, al-Banna starts his own discussion by putting the emphasis on 'sovereignty' whose *transcendental* nature the Brotherhood recognises and strives to affirm. The idea that 'sovereignty belongs to God' (*al ḥākimiyya li-l-lāh*) constitutes a central signifier in the articulation of most Islamist discourses, and is rooted in traditional legal procedures. Naturally, this evidences the relevance of tradition as an imaginary horizon embodying an entire universe of signification. *Fiqh* (jurisprudence of Islamic law), *shari'ah*, social and legal norms regulating the 'personal status' of Muslims, 'Islamic theology', 'Islamic ethics' (disciplining, for instance, sexual division and moral virtue, happiness), traditional discourses on *jihad*, traditional elements drawn from Sufism (spiritualism, organisational matters, etc.), references to the discourse of the caliphate, and Islamic universalism – all constitute 'traditional' discursive fields from which al-Banna draws on when articulating his own discourse. Besides the symbolic relevance of tradition, however, another scenario plays a central function since this very beginning: modernity. At a general level, in fact, al-Banna strives to pursue an Islamisation of modernity while, at the same time, modernising tradition.

In consideration of his assertion of God's sovereignty, for instance, its implementation by modern states is not only explained with the doctrinal argument of *shari'ah* incarnating the transcendental 'sovereign' power of God. It is also the self-sufficiency of Islam vis-à-vis competing systems of ideas that makes *shari'ah*, with its practical ability to solve human needs, a natural source of legislation for the 'nation':

> Every nation has a set of laws in which the people partake their ruling. These sets of laws must be derived from the proscriptions of the Islamic Sharee'ah (drawn from the Noble Qur'an, and in accordance with the basic sources of Islamic jurisprudence). The Islamic Sharee'ah and the decisions of the Islamic jurists are

---

[29] Ibid.

completely sufficient, supply every need, and cover every contingency, and they produce the most excellent results and the most blessed fruits.[30]

Transcendence is here shadowed by the immanent ability of jurists' 'decisions' to respond to concrete necessities, and to 'cover every contingency', a point that will be stressed in a much more energetic way in later writings. The goal of establishing 'Allah's sovereignty over the world' is thus translated into a gradualist agenda promoting Islamisation of individuals to solve concrete social needs. Gradualism and pragmatism mark al-Banna's conceptualisation of the aims of the Brotherhood. Al-Banna is careful in specifying that the Islamic goal does not work as a utopian project. Rather, it represents something that is *feasible*, and easy to realise practically; whose practicality is somehow even urged by the concrete circumstances affecting the colonised world:

> Perhaps they may say: 'What is wrong with this group is that they write about ideas which cannot even be achieved. What is the point of expressing utopian ideals except for floating around in a world of imagination and dreams?' My dear brother in Islam, take it easy! What you consider today as obscure and far away was commonplace to your predecessors.[31]

Al-Banna's urge for pragmatism was strictly related to his ability to understand the implications of the broader political and cultural context of those years. His references to God's sovereignty and the attempt to highlight the practical aspects of this principle were themselves a reflection of the discursive and cultural battle that was taking place in Egypt at that time. It should be noticed, for instance, that one of the most troubling effects of European influence across Islamic settings has been the introduction of a dual court system, with national courts applying Western-based civil law on the one hand, and religious courts (*shari'ah* courts) regulating personal status matters on the other (concerning marriage, family issues, heritage, and so on). An increasing limitation of the jurisdiction of religious courts in Egypt entailed the gradual replacement of *shari'ah* with European legal principles, thereby contributing to the general process of discursive desedimentation of Muslim societies through the colonial period. Hence, al-Banna's intervention into this desedimented space and his decision to draw upon the imaginary horizons of both tradition and modernity, using modern arguments in defence of traditional claims.

---

[30] Ibid.
[31] Ibid.

A second caveat is needed. In al-Banna's early writings, the tension between national and pan-Islamic drives remains largely unsolved. On the one hand, a national perspective is sometimes assumed, though the conceptualisation of the very idea of the nation remains mostly unexplored, acknowledged only as a matter of fact in the face of European imperialism. In an article written in 1933, al-Banna emblematically affirms the importance of the 'founding' of souls as functional primarily to the achievement of 'the nation's goals and aspirations':

> The solution is the education and moulding of the souls of the nation in order to create a strong moral immunity, firm and superior principles and a strong and steadfast ideology. This is the best and fastest way to achieve the nation's goals and aspirations, and it is therefore our aim and the reason for our existence. It goes beyond the mere founding of schools, factories and institutions, it is the 'founding' of souls. (insha' al-nufus)[32]

On the other hand, a strong and clearly defined pan-Islamic ethos is articulated in al-Banna's early discourse, superseding national forms of loyalty. The result is that, at this stage, pan-Islamism and nationalism are roughly combined together, with pan-Islamism very often playing a pre-eminent role both in terms of conceptualisation and celebration. In *To What Do We Invite Humanity?*, al-Banna proclaims, in traditional terms, the universalistic nature of Islam as founded upon a notion of 'brotherhood'. As mentioned above, a Sufi influence affected al-Banna's conceptualisation of the Society, largely as the result of the young al-Banna's involvement in a Sufi order.[33] Such influence can be seen in the focus on the spiritual notion of 'brotherhood', as well as on symbolism, rites, the obedience and discipline of adherents (through the traditional oath of loyalty, *bay'a*), the title and the strong charismatic tone assumed by al-Banna as the 'Supreme Guide' (*al-murshid al-'amm*), and the spiritual emphasis in al-Banna's message.[34] Tradition reflects therefore a central symbolic scenario at this stage. The notion of Islamic Brotherhood is particularly telling, because it informs the criteria according to which the 'horizon of the Islamic homeland' is defined. It

---

[32] Hasan al-Banna, 'Aghrad al-Ikhwan al-Muslimin', *Jaridat al-Ikhwan al-Muslimin*, no.7, 1352/1933, cited in Lia, *The Society of the Muslim Brothers in Egypt*, p. 67.

[33] Sufism is the tradition of Islamic mysticism, consisting of a highly heterogeneous system of beliefs, practices and rituals organised across an assorted range of organisations and sects.

[34] On the influence of Sufism in moulding the spiritual character of the Brotherhood, see Lia, *The Society of the Muslim Brothers in Egypt*, p. 116; for a discussion about al-Banna's early involvement in Sufi orders, see al-Husayni, *The Moslem Brethren*, pp. 28–30.

is the Islamic brotherhood, in the light of its intrinsic 'humanitarianism', that transforms the expansion of Islam into a movement for justice and equality, legitimising such expansion, and distinguishing it from those forms of conquest and aggression based on mere 'geographic', 'ethnic' or 'racial' factors such as 'nationalism' and 'patriotism'. In a section entitled, 'A Brotherhood Which Proclaims Humanitarianism', al-Banna states:

> Whenever the light of Muhammad's (Peace Be Upon Him) guidance shone upon the souls of people, all differences were obliterated, wrongs were wiped out, justice and equality prevailed in their midst, along with love and brotherhood. There was no question of a triumphant conqueror and a vanquished enemy, but simply one of affectionate and devoted brothers. The notion of nationalism thenceforth melts away and disappears just as snow disappears after bright, strong sunlight falls upon it. It is in contrast with the Islamic concept of brotherhood, which the Qur'an instils in the souls of all those who follow it.[35]

Being 'in contrast with the Islamic concept of brotherhood', the notion of nationalism is radically rejected here. Apparently, no attempt is made to integrate *local* nationalism within the broader universalistic framework expressed by the notion of Islamic homeland, as al-Banna will do later on. At this stage, a link is made instead between the notion of Islamic brotherhood and the need to preserve the 'territorial' integrity of Islam vis-à-vis its 'aggressors':

> Islamic brotherhood compelled every Muslim to believe that every foot of ground supporting any brother who held to the religion of the Noble Qur'an was a portion of the larger Islamic homeland ... For Islam, when it points this concept out to its people and fixes it firmly within their souls, imposes upon them the unavoidable obligation to protect the territory of Islam from the attack of the aggressor, to deliver it from occupation, and to fortify it against the ambitions of the transgressor.[36]

The strong anti-imperialist attitude that already marks the discussion at this stage reflects the embracing of a sort of *re-active* stance in al-Banna's words. The idea that the 'Islamic homeland', despite its transcendental and spiritual dimension is rooted in a 'territory' that its 'people' are 'obliged' to protect from 'the attack of the aggressor' indicates the adoption of a defensive stance vis-à-

---

[35] al-Banna, *To What Do We Invite Humanity?*
[36] Ibid.

vis the infiltration of the West. This reflects Muslims' awareness during colonial times of European powers as physically penetrating *into* the Islamic homeland.

A relevant discursive effect of this reactive stance is the adoption of an *Occidentalist* narrative in this phase. In Chapter 1, we described classic orientalist accounts as distinct forms of power and knowledge, mostly based on binaries and essentialisms, which were functional to colonial political control. Occidentalism entailed the attempt to reverse orientalist representations so redefining the Orient from a privileged position. Reductionisms and essentialisms were hence used to reverse the logocentric approach deployed by orientalist discourses. Such representations may be understood in terms of what Sartre called *the moment of the boomerang*, reflecting a sort of common pattern among anti-colonial movements. With this expression he referred to a strategy aimed at counterbalancing the positive dialectic of colonialism with an opposing revolutionary and *negative dialectic* (e.g., the *negritude* against white colonial oppression).[37] Consider the passage below where a reference to Western imperialism is put by al-Banna in sharp contrast with fundamental qualities of 'enlightenment', 'guidance', 'compassion', and 'benevolence' that adorn the Islamic 'civilisation':

> The Muslim, who has spread the word of Allah, was a guide and teacher adorned with enlightenment, guidance, compassion, and benevolence. Thus the civilized spread of Islam was one of preparing (for the future), of guiding, and teaching. Can this be compared with what Western imperialism is doing at this present time?[38]

In this frame, the *East* is not rejected on the ground of being a European and abstract concept. In the same pamphlet, statements such as 'the East would rise up and compete with the nations which have stolen its rights and oppressed its people' or 'the foundations of modern Eastern resurgence are built on the basic principles of Islam', evidence al-Banna's reactive emphasis towards the same linguistic categories that were used in orientalist fashion by colonial powers. The *East* is thus integrated in al-Banna's discourse and positivised in the face of the Western 'oppressor', becoming a space of 'resurgence' when infused with 'the principles of Islam'. This approach entails the counter-hegemonic attempt to dislocate the Western monopoly over modern political paradigms, Islamising

---

[37] Jean-Paul Sartre, 'Preface', in Frantz Fanon, *The Wretched of the Earth*, trans. Constance Farrington (New York: Grove Press, 1963), p. 20. For an interesting analysis on Occidentalism, see Larbi Sadiki, 'Occidentalism: The "West" and "Democracy" as Islamist Constructs', *Orient*, 39/1 (1998).

[38] al-Banna, *To What Do We Invite Humanity?*

modern 'signifiers', while reproducing, at a substantial level, the very dualistic mind-set that informed the colonial discourse.

In this attempt to appropriate the language of modernity from an anti-imperialist perspective, Western systems of ideas are not rejected on the ground of their *foreignness*; they are rather subject to a process of Islamisation, as al-Banna in keen in claiming their *Islamicity*. That is, if Islam needs to be modernised, modernity in turn will be Islamised:

> Globalism, nationalism, socialism, capitalism, Bolshevism, war, the distribution of wealth, the link between producer and consumer, and whatever is closely or distantly connected to the discussions preoccupying the statesmen and the social philosophers, we believe that all of these have been dealt with thoroughly by Islam, and that Islam has set forth the regulations assuring that the world employs all that is good, as well as avoiding whatever may lead to danger or disaster.[39]

Most of the signifiers delineated so far remain at the very core of al-Banna's discourse. Sovereignty, Islamic call ('da'wa'), Islamisation from below ('rebuild your self'), Islamic '*shari'ah*' as a form of good governance, 'universalism' (pan-Islamic 'brotherhood'), 'humanitarianism', 'anti-imperialism', feasibility of project (no 'utopian ideals'), Occidentalism ('Eastern resurgence', Western decline), 'Ideology', 'civilisation', 'territory', 'the people' – are all *moments* articulated around the master signifier Islam.

In this discursive context, although the idea of the nation is not celebrated by al-Banna – rather, as we saw earlier, it is sometimes even rejected – the hegemonic role that nationalist discourses play in the desedimented space of colonised populations is clearly acknowledged. In the 1935 pamphlet, *Our Message*, al-Banna recognises the ability of nationalism to provide Muslims with an important tool in the fight for the political emancipation of the colonised world, therein enabling subaltern subjects to deploy Western language against the West itself, e.g., in the form of Arab nationalism or Egyptian irredentism:

> People are at times seduced by the appeal to patriotism, at other times by that of nationalism, especially in the East, where they are aware of the abuse that the colonial West directs against them, abuse which has injured their dignity, their honor, and their independence ... The tongues of their leaders have been given a free rein, a stream of newspapers has gushed forth, their writers, their lecturers,

---

[39] Ibid.

and their broadcasters, are all working in the name of patriotism and the majesty of nationalism.[40]

In the attempt to appeal to the wide audience of nationalism, therein challenging the influence of the nationalist Wafd, al-Banna began in this pamphlet to come to term with the idea of the nation, for instance by listing those aspects that were compatible with Islam and those that were incompatible; then, by maintaining that those that were compatible were indeed 'prescribed' by 'Islam'. When describing 'patriotism' and 'nationalism', for instance, he stated that if these concepts mean 'affection' ('love for one's homeland'), 'freedom and greatness' ('every effort to free the land from its ravagers, to defend its independence'), 'community' ('to reinforce the bonds which unite individuals within a given country'), 'conquest' ('the conquest of countries and sovereignty over the earth') – then 'Islam has already ordained that'. He pointed out however that if patriotism and nationalism meant 'factionalism', 'aggression' ('racial self-aggrandizement to a degree which leads to the disparagement of Other races'), 'fanaticism' (the revival of Pre-Islamic customs) – then they were incompatible with Islam. As he put it:

> The bone of contention between us and them is that while we define patriotism according to the creed of Islam, they define it according to territorial borders and geographical boundaries.[41]

Although nationalism is not yet assumed as a central component in the discourse of al-Banna, we see here a first attempt to acknowledge the relevance of 'national' signifiers, showing that Islamism works on the side of national independence. National *elements* are therefore partially integrated, though still in an unbalanced manner. For instance, on the one hand al-Banna rejects here local forms of nationalism, like 'Pharaonism, Arabism, Phoenicianism, or Syrianism'; on the other, he states immediately after that:

> Nevertheless, we are not denying that the various nations have their own distinct qualities and particular moral characters … We believe that in these respects

---

[40] Hasan al-Banna, 'Da'watuna' (Our Message), in *Jaridat al-Ikhwan al-Muslimin* (1353/1935); also appeared as a pamphlet in 1937; available at http://thequranblog.files.wordpress.com/2008/06/_6_-our-message.pdf.
[41] Ibid.

Arabism possesses the fullest and most abundant share, but this does not mean that its peoples should seize upon these characteristics as a pretext for aggression.[42]

The strategic attempt to address a youth particularly sensitive to the national claim, as well as to a strong form of irredentism is evident.[43] It is emblematic that al-Banna, for instance, aims to reassure those nationalist sceptics that fear Islamism for its potential to divide the 'nation' because of religious issues:

> I would like to draw your attention to the glaring error in the leading figure who says: that acting on this principle [Islam] would tear apart the unity of the nation, which is composed of different religious elements. Now Islam, which is the very religion of unity and equality, maintains the ties of unity so long as the people continue to work for good … then, from what source could dissension spring? Do you not now see exactly how much we are in agreement with the most ardent patriots regarding love of the country's well being, sincere struggle for the sake of its liberation, its welfare, and its progress?[44]

Interestingly, other crucial elements are articulated in this pamphlet, *Our Message*. We find here the first attempt to define Islam as an '*all embracing* concept regulating every aspect of life' [emphasis added], which predisposes 'Islam' to play a hegemonic function as the master signifier of the Muslim community. Moreover, al-Banna defines his position towards those Muslims who have not yet embraced the vision of the Brotherhood:

> The difference between us and our people, although both of us agree on the same faith and principle, is that their faith is anaesthetized, lying dormant within their souls, one to which they do not wish to submit and act accordingly. Whereas it is a burning, blazing, intense faith fully awakened in the souls of the Muslim Brotherhood.[45]

---

[42] Ibid.
[43] The attempt to attract students and young adherents was also translated in the creation of a number of paramilitary bodies in these years, including a 'military wing' or 'secret section'; Lia, The Society of the Muslim Brothers in Egypt, pp. 170–75. For the influence of Fascist and Nazi paramilitary organisations in the creation of these bodies, see al-Husayni, The Moslem Brethren.
[44] al-Banna, 'Da'watuna'.
[45] Ibid.

The relevance of this passage lies not only in the fact that al-Banna defines his notion of Islamic revival, considering Islam as a dormant object of discourse that needs to be revitalised. Its interest also relates to the fact that those Muslims whose 'faith is anaesthetized' are not excluded from the ummah. The ummah in al-Banna's discourse is right there, physically existent; it just needs to be defended, 'rebuilt' and 'awakened'; hence the community's 'resurgent' character, so widespread among political discourses in Europe at that time (a resurgent fascist Rome or Germany). In contrast, we shall see in the next chapter that a potential upshot of a transitional trajectory of Islamism – as epitomised by Sayyid Qutb's descriptive vision – is the definition of the ummah as a missing good, as a mental attitude in a physical space dominated by the omni-presence of *jahiliyyah* (unbelief).

The alignment between al-Banna's notions of 'resurgence' and 'awakening' and concurrent modern nationalist discourses is evident, especially if one considers the popularity of fascist rhetoric in the Middle East in those decades (clearly, as an answer to British and French colonialism in the region) and fascist celebration of a *resurgent* golden past (e.g., Italian *Risorgimento*, Roma or Aryan glorious past). But al-Banna's alignment to modern discourses is also testified to by the emphasis put on the need to improve methods of 'propaganda' following the example of 'trained specialists, particularly in the Western countries', so urging the use of modern media ('publications, magazines, newspapers, articles, plays, films, and radio broadcasts').[46]

In sum, although in this early phase al-Banna discursive trajectory testifies to a growing reliance on the symbolic appeal of modernity, a universalistic ethos here is still privileged, allowing for an explicit criticism towards the more 'un-Islamic' aspects of nationalism (Western focus on ethnicity and borders vis-à-vis Islamic ability to preserve an inclusive spiritual fraternity).

The Late 1930s

It is in the late 1930s that al-Banna's drawing on the language of modernity was translated into a stronger integration and valorisation of national signifiers. This testified to a gradual 'nationalisation' of al-Banna's own premises, which reflected his growing awareness of the massive appeal of nationalism in a context where local populations were more and more frustrated by the persisting control of British over Egyptian affairs. It should be noticed, in fact, that a crucial event in these years had been the Anglo-Egyptian Treaty of 1936, which paved the

---

[46] Ibid.

way to the abolition of the capitulations in Egypt, reinvigorating the issue of a 'substantial' national independence as the centre of political debate.[47]

Traditional elements were, however, still combined with national elements, allowing for a counter-hegemonic connotation of nationalist language. As Lia puts it, the Brotherhood ideological vision in these years 'served in many ways as a bridge between the traditional and modernist camps by its insistence on Islam as its only ideological tenet, but incorporating at the same time many aspects of modern ideologies and thinking'.[48] This moderator function can be seen, for instance, in the notion of a multilevel identity elaborated by al-Banna in the 1937 pamphlet, *Towards the Light*.[49] We find here the first systematic integration of the idea of the nation within a harmonious multidimensional model where pan-Islamic views are merged together with national signifiers. For the first time, al-Banna defines the Islamic homeland as comprising:

1. The country itself.
2. The other Islamic countries, for all of them are seen as a home nation and an abode for the Muslim.
3. This extends to the first Islamic Empire.
4. Then the Homeland of the Muslim expands to encompass the entire world.[50]

This passage is of great significance inasmuch as it signals a formal integration of nationalism – even in its local forms of loyalty. The 'country' is taken here as a basic component of a wider 'homeland of the Muslim'. Al-Banna promotes therefore a first clear articulation of national signifiers, which are so 'reconciled' with the Islamic call: 'thus did Islam reconcile the sentiments of local nationalism with that of a common nationalism, in all that is good for mankind'. More than simply acknowledging the existence of nationalism or its importance vis-à-vis foreigner occupation, al-Banna here integrates nationalism as a new 'moment' in the discourse of Islam. By theorising identity as the complex overlapping of greater *concentric circles*, each one denoting a form of loyalty ('the country itself' denoting the national loyalty; 'the first Islamic Empire' denoting the

---

[47] Walid Mahmoud Abdelnasser, *The Islamic Movement in Egypt: Perceptions of International Relations 1967–1981* (London: Kegan Paul International, 1994).
[48] Lia, *The Society of the Muslim Brothers in Egypt*, p. 74.
[49] Hasan al-Banna, *Towards the Light* (Cairo: Dar al-Kitab al-Arabi, 1936); available at http://thequranblog.files.wordpress.com/2008/06/_1_-toward-the-light.pdf.
[50] Ibid. 'SWT' stands for 'Subhanahu wa ta'ala', which means 'May he be glorified and exalted'.

Arab circle, and then the 'other Islamic countries' entailing also an Eastern and a global conception of 'Islamic homeland'), al-Banna begins celebrating modern nationalism, interpreting it in the light of the purifying force of Islam:

> If the nation possesses all these reinforcements: hope, patriotism, science, power, health, and a sound economy, it will, without a doubt, be the strongest of all nations, and the future will belong to it. Especially, if to all this one adds that it has been purified of selfishness, aggressiveness, egotism, and arrogance, and has come to desire the welfare of the whole world.[51]

In this pamphlet al-Banna maintains and promotes most of the features that modern nations were expected to develop in that specific historical time, thereby rearticulating nationalist discourses in an Islamic fashion. For instance, he stated that a Muslim nation should be able to preserve and cultivate:

'National greatness':

> The upcoming nations need to find pride in their nationalism just as a superior nation does with its own merits and history, so that their image be imprinted on the minds of their sons, and they offer their blood and lives on behalf of this glory and nobility.[52]

'Militarism':

> The modern nations have paid close attention to this and have been founded on these principles: we see that Mussolini's Fascism, Hitler's Nazism, and Stalin's Communism are based on pure militarism. But there is a vast difference between all of these and the militarism of Islam, for the Islam which has sanctified the use of force has also preferred peace.[53]

'Public health':

> Nations which are up and coming need to excel in military force, and the buttress of such a force is physical health and strength ... And he [The Prophet] forbade urinating and defecating in stagnant water, and declared a quarantine against

---

[51] Ibid.
[52] Ibid.
[53] Ibid.

plague ridden countries, so that the inhabitants should not leave such a country nor any outsider enter it.[54]

'Science':

Just as nations need power, so do they need the science with which to support this power and direct it in the best possible manner, providing them with all that they require in the way of inventions and discoveries. Islam does not reject science; indeed, it makes it as obligatory as the acquisition of power, and gives it its support.[55]

'Economics':

The rising nation also needs to regulate its economic affairs. This has been the most important question of this recent age. Islam is not negligent of this aspect, but rather has laid down all the possible guidelines.[56]

Finally, by reasserting an Occidentalist stance, al-Banna points to a series of moral problems related to modernity that Muslim nations would be able to avoid when grounded on Islam:

Along the path of Europe are to be found enticement and glamour, pleasures and luxuries, laxity and license, and comforts that captivate the soul, for all of these things are loved by the soul ... But the path of Islam is one of glory and fortitude, truth, strength, blessing, integrity, stability, virtue, and nobility. Take the nation along this path, may Allah grant you success![57]

The increasing appropriation of the language of modernity is also manifest in the following pamphlet, *Between Yesterday and Today* (1939), where Islam itself appears as a unified nation satisfying both material and spiritual needs:

---

[54] Ibid.
[55] Ibid.
[56] Ibid.
[57] Ibid.

> There is no nation in the world that is held together by linguistic unity, participation in material and spiritual interests, and similarity of both suffering and hope that the Muslims are.[58]

Interestingly, a peculiarity of the Islamic nation is located here in its 'linguistic unity'. We see that despite al-Banna's criticism of Western racial and territorial nationalism, Arab language and ethnicity are somehow exalted and posited as the very foundation of the Islamic community. A passage best illustrates this point, where 'one of the most significant factors' leading to the dissolution of the Islamic nation is ascribed to:

> The transfer of authority to non Arabs: Persians at one time, the Mamluks, Turks, and others at another time who had never had a taste of genuine Islam, and whose hearts had never been illuminated with the light of the Qur'an because of the difficulty they encountered in trying to grasp its concepts, even though they read the Words of Allah.[59]

In a speech delivered during the Fifth Conference of the Brotherhood in 1939, also printed as a pamphlet under the title *Oh Youth*, al-Banna reiterates such points.[60] Besides reasserting his distance from any form of racial discrimination, and criticising those 'international agreements that have torn the Islamic nation into small and weak mini-states that can easily be swallowed by their aggressors', he directly calls for the 'national loyalty' of all Muslims for their homeland in their fight against foreign power.[61] Defence must follow then the multidimensional complexity of Muslim identity. This entails that a primary focus be put on the fight for independence of one's country, followed by broader loyalty towards the whole Islamic homeland:

> Muslims strive hard for a motherland such as Egypt, exert their utmost effort for its cause and exhaust themselves in the Jihad because Egypt is a part of the Islamic land and the leader of its nations. Moreover, Muslims do not confine these

---

[58] Hasan al-Banna, *Between Yesterday and Today* (Cairo, 1939); available at http://thequranblog.files.wordpress.com/2008/06/_7_-between-yesterday-today.pdf.
[59] Ibid.
[60] Hasan al-Banna, *Oh Youth* (pamphlet, 1939); available at http://thequranblog.files.wordpress.com/2008/06/_9_-oh-youth.pdf.
[61] Ibid.

sentiments within its limits, but they enjoin within these sentiments each Islamic land and nation.[62]

This passage well illustrates al-Banna's position at the end of the 1930s, with Egyptian nationalism acknowledged and combined with a pan-Islamic ideal: 'Egypt is a part of the Islamic land', yet, increasingly celebrated at the point of justifying the 'utmost effort for its cause' as 'the leader of its [Islamic] nations'. The juxtaposition of Egypt to the image of Islamic land serves here the crucial task of allowing a counter-hegemonic re-articulation of national signifiers. This point is further valorised by a tendency in al-Banna's writings to emphasise the sanctified character of a Muslim nation like Egypt, which suggests a possible inclination in assuming Egyptian 'territory' of as a form of *waqf*. The concept of *waqf* land or property was traditionally deployed to indicate the religious endowment that an owner made on behalf of the community. By offering a certain land as *waqf*, the owner decreed the unalienable property of God to that land, transposing the possession of it to the whole community. This traditional signifier had been creatively re-articulated throughout the Ottoman Empire where the symbolic appeal of *waqf* served crucial political purposes, contributing 'to impose competing definitions of legitimacy and community'.[63] Although never explicitly used, the recurrence of terms like sacredness, inviolability and sanctity to qualify the status of Muslim land denotes the influence that the notion of *waqf* played in al-Banna's conceptualisation of Islamic land.[64] The integration of national territory within the Islamic land served therefore the double effect of producing a further creative intervention in that tradition, while allowing for a counter-hegemonic re-articulation of national signifiers. This provided al-Banna with a further opportunity to Islamise the secular way of configuring space in the nation state discourse, accounting the entire ummah for its defence.

This increasing valorisation of modern signifiers and their combination with traditional concepts proved to be crucial to the Brotherhood's growing role in the political arena of the late 1930s, and its aspiration to challenge the main actors of Egyptian politics such as the British, the king, the sheikhs of al-Azhar, the ruling elite and the opposing party Wafd. This explains also, in *Oh Youth*, al-Banna's 'irredentist' tone, which resonates with populist and nationalist slogans

---

[62] Ibid.
[63] For a discussion about the political adaptations of the *waqf*, see Engin F. Isin, 'Ottoman waqfs as acts of citizenship', in Pascale Ghazaleh (ed.), *Held in Trust: Waqf in the Islamic World* (Cairo: American University in Cairo Press, 2011), pp. 253–79.
[64] Samantha May, 'God's Land: Blurring the National and the Sacred in Waqf Territory', *Politics, Religion* and *Ideology*, 16/3 (2014).

of the time (for instance, advocating the Islamic re-appropriation of 'Andalusia, Sicily, the Balkan, South Italy and Roman Sea Islands').[65] The publication of a pamphlet addressing the notion of *jihad*, with a significant section dedicated to the military aspect of this word, as the right to defence from aggression, also gives an indication of a certain radicalism in the tone of al-Banna characteristic of this period.[66] Naturally, this was also a response to the international arena and the difficult climate preceding the Second World War. In Egypt, the hope to exploit the tension among European nations to gain full independence had in fact contributed to stir nationalist feelings.[67] In the following years, it will be possible to observe an even greater valorisation of national signifiers.

Al-Banna's Discourse in the 1940s: The National Priority

At the end of the 1930s, the Brotherhood had become the most influential mass movement in Egypt, followed only by the Wafd whose political appeal, however, was gradually declining.[68] Since the beginning of 1940s, the idea of an Islamic government received more attention from al-Banna in a way that sometimes superseded the early emphasis on the Islamisation from below. In a pamphlet that appeared in the early 1940s, *The Message of the Teachings*, after having defined the aspirations of the Brotherhood as aimed at reforming the self, establishing Islam as an 'ideology' which calls for 'righteousness' and encourages 'virtue', and which strives to liberate the homeland 'from all un-Islamic or foreign control', al-Banna expressly advocates:

> Reforming the government so that it may become a truly Islamic government, performing as a servant to the nation in the interest of the people. By Islamic government I mean a government whose officers are Muslims who perform the obligatory duties of Islam, who do not make public their disobedience, and who enforce the rules and teachings of Islam ... Rebuilding the international prominence of the Islamic Umma by liberating its lands ... until once again the long awaited unity and the lost Khilafah is returned.[69]

---

[65] Ibid.
[66] Hasan al-Banna, *Al-Jihad* (Cairo, n.d.; appeared in the late 1930s), available at: http://thequranblog.files.wordpress.com/2008/06/_10_-al-jihad.pdf.
[67] Gorge Kirk, *The Middle East in the War* (London: Royal Institute of International Affairs, 1952).
[68] Lia, *The Society of the Muslim Brothers in Egypt*.
[69] Hasan al-Banna, *The Message of the Teachings* (Cairo, n.d.; appeared in the early 1940s), available at: http://thequranblog.files.wordpress.com/2008/06/_3_-the-message-

Besides the highly rhetorical and irredentist tone of this quote asking for the liberation of the Islamic homeland and the restoration of the caliphate ('the lost Khilafah is returned'), the significance of this passage is that al-Banna defines in clear terms what he means by Islamic government.[70] It is interesting to notice that while defining Islamic government as a Muslim administration, where officers are Muslims and where Islamic rules and teachings are enforced, the language used to articulate such an administration is a nationalist one, for 'a truly Islamic government' is the one 'performing as a servant' to 'the nation' in the 'interest' of the 'people'; that is, neither in the interest of Islam itself, nor in that of shari'ah. This is a point of pivotal importance for its signals a sort of adaptation of the Islamic government to the nation state model in al-Banna's discursive trajectory, though this adaptation was not new in absolute terms.

Since the late nineteenth century the encounter between the language of modernity and the language of tradition had given rise to an ongoing debate about the nature of the Islamic government. Crucially, prominent reformist Muhammad 'Abduh (1849–1905) had used the legal notion of *maslaha*, the 'common good' in Islamic jurisprudence, to reconsider the traditional prerogatives of the government, influencing the cultural climate preceding the foundation of the Brotherhood in the 1920s.[71] Since the thirteenth century the concept of *maslaha* had undertaken important conceptual shifts, allowing for doctrinal innovations (we mentioned in Chapter 2, for instance, that the principle of *maslaha* was used by Shafi'i jurists to moderate universalistic polarity introducing the domain of *dar al-'ahd*).[72] Al-Banna's emphasis on 'the interest of the people' came forth from these enduring cultural transformations, bringing the Islamic notion of 'common good' – which had to maintain some moral and theological characterisation as expression of the will of God – close to the liberal concept of 'public interest' or 'general welfare', to use Robert Mitchell's translation of this term.[73]

When describing the constitutive features of the discourse of the nation, we mentioned that a common juridical tendency among modern doctrines of sovereignty had been to conceptualise the supreme power of political order

---

of-the-teachings.pdf.

[70] On al-Banna's ideas on the caliphate see Bertier, 'L'idéologie politique des frères musulmans'.

[71] Wael B. Hallaq, *A History of Islamic Legal Theories: An Introduction to Sunni Usul al-Fiqh* (Cambridge: Cambridge University Press, 1997).

[72] Felicitas Opwis, 'Maslaha in Contemporary Islamic Legal Theory', *Islamic Law and Society*, 12/2 (2005): 182–223.

[73] Mitchell, The Society of the Muslim Brothers, p. 239.

as an absolute and exclusive power which does not recognise any principle of legitimacy outside itself (*summa potestas*). In particular, modern sovereignty entailed the passage of this exclusive and absolute power from the transcendent dimension of God to the immanent authority of the state, though differences among theorists regarded the locus of sovereignty: the king, the people, the law, and so forth. We mentioned earlier that while acknowledging the transcendent power of God in principle, this transcendent trait was shadowed by al-Banna on a practical level, justifying that claim through an emphasis on the immanent ability of jurists' 'decisions' to 'cover every contingency'.[74] The quote above shows an intensification of this early emphasis, defining a 'truly Islamic government' 'as a servant to the nation *in the interest of the people* [emphasis added]'. It is not God or shari'ah that defines the ultimate 'interest' of which the Islamic government is an expression, but 'the people', here incarnating the locus of sovereignty and the space of *public interest*. This signals the integration and re-elaboration of modern national signifiers and the substantial resonance with modern theories of sovereignty of the state, in itself a further expression of al-Banna's reliance on the modern symbolic scenario.

This transition defines al-Banna's representation of the Islamic order as a sort of modern nation state, deprived of its secular characterisations, with shari'ah inspiring legislative provisions rather than literally supplanting them. Such a position is accompanied by al-Banna's increasing opening to Western parliamentary political and institutional procedures in the early 1940s. Although on several occasions al-Banna had rejected the party system as a factor of social and political division ('we do not support these political parties'), and invited Muslims 'to boycott non-Islamic courts and judicial systems' that draw on Western juridical principles, he acknowledged liberal tools in principle (for instance the separation of powers, or state institutions such as the parliament).[75] He formally engaged, for instance, in the mainstream political process, even advancing his candidature to the parliamentary election of 1942.[76] Although the candidature was withdrawn under pressure from the king and the Wafd in exchange for the promise to introduce some 'Islamic laws' prohibiting gambling and prostitution, this event reveals that al-Banna had begun considering the modern state as offering all the tools needed for the implementation of an Islamic system. More precisely, the *Islamisation* of the modern *statist* structure was seen as an antidote against the dangers of the secular state. Later on in

---

[74] al-Banna, *To What Do We Invite Humanity?*
[75] al-Banna, *The Message of the Teachings*. See M. Borrmans, 'Les Fréres Musulmans', in *Comprendre* 70/14 (1969).
[76] Mitchell, The Society of the Muslim Brothers, pp. 27–8.

the 1940s, al-Banna while describing the 'course of modernity' praised the emancipatory nature of the democratic system, alerting the reader, however, to the risks entailed by modernity:

> The democratic system led the world for a while, encouraging many intellectuals as well as the masses to think of it as the ideal system. Nobody can ignore the freedom it has secured for peoples and nations alike, and the justice it has introduced to the human mind in allowing it to think freely ... However, it was not long before people realized that individuality and unlimited liberty can lead to chaos and many other short-comings, which ultimately led to the fragmentation of the social structure and family systems, and the eventual re-emergence of totalitarianism.[77]

Al-Banna's use of modern language is exemplary here. Central to the point is al-Banna's emphasis on the risks of modern *individualism* (here described in terms of 'individuality') and the ultimate 'fragmentation of the social structure and family systems' – all features we assumed in Chapter 2 as constitutive of a *moral connotation* of modernity. In this sense, al-Banna fully reflects the attempt to appropriate the language of modernity for counter-hegemonic purposes, pointing to the modern loss of sociability that had hitherto been associated with the emergence of industrial societies. Hence, al-Banna's emphasis on Islamic 'brotherhood' as a remedy against the 'fragmentation' of 'family systems', 'social structure' and community.

In this broader context, Islam is more than simply an *element* amongst others, standing as the very core of a universe of signification. It is the master signifier that gives traditional and modern signifiers their *new* semantic connotation. So far, we have emphasised that in order for Islam to exert its hegemonic function, and assume the metonymic representation of a whole discursive universe, it must work as an empty signifier. This implies a partial loss (emptiness) of meaning. In order to embody and represent a growing range of elements, Islam, as a master signifier, needs to become more and more abstract, extending its semantic domain as much as possible. This process is best exemplified by al-Banna's reiterated emphasis on Islam as an *all embracing* concept or, as he put it again in the above-mentioned *Oh Youth* in the late 1930s, as an 'all-encompassing' system:

---

[77] Hasan al-Banna, *Peace in Islam* (Cairo, 1948), available at: http://thequranblog.files.wordpress.com/2008/06/_4_-peace-in-islam1.pdf.

Creed as well as worship, 2. Homeland and nationalism, 3. Behavior and matter, 4. Culture and law, 5. Leniency and harshness. Islam is a Divine Comprehensive way of life that imposes itself upon all aspects of life and regulates the worldly matters as well as matters of the hereafter. Islam combines the Practical as well as Spiritual aspect of life. For them, Islam is: 1. Both Religion and State. 2. Both Scripture and Sword.[78]

In the 1940s, the emphasis on the 'comprehensive and universal' nature of Islam, and its ability to absorb external ideologies by way of an osmotic process that purifies them of their negative aspects, remains at the very core of al-Banna's discourse. In *Our Message in a New Phase* (n.d., but appeared in the 1940s), al-Banna states:

> Nowadays both people and leaders use many slogans to convey their thoughts and ideologies. What is the place of such slogans in our message? Every sentence and idea has a special place in our invitation.[79]

At this stage, al-Banna's recognition of local nationalism as an integral part of the Islamic system is fully achieved. In a passage, al-Banna makes explicit as never before his own devotion towards Egyptian nationalism:

> Egyptian nationalism has a definite place in our call. It is its right that it should be defended. Surely we are Egyptians; the most honourable place on this Earth to us, we were born and raised up here. Egypt is the land, which has been an abode of belief. It gladly embraced Islam and gave it a new territory … In light of the present circumstances, the responsibility for the safeguarding of Islamic thinking is upon its shoulders. So how can we not work for Egypt and its welfare? Why shall we not defend it with all of our energy and strength? How can it be said that the Egyptian Nationality can not fit in with the demands of the belief of a Muslim? … This is only a part of the entire Arab homeland. Therefore, whatever effort we make for the welfare of Egypt, would in reality be for Arabia, The East and Islam.[80]

---

[78] al-Banna, *Oh Youth*.
[79] Hasan al-Banna, *Our Message in a New Phase* (Cairo, n.d.; appeared in the 1940s), available at: http://thequranblog.files.wordpress.com/2008/06/_5_-our-message-in-a-new-phase.pdf.
[80] Ibid.

We see that al-Banna re-articulates nationalism preserving the idea of the nation, and transforming it into an expression of Islamic loyalty: 'whatever effort we make for the welfare of Egypt, would in reality be for Arabia, The East and Islam'.

In the 1940s, the idea of the growing concentric circles (each one referring to a specific form of identification, e.g., Egyptian, Arab, Eastern, Islamic) that was first expressed in *Towards the Light* in 1937 had become an integral part of al-Banna's discursive articulation. We have just seen in the previous quote that al-Banna clearly links Egyptian nationalism, and the effort made for the sake of national independence, to the upper levels of loyalty, to the upper strata of the Islamic homeland. Each of these circles maintains its modern binary structure when defining space and subjectivity, for instance by relying on an exclusionary notion of 'territory' or defining 'people' as a unified community grounded on common 'history', 'religion' and 'language'. This is best demonstrated by al-Banna's conceptualisation of Arab subjectivity in the *Arab circle*:

> Islam cannot be revived, unless the Arabs start to revive and become a unified force. It is for this reason that we regard every inch of the native land of the Arabs as part of our own homeland. How can these geographical boundaries and political divisions, terminate the value and feelings of the Arabic/Islamic Unity, which united in the hearts of myriads, one hope and one goal, turning all these countries into one nation?[81]

In Chapter 2, we argued that the dualistic structure organising the nation state discourse in Europe entailed the transformation of local populations into a nation; that is, the subsumption of all differences into a unified 'self', the national people, which was furthermore put in radical opposition with its outside (competing nations). The passage above is particularly telling in this respect. Al-Banna acknowledges that differences inform the contemporary reality of 'Arabs', but he advocates the need to overcome such divisions becoming 'a unified force', to 'unite in the hearts of myriads, one hope and one goal, turning all these countries into one nation'. It is the movement of national unification that transforms the various Arab populations into a people, and that allows Islam to 'be revived'.

In *Peace in Islam* (1948), the role of language in defining the nationality of Arabs is furthermore emphasised; so are the merits of linguistic ties when compared with Western exaltation of race and ethnicity:

---

[81] Ibid.

> Sociologists confirm that language is one of the strongest binding factors in any society and the easiest way to bring people together. Islam has recognized this fact, and obliged the Believers to use the Arabic language in their prayers and all other forms of worship. Hence the Arab nationality is not based on race, but language, and it encompasses all those who come to speak it.[82]

Although the importance ascribed to Arabic language is largely motivated by Muslims on the basis of Arabic being the language of the Qur'an, the language chosen by Allah to communicate the message of Islam, it is interesting to note in this passage that linguistic unity is deployed to define a nationality rather than the 'spiritual brotherhood' of the early writings. In the aftermath of the Second World War, the nationalist link between race and people had led to the most disastrous consequences in Europe. This, in part, explains al-Banna's attempt to bypass the Western focus on ethnic factors on behalf of linguistic commonalities.

Yet, we mentioned in Chapter 2 that a basic feature of early narratives about nationalism was to define national belonging in relation to a common language. By asserting the 'Arabness' of all those who speak Arabic, and by underlining the link between Arabism and Islam, al-Banna re-articulates nationalist paradigms of language and race, thereby fostering a sort of 'nationalisation' of the Muslim community.

The ultimate adoption of a binary logic in this phase is also reflected in the Occidentalist representation of the 'East' as a *unified Self*, opposed to a Western *outside* accused of invading the 'orient'. In the 1940s, the strategic and reactive function of Occidentalism that aimed at reversing orientalist discourses is openly professed:

> Orientalism: This also has a position in our invitation, although it is based entirely on ephemeral and transitory things. It so happened that the West became unduly proud of its civilisation. Accordingly, it abandoned and isolated the Eastern nations, dividing the world into two parts: one was named the East, and the other, the West. It called it by such divisions until an influential poet went to the extent of saying: 'East is East and West is West And never the Twain shall meet.' This made the Easterners feel that they were one battalion, ready to meet the ranks of the West.[83]

---

[82] al-Banna, *Peace in Islam*.
[83] al-Banna, *Our Message in a New Phase*.

In the attempt to reverse the logocentric approach of orientalist discourses, the 'East' is here positivised against the West from which it was 'abandoned and isolated'. This is done, again, by subsuming differences within a higher unity set against an outside; that is transforming a plurality of Eastern manifestations into 'one battalion'. Occidentalism provides then a further example of the growing importance that al-Banna ascribed to binary representations.

Final Remarks

By inquiring into the discourse of Islamist thinker and militant Hasan al-Banna, the aim of this chapter has been to show that, while initially caught between nationalism and pan-Islamism, two discourses that defined al-Banna's genealogical discursive context and characterised the desedimented space of Middle Eastern colonised settings, in the end, it was the modern symbolic scenario that acquired every growing importance for him. In the last pamphlet written by al-Banna in 1949, which remained unfinished because of his assassination, al-Banna provides clear evidence of this, citing a number of Western physicists and modernist discourses in support of the existence of God and His attributes.[84] In uncovering al-Banna's reliance on the modern reservoir, however, we have given special attention to the increasing symbolic appeal that the nation state discourse acquired in his trajectory. We mentioned al-Banna's late acknowledgment of the benefits of democratic systems and parliamentary institutions, though it should observed that sections of the Brotherhood remained eager to adopt violent strategies in politics, as was the case with most political formations in the turbulent times of the 1940s in Egypt. Al-Banna's immanent approach to sovereignty, with the 'interest of the people' posed as the ultimate requirement for any 'truly Islamic government', the celebration of local nationalism as a first, more intimate circle within broader forms of loyalty (Arab, Eastern, Islamic) as well as the very dualistic structure used to construct any of the identity circles that al-Banna foresaw in his idea of loyalty (as if the Arab, the Eastern and the Islamic circles were *national* circles in their own right) – all this denoted the delineation of a *territorial trajectory*. This entailed the adoption of a binary logic defining forms of space (territory) and subjectivity (people), with tradition maintained nonetheless as a moderator principle in the counter-hegemonic process of re-signifying the space of modernity.

---

[84] Hasan al-Banna, *Al-Aqaa'id (Islamic Creed)* (Cairo, 1949), available at: http://thequranblog.files.wordpress.com/2008/06/_8_-al-aqaaid.pdf.

Al-Banna's notion of Islamic 'government' or 'system' (*al-nizam al-Islami*) paved the way for the theorisation of an Islamic state that was central in the political agenda of Islamist groups in the following decades, the Brotherhood included. The nationalisation of al-Banna's discourse, however, signalled that the target was not the restoration of a traditional Islamic government but, rather, a sort of counter-hegemonic appropriation and Islamisation of the nation state structure, with *shari'ah* maintained as an ethical source for state legislation.

From a broad perspective, al-Banna's trajectory reveals that the nationalisation of the Islamist message was somehow intrinsic to the discursive development of early Islamist representations, rather than emerging as a sort of political expedient in recent decades. Al-Banna has certainly been one of the most influential figures of the modern Muslim world. He founded the Brotherhood as early as 1928, at a time when discourses such as fascism, communism and exacerbated forms of nationalism were gaining increasing relevance in the West. Although al-Banna inherited a sense of mission for social transformation from important Muslim reformists of the nineteenth century such as Jamal al-Din al-Afghani (1838–1897) and Muhammad 'Abduh (1849–1905), he also introduced an important innovation to the history of Islamic activism. In founding the Muslim Brotherhood, he merged an ideological vision into a mass social movement challenging Western discursive narratives, and showing the same ability as modern political movements in Europe to mobilise entire sections of society.

From a theoretical and political perspective, we mentioned that al-Banna reflected the official position of the Brotherhood until his death, remaining a central point of reference for the Society. The Brotherhood itself, modelled around al-Banna's vision, reflected a 'proto-typical Islamist movement'.[85] It expanded beyond Egyptian borders, branching out in Palestine, Syria and Jordan, giving rise to organisations such as Hamas (resulting from the Palestinian wing of Brotherhood) or the *Islamic Action Front* (the political branch of the Brotherhood in Jordan). Moreover, a number of political parties and movements found explicit inspiration in the activities of the Brotherhood after the 1950s. This can been seen in Tunisia, Sudan, and Morocco where contemporary Islamist figures, such as the exiled leader of the Tunisian Islamist movement *al-Nahda*, Rashid al-Ghannushi, and the leader of the *National Islamic Front* in Sudan, Hasan al-Turabi, openly acknowledged their intellectual debt to the Brotherhood.

---

[85] Peter G. Mandaville, *Global Political Islam* (London: Routledge, 2007), p. 85. MB stands for Muslim Brothers.

Certainly, the reference to al-Banna was not always a direct one. As we shall see in the Conclusion of this study, the term 'resonance' best describes the analogical relation between al-Banna's distinct articulation and the discursive route that other Islamist actors pursued later on. While the afore-mentioned groups displayed a pretty explicit reliance on al-Banna's ideas, especially with regard to his progressive integration of national signifiers and his bottom-up approach to Islamisation, other theorists and movements, for instance in countries such as Turkey, Malaysia, or the Shi'a context of the Islamic Republic of Iran, came to share similar perspectives about the nation, without any direct or comprehensive reference to al-Banna's discourse. Despite the significant differences that have come to characterise these organisations, al-Banna's vision remained an 'exemplary' way of engaging with the symbolic scenarios of modernity and tradition, constituting something akin to a foundational discourse as far as a territorial trajectory of Islamism is concerned. Of relevance to all these movements is Peter Mandaville's observation in his analysis of contemporary Islamism, that: 'in so far as the MB represented the first sustained and successful articulation of a modern Islamist method, all of these groups owe a debt to the project Hasan al-Banna initiated in 1928'.[86]

---

[86] Ibid.

Chapter 5

The Discourse of Sayyid Qutb: A Transitional Trajectory

> This marvellous civilization was not an 'Arabic civilization', even for a single day; it was purely an 'Islamic civilization'. It was never a 'nationality' but always a 'community of belief'.[1]

Following our inquiry of Hasan al-Banna's discourse, which contributed to outlining a 'territorial' trajectory of Islamism, this chapter attempts a first differentiation of Islamist articulations. In the previous chapter we traced the path of an increasing valorisation of national signifiers, with tradition maintained by al-Banna as a moderator principle in the counter-hegemonic appropriation of modernity. In an attempt to present the internal complexity of Islamism, this chapter will now identify the articulation of an alternative discursive route, one that drew creatively on the traditional appeal of Islamic universalism, rejecting the dominant role that modern discourses had maintained in the aftermath of Hasan al-Banna's assassination. This will be done by examining the discourse of Sayyid Qutb (1906–1966), together with al-Banna, one of the most significant thinkers of the twentieth-century Sunni Islamic political movement. This analysis will allow us to identify a *transitional* trajectory of Islamism, unpacking the way in which antagonistic relations have variously been articulated by this thinker.

The term 'transitional' is not used here with the meaning of marginal, 'transitory' or minor. As we shall see in the next pages, Qutb's intellectual contribution to the development of contemporary Islamism has been strong, anticipating a number of key discursive features that will be either adopted or re-elaborated in the following decades. In a way, it is precisely this anticipatory character that we want to emphasise: its being in-between different historical phases and discursive strategies of Islamism. In historical terms, Qutb represented a period, between the 1950s and the 1960s, characterised by the wide repression of Islamist movements by Arab regimes, and by the quasi-dormancy of Islamist

---

[1] Sayyid Qutb, *Milestones* (Birmingham: Maktabah Booksellers & Publishers, 2006), p. 60.

action. Situated between the dismantling of the Brotherhood in the early 1950s and the revival of Islamist groups in the 1970s, Qutb's discourse gained increasing relevance in this intermediate post-colonial phase. This position also reflects the kind of discursive structure that has been adopted in this book, where a speculative examination of Qutb's vision has been proposed just after al-Banna's opening discourse in a colonial context and immediately before a representative version of contemporary global jihadism in the form of bin Laden's discourse.

While located in different historical phases, this positioning entails an overlapping of different discursive strategies. Although chronologically belonging to subsequent periods, their visions have in fact continued to cohabit within the Islamist discursive universe, working as 'co-existing' speculative models for understanding spatial arrangements and subjective constructions. We will see that Qutb's transitional trajectory abandons al-Banna 'territorial' way of engaging with the symbolic scenario of modernity. His approach is, rather, to re-activate the traditional ideal of Islamic universalism as the sole imaginary horizon for a just society, thereby 'anticipating' the kind of pan-Islamic perspective subsequently mobilised by bin Laden. But while Qutb's reliance on tradition is functional to his rejection of modernity, we will see that bin Laden's re-elaboration of a universalistic ideal evidences some kind of engagement with the transmodern symbolic scenario in what we define a *transterritorial* trajectory.

An Historical Framework

Defined as the 'ideologue of Islamic revival', Sayyid Qutb's intellectual activity began in the 1930s when he wrote a series of articles on literary criticism and a number of short commentaries on the Qur'an, highlighting its aesthetic, rhetorical, and literary dimension.[2] Although politically committed to an anti-imperialist ethos, exacerbated by the long years of British control, his gradual move toward Islamist activism intensified in the following decade. During the 1940s, Qutb completed one of his most important contributions, *Social Justice in Islam* (*Al-'adala al-Ijtima'iyya fi-l-Islam*), a work reverberating with the Brotherhood's leitmotif of Islam as a complete and self-sufficient system of

---

[2] Yvonne Y. Haddad, 'Sayyid Qutb: Ideologue of Islamic Revival', in John Esposito (ed.), *Voices of the Islamic Revolution* (Oxford: Oxford University Press, 1983); Adnan A. Musallam, *From Secularism to Jihad: Sayyid Qutb and the Foundations of Radical Islamism* (Westport, CT: Praeger, 2005); Issa J. Boullata, 'Sayyid Qutb's Literary Appreciation of the Qur'an', in Issa J. Boullata (ed.), *Literary Structures of Religious Meaning in the Qur'ān* (Richmond: Curzon, 2000).

ideas able to ensure justice and virtue.[3] In these years, Qutb's criticism of Western culture, which was fuelled by a short research visit to the United States between 1948 and 1950, targeted most of those moral concerns, such as individualism, materialism, lack of social bonds, that were often associated with modernity. In line with the kind of occidentalist reaction that we examined in relation to al-Banna's discourse, the modern predicament in the West was contrasted with the ideal of spirituality, morality and justice in Islam.

The intellectual, spiritual and political proximity to the Brotherhood reached symbolic highpoint when the Free Officers seized power in 1952. A year earlier, Qutb had joined the Muslim Brotherhood, becoming editor-in-chief of the Brothers' weekly journal and head of its propaganda section.[4] He then participated in the Brotherhood's increasing criticism of the Free Officers and the dramatic and intense events that led to the dismantling of the Society in 1954. As we mentioned in Chapter 4, despite the initial material and moral support of the coup, the Brotherhood soon began to criticise the Free Officers as they appeared to reject the role of 'moral tutor' of the Society, resisting the increasing pressure to infuse the new regime with Islamic principles.[5] As tensions intensified – with the Society aspiring to play a stronger role in the transition, defending its position of independence, and the new regime being more and more inclined to silence political opponents – events came to a head.

In 1954, a member of the Muslim Brotherhood attempted to kill Nasser. In response, the leader of the Free Officers ordered a major crackdown on political adversaries, the disbandment of the Society, and the dismissal of a number of officers whose loyalty was doubted.

Over his following nine years of prison, Qutb, who had been arrested with thousands of other Islamists and political opponents, witnessed the harsh Nasserite response to political opposition. The hanging of a number of

---

[3] Sayyid Qutb, *Social Justice in Islam* (Oneonta, NY: Islamic Publications International, 2000).

[4] Ishaq Musa al-Husayni, *The Moslem Brethren: The Greatest of Modern Islamic Movements* (Beirut, Khayat's College Book Cooperative, 1956), pp. 145–6. In his recent work on Qutb, John Calvert dates Qutb's entrance in the Society in 1953; see John Calvert *Sayyid Qutb and the Origins of Radical Islamism* (New York: Columbia University Press, 2010). Gilles Kepel anticipates his enrolment at 1951; see Gilles Kepel, *The Prophet and Pharaoh: Muslim Extremism in Egypt* (Berkeley, CA: University of California Press, 1985).

[5] Gilbert Delanque, 'Al-Ikhwan al-Muslimun', *Encyclopaedia of Islam* (Leiden: E.J. Brill, 1960; new edn, vol. 3, 1969); see also early historical accounts on these events in Robert Mitchell, *The Society of the Muslim Brothers* (London: Oxford University Press, 1969) and Christina Phelps Harris, *Nationalism and Revolution in Egypt: The Role of the Muslim Brotherhood* (The Hague: Mouton & Co., 1964).

Brotherhood leaders, the physical and psychological torture of inmates in Egyptian prisons, and the need for thousands of political activists to expatriate contributed to radicalising his position. Released from prison at the behest of the then Prime Minister of Iraq in 1964, he joined a secret organisation in the attempt to reconstitute the Islamist movement and re-activate an Islamist agenda.[6] The organisation, however, was immediately suppressed, and Qutb was rearrested a few months later, charged with plotting to overthrow the regime along with two other members, and executed in 1966.

During these years, the Islamist movement in Egypt faced increasing difficulties, both because its leaders had been exiled and imprisoned, and because, as Kepel observes, 'despite Nasser's propaganda and coercive methods, the Egyptian people were firmly behind him.'[7] Political repression following the abolition of the Brotherhood in 1954 and the increasing relevance of nationalism and pan-Arabism between the 1950s and the 1960s curtailed the ability of Islamism to compete with nationalist and pan-Arab discourses in the battle of Arab minds.

At this time, Egypt had substantially freed itself from the direct interference of the British, with Nasser, in the aftermath of the Suez Crisis in 1956, guiding the country toward a post-colonial era. By drawing on nationalism, Arabism and socialism in the articulation of a new type discourse, *Nasserism*, which succeeded in winning over wide sections of the Arab population well beyond the Egyptian borders, Nasser allowed Egypt to play a major role in the region. In this broader scenario, Islamist discourses between the 1950s and the 1960s were espoused by only a limited number of parties and organisations in the Middle East and North Africa, whose freedom of action was furthermore curtailed by the increasing suspicion of domestic regimes. With nationalist post-colonial elites willing to pursue a lay and Westernised way of life in the administration of the state, tensions led to the imprisonment of Islamist militants, thereby reducing the visibility of Islamism in general.

There were exceptions to this general trend, which, between the late 1950s and 1960s, included the development of a number of Islamist organisations resonating with the kind of territorial trajectory outlined by Hasan al-Banna, including, by way of example, the foundation of some international branches of the Muslim Brotherhood, the emergence of various Islamist parties and associations in North Africa and East Asia, and the increasing influence played by the Pakistani Islamist movement *Jamaat-e-Islami*.

---

[6] John Calvert, *Sayyid Qutb and the Origins of Radical Islamism*.
[7] Gilles Kepel, *Jihad: The Trail of Political Islam* (London: I.B. Tauris, 2002), p. 31.

Sayyid Qutb's discourse is mostly associated with this post-colonial period, bearing its inheritance of the counter-hegemonic passion that al-Banna had aroused in his colonial context. While Qutb's execution was testament to the difficulty of this phase, his discourse anticipated, beyond any ambiguity, the attempt to revitalise the Islamic tradition in what has been called the 'rejuvenation', 'revival' or 'return' of Islamism in the 1970s.[8] His vision was central in challenging 'the imposition of a monolithic Arab nationalist-socialist discourse on Egyptian society', thereby countering the dominant role that nationalism played during this time.[9]

The exemplary value of his thought, however, transcended his national, social and historical context. His last work, translated either as *Signposts on the Road* or *Milestones*, (*Ma'alim fi-l-Tariq*) and published in 1964 (Qutb 1964/2006), has had a massive impact on several generations of Muslim activists and believers, influencing the way in which antagonistic relations have been articulated by many Islamist groups. This has been true, to some extent, for organisations such as the Muslim Brothers, whose political focus, however, has rested primarily on the reformation of domestic politics rather than a universal Muslim community. But the influence of *Milestones*, as we shall see in Chapter 6, was also felt in the formation of the Awakening movement (*Da'wa*) in Saudi Arabia in the 1980s, subsequently contributing to the emergence of transnational views of those such as bin Laden, and inspiring the particular antagonistic position that so-called 'neo-fundamentalist' groups have assumed in recent decades in what they often perceive as a globalised and post-national world.[10] Described as 'one of the most widely read and controversial Arab books of the twentieth century', *Milestones* stands as Qutb's political manifesto.[11] In both its concision and clarity of argumentation, the text has been a potent tool for political mobilisation. As Roxanne L. Euben puts it: 'Qutb's thought can serve as a window into the world of contemporary Islamic fundamentalist political practice; as Qutb's most influential and radical book, *Signposts* is the text that has significantly influenced

---

[8] Bernard Lewis, 'The Return of Islam', *Commentary*, 61/1 (1976): 39–49; Peter G. Mandaville, *Global Political Islam* (New York: Routledge, 2007).

[9] Mansoor Moaddel, *Islamic Modernism, Nationalism, and Fundamentalism: Episode and Discourse* (Chicago, IL: University of Chicago Press, 2005), p. 218.

[10] Olivier Roy, *Globalized Islam: Fundamentalism, Deterritorialization and the Search for a New Ummah* (London: Hurst & Company, 2004).

[11] Gregory Starrett, 'Islam after Empire: Turkey and the Arab Middle East', in R. Michael Feener (ed.), *Islam in World Cultures: Comparative Perspectives* (Oxford: ABC-CLIO, 2004), p. 55.

such practice.'[12] This influential book reprises most of the arguments presented in earlier major writings, drawing, for instance, on certain antagonistic elements already discussed in *Social Justice in Islam*, or re-proposing sections taken from *In the Shade of the Qur'an* (*Fi Zilal al-Qur'an*, first instalment 1954–1959), another major work written by Qutb in the years in prison, and consisting of a multi-volume commentary on the Qur'an, which partly re-elaborates early hermeneutic works.

Compared with the more disperse and uneven nature of al-Banna's work, Qutb's overall literary production shows remarkable coherence and structural consistency. The strong appeal exerted by *Milestones* over the years, despite its density, suggests that this text can be taken as a sort of general summa of his vision. Its impact on the subsequent development of Islamist thought, and the power with which it summarises Qutb's political reflections over the years, give us a clear picture of his modalities of engagement with broader symbolic scenarios. The following pages will present a focused analysis of this crucial text. This will allow us to appreciate the spatial complexity of Qutb's eschatological vision, revealing the multilayer dimension of his antagonistic perspective, which has played such an important role in the history of the twentieth-century Sunni Islamic political movement.

Sayyid Qutb's Articulatory Practice: A Discursive Inquiry[13]

In her noteworthy study of Qutb's political theory, Euben interprets *Milestones* as a tripartite analysis of contemporary political communities. According to Euben such an analysis would consist of a 'diagnosis of the ills of modernity (*jahiliyyah*), a cure (rebellion, followed by the establishment of sovereignty based on Islamic law), and a method of implementing the cure (organising a counter-community, *jama'a*, and spreading it through *jihad*'.[14] In the following examination of *Milestones* a different organisation of this structure is proposed, entailing critical differences in terms of spatial and subjective configurations. According to the proposed reading, a twofold dimension, embodying both a

---

[12] Roxanne L. Euben, *Enemy in the Mirror: Islamic Fundamentalism and the Limits of Modern Rationalism* (Princeton, NJ: Princeton University Press, 1999), p. 56.
[13] Italics will be used in this section to emphasise specified terms or concepts, or, alternatively, when typing words in languages other than English, single quotation marks will be deployed to quote Qutb's own words as found in the original text, and should be taken to express potential *signifiers* in the articulation of his discourse.
[14] R.L. Euben, *Enemy in the Mirror*, p. 56.

descriptive and a *normative* register, informs Qutb's view of the human condition in *Milestones*. On the one side, Qutb provides a critical description of the contemporary predicament in which mankind lives, something akin to the level of diagnosis in Euben's analysis. On the other side, a discussion of how humanity *should* be and live according to human nature, as it was created by God, intersects with the descriptive level. This latter register entails a dimension somewhat irreducible to the former, and placed on a different temporal and spatial 'plane'. An inquiry into these two spatial dimensions is essential to distinguish between different forms of antagonism in Qutb's discourse.

A sense of critical, if not apocalyptic, determination characterises the first observation in the incipit of the book:

> Mankind today is on the brink of a destruction, not because of the danger of complete annihilation, which is hanging over its head – this being just a symptom and not the real disease – but because humanity is devoid of those vital values which are *necessary* [emphasis added] not only for its healthy development but also for its real progress.[15]

Such a descriptive state of affairs is followed by a series of statements suggesting the increasing loss of vitality of modern discourses, whose hegemonic role, then, needs to be challenged in this critical age:

> Democracy in the West has become infertile to such an extent that it is borrowing from the systems of the Eastern bloc, especially in the economic system, under the name of socialism. It is the same with the Eastern bloc. Its social theories, foremost among which is Marxism, in the beginning attracted not only a large number of people from the East but also from the West, as it was a way of life based on a creed. But now Marxism is defeated on the plane of thought, and if it is stated that not a single nation in the world is truly Marxist, it will not be an exaggeration ... All nationalistic and chauvinistic ideologies which have appeared in modern times, and all the movements and theories derived from them, have also lost their vitality. In short, all man-made individual or collective theories have proved to be failures and unsustainable.[16]

A well-defined range of signifiers frames Qutb's articulation from the start. Decadence and an apocalyptic sense of crisis ('destruction'), accompanies

---

[15] Qutb, *Milestones*, p. 23.
[16] Ibid., pp. 23–4.

Qutb's awareness of the 'global' (from 'the West' to the 'Eastern bloc') discursive desedimentation informing modern social space. Such a critical state of 'annihilation' in fact is taken as a 'symptom', rather than as a cause, while the 'real disease' is expressly identified with the deprivation of those vital values which are *'necessary'* for human 'development' and 'progress'. That is, necessary for the achievement of those very ideals that have informed all 'ideologies which have appeared in modern times'. Hence the first bifurcation established by Qutb: between a necessary order for mankind – which encompasses ideal human values and reflects a necessary vision of humans – and the actual conditions in which mankind live, which entails the deprivation of those necessary values and reflects a descriptive vision of history and the contemporary world.

In the passage above, it is interesting to notice that Qutb is fully aware of the relevance that modern discourses ('the ideologies of modern times') have played on a global level, but is similarly convinced of the increasing inability of such discourses to maintain their hegemonic function. In a way, we can say that Qutb anticipates some sort of transmodern assessment about the declining force of modernity, valorising, furthermore, those universalistic signifiers that will be – likewise transmodern ones – particularly suitable to a global scenario. This process of anticipation and alignment between tradition and transmodernity will become clearer when tackling Osama bin Laden's transterritorial trajectory in Chapter 6. From these early statements, however, we can also trace a first important distinction from al-Banna's territorial trajectory.

When considering Hasan al-Banna's discourse we noticed that a major concern for this early Islamist thinker was that, in the face of the cultural, social and discursive desedimentation brought about by colonialism, tradition was increasingly challenged by the *incoming* dissemination of modern discourses, which were hegemonising the social space. The vigour of modern discourses, and nationalism *in primis*, was acknowledged as an *ascendant* force, which needed to be purified by Islam, not rejected. Qutb's discourse, in this respect, is situated in a different (post-colonial) context. His impression is that modern discourses reflect a *descendant* force, no longer able to provide the necessary vitality for 'the guidance of mankind'.[17] Their 'present decline' justifies their rejection, opening up new space for contestation:

> The leadership of mankind by Western men is now on the decline, not because
> Western culture has become poor materially or because its economic and military

---

[17] 'Even the Western world realises that Western civilization is unable to present any healthy values for the guidance of mankind'; Qutb, *Milestones*, p. 23.

power has become weak. The period of the Western system has come to an end primarily because it is deprived of those life-giving values, which enabled it to be the leader of mankind.[18]

It is at the heart of such a *critical* stage that Qutb poses the discourse of Islam as the only possible ethical alternative: 'At this crucial and bewildering juncture, the turn of Islam and the Muslim community has arrived.'[19]

In pointing to the loss of 'vitality' of modern discourses and the need to return to the original spirit of Islam, Qutb is keen in rejecting those innovations that render tradition itself a fluid concept, a cumulative and dynamic matrix of experiences:

> If Islam is again to play the role of the leader of mankind, then it is necessary that the Muslim community be restored to its original form. It is necessary, to revive that Muslim community which is buried under the debris of the man-made traditions of several generations, and which it crushed under the weight of those false laws and customs which are not even remotely related to the Islamic teachings, and which, in spite of all this, calls itself the '*world of Islam*.'[20]

Qutb's return to the origin, however, is not translated into a quietist or nostalgic attitude. On the contrary, he is adamant about maintaining an assertive position; that is, the return to Islam needs to be translated into practical political action. As he puts it: 'the requirement of Islamic belief is that it takes shape in living souls, in an active organization, and in a viable community'.[21]

If Qutb's major target is a return to Islam, then, and if such a revival needs to be accompanied by a concrete strategy, the strategic route is to identify those positive elements that competing discourses fail to valorise: namely, the core of ethical values that define the 'Muslim society':

> Hence we must have some other quality, that quality which modern civilization does not possess ... To attain the leadership of mankind, we must have something to offer besides material progress, and this other quality can only be a faith and a way of life which, on the one hand conserves the benefits of modern science and technology, and on the other fulfils the basic human needs on the same level of excellence as technology has fulfilled them in the sphere of material comfort. And

---

[18] Ibid., p. 23.
[19] Ibid., p. 24.
[20] Ibid., p. 25.
[21] Ibid., p. 51.

then this faith and way of life must take concrete form in a human society – in other words, in a Muslim society.[22]

But, how should a Muslim society be defined? It is here that the normative register clearly emerges as a theoretical level of discussion in Qutb's articulation.

Sayyid Qutb's Normative Vision

The basic *norm* to establish how a society *should be*, therein acceding a *normative* level of analysis, is best exemplified by a passage where Qutb defines Islamic society as 'that which follows Islam in belief and ways of worship, in law and organization, in morals and manners'.[23] At a first general level, the realm of Islam is qualified by a particular definition of 'sovereignty' (*hākimiyya*) as derivative of God's will on earth, and its fundamental equation with two other main signifiers: 'freedom' and 'human civilisation':

> When, in a society, the sovereignty belongs to Allah alone, expressed in its obedience to the *Shari'ah* – the Divine Law – only then is every person in that society free from servitude to others, and only then does he taste true freedom. This alone is *'human civilization'*, as the basis of a human civilization is the complete and true freedom of every person and the full dignity of every individual of the society.[24]

This passage evidences the central position played in Qutb's articulation by the notion 'sovereignty', and by the particular semantic relation that such a signifier establishes with 'Allah'.[25] It is this relation that gives 'sovereignty' its specific connotation, differentiating it from Westernised approaches to political power, and thereby enacting the possibility for 'freedom' and 'human civilisation' to be realised at all. In Chapter 4, we evidenced al-Banna's inclination to re-articulate the notion of 'sovereignty' along modern lines. This implied depriving 'sovereignty' of its transcendental character and re-directing it from God to the immanent power of the people of the nation (Islamic government serving 'the nation in the interest of the people').[26]

---

[22] Ibid., p. 26.
[23] Ibid., p. 106.
[24] Ibid., p. 108.
[25] Sayed Khatab, *The Power of Sovereignty: The Political And Ideological Philosophy of Sayyid Qutb* (London: Routledge, 2006).
[26] Hasan al-Banna, *The Message of the Teachings*.

Unlike al-Banna, Qutb articulates God's sovereignty in purely transcendental terms. This means that even in cases where Islamic society takes the form of a state, such a juridical construction would remain substantially alien to the model of the nation state, with the Islamic government finding its inner legitimisation outside itself; that is, in God rather than in the *immanent* power of the state or the people of the state (as with modern sovereignty). Hence, a certain downplaying of the very notion of Islamic state in Qutb and the prioritisation of an Islamic community devoted to the direct application of the *shari'ah*.

The definition of sovereignty in transcendental terms entails a double movement. On the one hand, his traditional reading implies an upward re-directing of sovereignty from humankind to God:

> They [Arabs] knew that '*Uluhiya*' means sovereignty and they also realized that ascribing sovereignty only to Allah meant that the authority would be taken away from the priests, the leaders of tribes, the wealthy and the rulers, and would *revert* [emphasis added] to Allah. It meant that only Allah's authority would prevail in the heart and conscience, in matters pertaining to religious observances and in the affairs of life such as business, the distribution of wealth and the dispensation of justice; in short, in the souls and bodies of men.[27]

This position is reinforced by another statement in which Qutb expressly rejects the possibility of having not only lay but also religious authorities incarnating or interpreting Islamic law, while suggesting a strict and literalist application of the *shari'ah*.

> The way to establish Allah Almighty's rule on earth is not that some consecrated people, the priests, be given the authority to rule, as was the case with the rule of the Church, nor that some spokesmen of Allah Almighty become rulers, as is the case in a '*theocracy*'. To establish Allah's rule means that His laws be enforced and that the final decision in all affairs be according to these laws.[28]

On the other hand, an extensive and horizontal movement allows Qutb to state the traditional Islamic significance of sovereignty as embodied by Islamic law, depriving it of all modern interpretations that have reduced *shari'ah* to a matter of legal injunction:

---

[27] Qutb, *Milestones*, p. 38.
[28] Ibid., p. 68.

> In Islam the meaning of the '*Shari'ah*' is not limited to mere legal injunctions, but includes the principles of administration, its system and its modes ... Similarly, it includes political, social and economic affairs and their principles, with the intent that they reflect complete submission to Allah alone. It also includes legal matters (this is what today is referred to as the '*Shari'ah*', while the true meaning of the '*Shari'ah*' in Islam is entirely different). It deals with the morals, manners, values and standards of the society, according to which persons, actions and events are measured. It also deals with all aspects of knowledge and principles of art and science.[29]

When defined in this way, *shari'ah* expresses an all-inclusive and integral conception of life. This is particularly important considering that Qutb is adamant in defining an Islamic society in traditional terms assuming a universal conceptualisation of ethics, which is not reduced to the logic of public interests:

> In all modern *jahili* societies, the meaning of 'morality' is limited to such an extent that all those aspects which distinguish man from animal are considered beyond its sphere ... The meaning of ethics is limited to economic affairs or sometimes to political affairs which fall into the category of 'government interests'. For example, the scandal of Christine Keeler and the British minister Profumo was not considered serious to British society because of its sexual aspect; it was condemnable because Christine Keeler was also involved with a naval attaché of the Russian Embassy.[30]

A society in which sovereignty is taken to express God's will, needs then to be articulated in an ethical model involving every aspect of human life, rejecting the secularist organisation predicated around the public–private divide.[31] Such a society will be recognised not only for the Islamic quality of its political institutions, but also, and more importantly, for the way social relations are

---

[29] Ibid., p. 120.

[30] Ibid., p. 111. The term '*jahili*' comes from '*jahiliyyah*', the state of 'ignorance of divine guidance' that was traditionally ascribed to the pre-Islamic Arab society living prior to the revelation of the Qur'an. Extensively, it has also been used so as to include contemporary forms of unbelief. We shall examine Qutb's notion of *jahiliyyah* in detail in the next pages.

[31] Sayed Khatab, 'Hakimiyyah and Jahiliyyah in the Thought of Sayyid Qutb', *Middle Eastern Studies*, 38/3 (2002): 145–70; Ahmad S. Moussalli, *Radical Islamic Fundamentalism: The Ideological and Political Discourse of Sayyid Qutb* (Beirut: American University of Beirut, 1992).

constructed and the role ascribed to 'the family system and the relationship between the sexes':[32]

> If the family is the basis of the society, the basis of the family is the division of labor between husband and wife, and the upbringing of children is the most important function of the family, then such a society is indeed civilized. In the Islamic system of life, this kind of a family provides the environment under which human values and morals develop and grow in the new generation.[33]

This, however, requires for 'humanity' and 'morality', when infused with the true spirit of Islam, to be enfranchised by all those material aspirations that have ended up marking the modern predicament:

> A society which places the highest value on the 'humanity' of man and honours the noble 'human' characteristics is truly civilized. If materialism, no matter in what form, is given the highest value, whether it be in the form of a 'theory', such as in the Marxist interpretation of history, or in the form of material production, as is the case with the United States and European countries, and all other human values are sacrificed at its altar, then such a society is a backward one, or, in Islamic terminology, is a '*Jahili society*'.[34]

A society where 'morality' informs the way social relations are structured is a society where 'humanity' and 'freedom' are asserted, and where the sovereignty of God replaces materialistic conceptions of life. It is on the basis of this ethical framework alone that the Islamic society can be thought of, and strategically counterposed to modern discourses.

In his outstanding work on Qutb, John Calvert argues that Qutb's reliance on a 'Qur'anically justified concept of God's judgment and dominion' aimed to 'undermine the theory and practice of state sovereignty which undergirded the Western-dominated global order'.[35] From this perspective, Qutb's eschatological vision is intimately related to the political dimension of his universalism. The counter-hegemonic potential that Qutb ascribes to his universalistic conception of human society vis-à-vis the discourse of the nation is therefore central to understand the specificity of his vision.

---

[32] Ibid.
[33] Qutb, *Milestones*, p. 110.
[34] Ibid., p. 109.
[35] J. Calvert, *Sayyid Qutb and the Origins of Radical Islamism*, p. 215.

From a general perspective, we examined nationalist discourses on the ground of the fundamental link they establish between three key signifiers, whose articulation is intimately related to a binary conceptualisation of space and subjectivity: 'sovereignty', 'territory' and 'the people'. In spite of this national framework, we have seen that Qutb's approach to 'sovereignty' enacts a transcendent *reversion* from humankind to God, and that this movement also implies an integral and horizontal expansion of sovereignty so as to include also the non-political. This move, we observed, undoes modern dualistic conceptions of sovereignty that ended up celebrating the priority of state immanence over a divine transcendent, and the ultimate primacy of the political over the religious. Qutb's rejection of modern symbolic coordinates, however, is also evidenced by his dismissal of nationalist conceptions of 'territory' and 'people' in favour of a universalistic approach to traditional notions of *dar al-Islam* and the *ummah*.

Qutb's alignment to a universalistic understanding of *ummah*, which in its vocabulary is also called the 'Islamic society', is unequivocal. In a short passage, he formulates his position in explicit terms:

> Islam based the Islamic society on the association of belief alone, instead of the low associations based on race and colour, language and country, regional and national interests. Instead of stressing those traits which are common to both man and animal, it promoted man's human qualities, nurtured them and made them the dominant factor. Among the concrete and brilliant results of this attitude was that the Islamic society became an open and all-inclusive community in which people of various races, nations, languages and colours were members, there remaining no trace of these low animalistic traits.[36]

From a normative perspective, the ummah figures as a universal community predicated upon a principle of spatial inclusivity. Unlike the concept of the 'people', a perfect Islamic society *should be* 'an open and *all-inclusive* community' [emphasis added] integrating all differences within its multiplicity, rather than a closed *us* intrinsically opposing an *outside*. Defined like this, such a conceptualisation of the *ummah* reflects a *state of necessity*. That is, Islamic society alone allows 'humanity' to emerge and develop. It figures as a *necessary condition* for the very realisation of 'humanity'; the absence of this condition would qualify human life as a mere 'animalism':

---

[36] Qutb, *Milestones*, p. 59.

> In whatever society Islam is dominant, whether it is an agricultural or industrial society, nomadic and pastoral or urban and settled, poor or rich, it implants these human values and morals, nurtures them and strengthens them; it develops human characteristics progressively and guards against degeneration toward animalism.[37]

In his recent analysis of Qutb's ethical model, Andrew March drew from Rawls the concept *realistic utopia* to describe a comprehensive theory of political life that 'not only posits a true doctrine of the good or the right (i.e., the substance of moral obligation for persons and societies), but also contains an account of how that theory does not contradict what we know about human moral psychology'.[38] From this perspective, to define Islamic society as a necessary condition means to point to the immediate adaptability and convergence that Qutb instantiates between humanity and the ethical and normative framework that God has reserved for it. This permits enacting a crucial disjuncture between the uniqueness of the Islamic normative system, which only responds to humans' own characteristics, and other normative systems that alter the very 'human' quality of mankind. The state of necessity that Islamic society incarnates entails in fact the assumption of a universalistic and inclusive approach to subjectivity, which overcomes the particularistic features that nationhood is said to involve with its emphasis on 'low animalistic traits'. It only preserves the spirit of the human *genre* preventing its *degeneration* into animalism. From this perspective, the refusal of national affiliations, from local forms of belonging to pan-Arab or pan-continental loyalties implies, for Qutb, formulating communitarian ties not on the basis of geographical adjacency or biological traits (lineage or race), but as a commonality of choice and belief.

> In this great Islamic society Arabs, Persians, Syrians, Egyptians, Moroccans, Turks, Chinese, Indians, Romans, Greeks, Indonesians and Africans were gathered together – in short, peoples of all nations and all races. Their various characteristics were united, and with mutual cooperation, harmony and unity, they took part in the construction of the Islamic community and Islamic culture. This marvellous civilization was not an 'Arabic civilization', even for a single day; it was purely an '*Islamic civilization*'. It was never a 'nationality' but always a 'community of belief'.[39]

---

[37] Ibid., p. 110.
[38] Andrew F. March, 'Taking People as They Are: Islam as a "Realistic Utopia" in the Political Theory of Sayyid Qutb', *American Political Science Review*, 104/1 (2010): 192.
[39] Qutb, *Milestones*, p. 60.

While the rejection of 'nationality', even in its pan-Arab form, is made here in unambiguous terms, an important remark is needed in relation to Qutb's articulation of the signifier 'ummah' vis-à-vis its nationalist counterpart 'the people'. We argued that the people was conceptualised through the double connection of 'blood' and 'territory' as discriminatory criteria for the inclusion/exclusion of national citizenship (via the juridical principle of *jus soli* and *jus sanguinis*). By formulating the ummah in universal terms, as a 'community of belief', Qutb is adamant in downplaying the relevance of both 'geography' and 'blood' as privileged signifiers within the ummah: 'when their hearts became free of pride of lineage, of nationality, of country, of tribe, of household – in short, when Allah Most High saw them to be morally pure – then He granted them the great trust, the conscious assumption of being Allah's representative on earth'.[40] More radically, this means re-signifying the meaning of blood and cultural connections. Although the family is thought of as the heart of the Islamic society, feelings and bonds in this intimate environment are subsumed within the higher logic of the ummah and its relation with God. It is Allah, or Islam (God's emanation) who, by functioning as the master signifier of Qutb's discourse, gives the family its actual *connotation*:

> A Muslim has no relatives except those who share the belief in Allah, and thus a bond is established between him and other Believers through their relationship with Allah Almighty. A Muslim has no relationship with his mother, father, brother, wife and other family members except through their relationship with the Creator, and then they are also joined through blood.[41]

A further element of differentiation from the discourse of the nation is reflected in Qutb's reactivation of the traditional concept of *dar al-Islam* vis-à-vis the idea of national *territory*. Again, in considering the historical process leading to the formation of the modern nation state, we pointed to the binary and exclusivist model organising the construction of national space, and the delineation of borders (Figure 2.2, Chapter 2). We then contrasted this model with the traditional idea of Islamic territoriality, where the outside, the *dar al-harb*, is not so much a constitutive and necessary moment for the very articulation of *dar al-Islam* as it could be the case with a national construction, but rather reflects a contingent factor to be subsumed and integrated within the inclusive space of Islamic universalism (Figure 5.1).

---

[40] Ibid., p. 44.
[41] Ibid., p. 133.

In Qutb's normative vision, we find a clear attempt to recover the category of *dar al-Islam*, re-elaborating its universalistic premises. We saw that a full realisation of humanity necessitates the universalisation of Islam and the rejection of animalism and unbelief. This is the path that mankind should follow in order to abide by the supreme law of God as well as to its own humanity. The universal implementation of Islam as being consubstantial to the full realisation of humanity expresses what we define as a *state* or *plane of necessity* – where Islam is taken here to reflect the *ideal* of both the Islamic *ummah* (subjective formation) and its territorial and juridical transposal in the *dar al-Islam* (spatial representation).[42] Now, if the *state of necessity* presupposes the ideal universalisation of *dar al-Islam*, the contingency of history entails that such universalisation is hampered by the very presence of non-Muslims. Here, *dar al-Islam* figures in the contingency of history as a partial reality competing with some sort of outside, the *dar al-harb*. This plane where historical events take place and where *dar al-Islam* and *dar al-harb* appear as historical particular or partial manifestations we call the *state of contingency*.

Since in Qutb's eschatological vision the full realisation of humanity requires establishing Islam as a totality, *dar al-harb* can only appear as a temporary historical manifestation that *dar al-Islam* should be able to absorb. Such an inclusive movement would allow *dar al-Islam* to dismiss its particular character in the state of contingency assuming a permanent and universal dimension and thereby affirming the state of necessity. The ability of *dar al-Islam* to subsume the *dar al-harb* in the contingency of history, in fact, would allow *dar al-Islam* to figure as an all-encompassing totality. But should this happen, it would mean that the state of contingency and the state of necessity coincide and that the necessary ideal of Islamic universalism would have found a breach in history. Hence, *in principle*, it is the inclusive nature of the pan-Islamic theoretical model that connects necessity and contingency. In this respect, *dar al-harb* stands as a *simulacrum* that appears on the surface of an *inclusive dynamic*. By dynamic, we mean quite literally the force that sustains change within a certain process. The term simulacrum refers then to the very existence of *dar al-harb* as a transient historical phenomenon in the inclusive movement leading to the universalisation of Islam. This implies that *dar al-harb* is seen by the viewpoint of Islamic universalism as something that appears temporarily but that, sooner or later, will necessarily be absorbed by *dar al-Islam*. It can thus be said that,

---

[42] Terms such as 'state' or 'plane' are used here interchangeably for illustrative and heuristic purposes, facilitating the temporal and spatial representation of necessity and contingency when using topological figures.

despite the fact that it figures as a contingent manifestation, *dar al-harb* already expresses the Islamic universality as a form of *potentiality*.

Such a movement can best be illustrated by resorting to the topology of the Möbius strip that we have first encountered in Chapter 2 when discussing Islamic territoriality (for the reader's convenience, we reproduce in this chapter a more explanatory re-articulation of Figure 5.1 in the figure below).

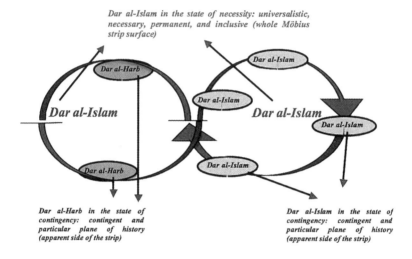

Figure 5.1   Qutb's normative vision

In attempting to offer a heuristic and illustrative representation of Islamic territoriality in Chapter 2, we mentioned that the topology of the Möbius strip helps us denoting the delineation of a non-binary *structuring*, standing as an uninterrupted and self-rearticulating territorial surface. The apparent two-sided structure is, in fact, a one-level, contiguous and open configuration, for the Möbius strip has only one side and only one boundary component (by travelling on one side, one ends up on the other side of the strip). What is distinctive about the Möbius is that although the very organisation of space through referents of interiority and exteriority is preserved, this is done exposing it to change, inclusivity and contingency. While the two sides of the Möbius can be clearly distinguished at any one point, in their local dimension, when the strip is traversed and assumed as a whole it becomes clear that they are in fact continuous. In spite of the static dimension of Euclidian figures, such as the circle that we used to represent the binary space of the nation, it is time that allows here the two sides of the Möbius both to emerge and to become indistinguishable along the movement employed to traverse the strip.

When using this topological model, *dar al-harb* emerges as a transient, particular, contingent and historical manifestation lying on one of the two *apparent* sides of the strip. The other apparent side of the strip is incarnated by *dar al-Islam* which, similarly, figures here as a transient, particular, contingent and historical manifestation. Both *dar al-harb* and *dar al-Islam* express – as the two *apparent* sides of the strip – the state of contingency. *Dar al-harb* figures, however, as a *simulacrum*, which is deemed to disappear because the movement along the strip allows *dar al-Islam* to emerge clearly, thereby absorbing *dar al-harb* and enacting the inclusive, necessary, and permanent movement of Islamic universalism. *Dar al-Islam* therefore reflects a twofold dimension. On the one hand, it coincides with one of the two apparent sides of the strip, continuously competing with and striving to absorb *dar al-harb* at the level of contingency. On the other hand, it also coincides with the overall inclusive *surface* of the Möbius strip itself, which reflects the state of necessity permanently incorporating historical contingency. The *dar al-Islam* thus functions as a connecting point between necessity and contingency. The integration of *dar al-harb* within the contingent domain of *dar al-Islam*, and the consequent subsuming of contingency by necessity within a permanent and inclusive movement constitutes what we define as *Islamic inclusive universalism*. Given Qutb's normative formulation of Muslim subjectivity in the form of the Islamic society, how is territoriality defined in relation to such a speculative framework?

In line with traditional universalistic discourses, Qutb's spatial re-articulation of *dar al-Islam* maintains an inherently universal and necessary character, paralleling and sustaining the fluid and universal notion of the Islamic community. At first stance, Qutb asserts *dar al-Islam* as the only possible form of territoriality that Muslims should conceive as acting against communal or national forms of identification:

> A Muslim has no country except that part of the earth where the Shari'ah of Allah is established and human relationships are based on the foundation of relationship with Allah Almighty; a Muslim has no nationality except his belief, which makes him a member of the Muslim community in *Dar-ul-Islam*.[43]

---

[43] Qutb, *Milestones*, pp. 132–3.

Since, as we have seen, the establishment of God's sovereignty alone allows 'humanity' and 'freedom' to be expressed, then *dar al-Islam* reflects the *necessary* condition for mankind *to exist*; that is, to develop, collectively, its very qualities of 'humanity' and 'civilisation'. This entails, however, that the very meaning and the value of territoriality are re-signified through a direct association with the master signifier 'God':

> The soil of the homeland has in itself no value or weight. From the Islamic point of view, the only value which the soil can achieve is because on that soil Allah's authority is established and Allah's guidance is followed; and thus it becomes a fortress for the belief, a place for its way of life to be entitled the '*homeland of Islam*', a centre for the movement for the total freedom of man.[44]

Such an understanding of *dar al-Islam* renounces any physical conceptualisation of territoriality and stands as the immaterial surface of a new communitarian and ethical linkage. The ecumenical reference to 'God' or 'Islam' now subsumes old distinctions of blood, culture and geography:

> Only this is Islam, and only this is *Dar-ul-Islam* – not the soil, not the race, not the lineage, not the tribe, and not the family ... The homeland of the Muslim, in which he lives and which he defends, is not a piece of land; the nationality of the Muslim, by which he is identified, is not the nationality determined by a government; the family of the Muslim, in which he finds solace and which he defends, is not blood relationships; the flag of the Muslim, which he honours and under which he is martyred, is not the flag of a country; and the victory of the Muslim, which he celebrates and for which he is thankful to Allah, is not a military victory.[45]

This connection among three main signifiers, 'necessity', 'spirituality' and 'universality' sustains the particular *connotation* that the *dar al-Islam* assumes vis-à-vis the national concepts of 'territory'. Although Qutb acknowledges the attempts made by imperial, national or other alternative political systems to supersede divisions among their constituencies, such experiences are rated as failures, which produced new discriminatory distinctions. The domain of Islam alone can succeed in the realisation of a universal message:

---

[44] Ibid., p. 82.
[45] Ibid., p. 140.

> Various societies have also appeared in modern times. For example, consider the British Empire. It is like the Roman society to which it is an heir. It is based on national greed, in which the British nation has the leadership and exploits those colonies annexed by the Empire. The same is true of other European empires. The Spanish and Portuguese Empires in their times, and the French Empire, all are equal in respect to oppression and exploitation. Communism also wanted to establish a new type of society, demolishing the walls of race and colour, nation and geographical region, but it is not based on 'human relationship' but on a 'class system'. Thus the communist society is like the Roman society with a reversal of emphasis; there nobles had distinction, while here the proleteriat has distinction ... Islam, then, is the only Divine way of life which brings out the noblest human characteristics, developing and using them for the construction of human society.[46]

If 'necessity', 'spirituality' and 'universality' define the meaning of *dar al-Islam*, how does Qutb characterise the very existence of *dar al-harb*? We have seen that Qutb unambiguously rejects the notion of nationality and its inner dichotomous distinction based on race, lineage and geography, constructing *dar al-Islam* as an *immediate presence* whose nature is *necessary* and *self-asserting*. It is true that an outside, *dar al-harb*, is also represented here, but it emerges by way of a secondary movement, and not as a necessary condition for the very presence of Islam. This is an important difference, as we observed that the binary articulation of the national territory entails a primary delineation of the outside against which, in the guise of an absolute opposition, it is possible to think of the inside as a closed totality. While the national territory assumes its respective outside as a constitutive and irreducible exteriority, the *dar al-harb* remains a contingent and transient manifestation within history to be integrated, at some point in time, by Islam.

In a crucial passage, Qutb reasserts the traditional 'inclusive' notion of *dar al-Islam* as able to integrate and articulate internal differences while, at the same time, stating the presence of non-Islamic domains, the *dar al-harb*, on a very factual level:

> The Muslim's country has not been a piece of land, but the homeland of Islam (*Dar-ul-Islam*) – the homeland where faith rules and the *Shari'ah* of Allah holds sway ... This Islamic homeland is a refuge for any who accepts the Islamic *Shari'ah* to be the law of the state, as is the case with the *Dhimmis*. But any place where

---

[46] Ibid., p. 61.

the Islamic *Shari'ah* is not enforced and where Islam is not dominant becomes the home of hostility (*Dar-ul-Harb*) for both the Muslim and the *Dhimmi*. A Muslim will remain prepared to fight against it, whether it be his birthplace or a place where his relatives reside or where his property or any other material interests are located.[47]

It is clear from the passage above that Qutb acknowledges traditional views of Islamic territoriality, for the *dar al-Islam* is said to embody within its jurisdictional domain not only Muslim constituencies but also the *dhimmi*: non-Muslims living in Islamic-ruled countries and enjoying forms of legal protection behind special taxation. At the same time, the *dar al-harb* of non-Islamic-ruled countries is acknowledged as a matter of fact. Since the *dar al-Islam* must reflect the universality of Islam, no outside would be possible on a *necessary* level. Thus *dar al-harb* can only appear as a *contingent* manifestation that, sooner or later, will need to be subsumed within the universality of Islam, so losing its *external* character and becoming either an internal difference in the form of the *dhimmi* or a form of Muslim singularity.[48]

In Chapter 2 we mentioned, however, that within the multiplicity of discourses informing the Islamic jurisprudential thought, a middle ground – the *dar al-'ahd* (land of truce) – was acknowledged as a practical device to ensure peace and stability with non-Muslim lands and reduce the cost of a permanent *jihad*. It consisted of those lands with which a formal agreement was made, guaranteeing the protection of Muslims under foreign rule or the protection of non-Muslim regions behind tributary taxation or within any area in which open warfare was absent.[49] This third temporary division remained subject to perpetual renewal as the limits between *dar al-Islam* and *dar al-'ahd* were never formalised, thereby moderating the polarity between *dar al-Islam* and *dar al-harb*. Moreover, a series of administrative devices were elaborated across time to substantiate the inclusive and universal character of *dar al-Islam*, tempering its potential antagonism, and ensuring a form of harmonious stability. This is best demonstrated by the *millet system*, consisting of non-Muslim communities in the Ottoman Empire – such as the Greek, the Armenian Orthodox, and the

---

[47] Ibid., pp. 139–40.
[48] Majid Khadduri, *War and Peace in the Law of Islam* (Clark, NJ: The Lawbook Exchange, 1955, 2006), p. 145.
[49] Shahrul Hussain, *Dar Al-Islam and Dar Al-Harb: An Analytical Study of its Historical Inception, its Definition by the Classical Scholars and its Application to the Contemporary World* (Manchester: Al Hikma Publishing, 2012); Ralph H. Salmi, *Islam and Conflict Resolution: Theories and Practices* (Lanham, MD: University Press of America, 1998).

Jews – that were incorporated into the institutional system of the Empire and provided with the right to observe their religious affiliations and govern their internal affairs.[50] These devices allowed for official recognition of possible spaces of exteriority that were constantly reproduced and formally acknowledged. In principle, they did not undermine the inclusive structure of Islamic universalism as their inclusion in the domain of Islam was maintained ideally and postponed somewhere in the future, as if time would have naturally allowed, at some indefinite point, the dynamic shift from contingency to necessity. Although Qutb expresses a more radical stance in this regard, as no mention is made of the existence of *dar al-'ahd*, the inclusive structure of this dynamics remains a potential offshoot of this model. A form of inclusive differentiation here is constantly reproduced in the antagonistic form of *dar al-harb* or in the more compromising and mediating form of *dar al-'ahd*, which does not obstruct the universalistic *projection* of a full-humanity.

With this overall structure in mind, it is crucial to highlight that an even stronger polarisation could mark the *contingent* tension that Qutb's normative vision instantiates between *dar al-Islam* and *dar al-harb*. This could happen if the temporary antagonism between *dar al-Islam* and *dar al-harb* 'freezes' into a definitive and irremediable counter-position that would ultimately interrupt the inclusive relation between necessity and contingency. We contend that such a risk clearly emerges when Qutb introduces his notion of *jahiliyyah* and undertakes a critical assessment of the contemporary human condition.

Qutb's Descriptive Vision of Jahiliyyah

As we mentioned above, what appears to be a dynamic form of antagonism in Qutb's normative vision is somehow frozen as Qutb switches his focus to an analysis of his times. It is here that a 'descriptive register' is adopted:

---

[50] Cf. Inoue Tatsuo, 'Liberal Democracy and Asian Orientalism', in Joanne R. Bauer and Daniel A. Bell (eds), *The East Asian Challenge for Human Rights* (Cambridge: Cambridge University Press, 1999), and Kemal H. Karpat, 'Millets and Nationality: The Roots of the Incongruity of Nation and State in the Post-Ottoman Era', in Benjamin Brad and Bernard Lewis (eds), *Christians and Jews in the Ottoman Empire: The Functioning of a Plural Society* (New York: Holmes & Meier Publishers, 1980). For a more critical reading, which problematises some of the limits in the recent literature on the millet system, see Engin F. Isin, 'Citizenship after Orientalism: Ottoman Citizenship', in Fuat Keyman and Ahmet Icduygu (eds), *Citizenship in a Global World: European Questions and Turkish Experiences* (London: Routledge, 2005), pp. 31–51.

> If we look at the sources and foundations of modern ways of living, it becomes clear that the whole world is steeped in *Jahiliyyahh*, [Ignorance of the Divine guidance] and all the marvellous material comforts and high-level inventions do not diminish this ignorance. This *Jahiliyyahh* is based on rebellion against Allah's sovereignty on earth. It transfers to man one of the greatest attributes of Allah, namely sovereignty, and makes some men lords over others. It is now not in that simple and primitive form of the ancient *Jahiliyyahh*, but takes the form of claiming that the right to create values, to legislate rules of collective behaviour, and to choose any way of life rests with men, without regard to what Allah Almighty has prescribed.[51]

A few caveats are needed in respect to the crucial passage above. First, it is clear that Qutb is no longer defining how humanity *should be* on an ideal and normative level, but is indeed describing how things on a factual and historical level *are* or *appear* ('If we look at' ... 'it becomes clear that the whole world is'). The ideal of the Islamic society with all its creativity, humanity, and ability to integrate difference (e.g., through the legal recognition of the *dhimmi*) is here contrasted with the acknowledgment that 'reality' is completely un-Islamic (*jahili*), animalistic, and primitive. The difference between the ideal and reality, the Islamic society and *jahiliyyah* is best represented through the distinction between a normative and a descriptive level in Qutb's work. A second point to be stressed from the passage above regards the very notion of *jahiliyyah*. Unlike pre-Islamic ignorance, contemporary *jahiliyyah* is described first and foremost by its immanent character.[52] That is, *jahiliyyah* figures as the social condition under which God's will is replaced with the immanency of human decisions, with the claim that 'the right to create values ... rests with men'. Finally, and critically, the *transient* and *particular* appearance that *dar al-harb* covers in Qutb's normative vision undergoes a sort of crystallisation and pervasive expansion to the extent that 'the whole world' is now 'steeped in *Jahiliyyah*'.

The notion of *jahiliyyah* to describe contemporary reality had already been used within the realm of Islamist discourse. For instance, the Pakistani Islamist thinker Syed Abul A'ala Mawdudi (1903–1979) had deployed the classic concept of *jahiliyyah* to describe the domain of what, in traditional terms, was dubbed *dar al-harb*. Equated with the notion of *dar al-harb*, *jahiliyyah* stood

---

[51] Qutb, *Milestones*, pp. 26–7.
[52] Sayed Khatab, *The Political Thought of Sayyid Qutb: The Theory of Jahiliyyah* (London: Routledge, 2009).

for Mawdudi as a historical, partial and transient manifestation of unbelief to be challenged by *dar al-Islam* through the very revival this thinker was advocating.

Although Qutb was 'an avid reader' of Mawdudi and there is common tendency among scholars to emphasise Mawdudi's genealogical influence on Qutb's more radical aspects as developed during his time in prison, a difference needs to be emphasised between the two, which strongly affects the way in which forms of political antagonism are considered.[53] Unlike Mawdudi, Qutb's understanding of *jahiliyyah* should not be seen as a condition somehow informing the space of *dar al-harb*. We saw that in Qutb's normative vision, *dar al-harb* stands as a transient and partial manifestation competing with *dar al-Islam* in the plane of contingency. On a descriptive level, instead, Qutb's notion of *jahiliyyah* implies that the Islamic community itself is erased and *replaced* by an overarching and absolute un-Islamic surface, thus disappearing from the plane of contingency. In this sense, *jahiliyyah* stands as an *all-encompassing* reality in the contingency of history *supplanting* the Islamic society entirely and becoming a sort of totality, a *universality* whose omnipresence does not acknowledge any outside:

> The *Jahili* society is any society other than the Muslim society; and if we want a more specific definition, we may say that any society is a *Jahili* society which does not dedicate itself to submission to Allah alone, in its beliefs and ideas in its observances of worship, and in its legal regulations. *According to this definition, all the societies existing in the world today are Jahili.* (emphasis added)[54]

This 'all-encompassing' character of *jahiliyyah* provides us with an important element of differentiation with al-Banna's territorial trajectory, for, as noted in Chapter 2, al-Banna assumes the un-Islamic (colonial and secular) forces of *dar al-harb* to be in the process of penetrating *into* Islamic land, rather than supplanting it in its entirety.

Interestingly, Qutb differentiates between several kinds of *jahili* societies, each one dominated by a particular discourse ('communism', 'paganism', 'nationalism', etc.). Hence, in the list of *jahili* societies, we find the communist society:

---

[53] J. Calvert, *Sayyid Qutb and the Origins of Radical Islamism*, p. 213; on this point, see also Adnan A. Musallam, *From Secularism to Jihad: Sayyid Qutb and the Foundations of Radical Islamism* (Westport, CT: Praeger, 2005); Peter R. Demant and Asghar Ali Engineer, *Islam vs. Islamism: The Dilemma of the Muslim World* (Westport, CT, and London: Praeger, 2006); Suha Taji-Farouki and Basheer M. Nafi (eds), *Islamic Thought in the Twentieth-Century* (London: I.B. Tauris, 2004).

[54] Qutb, *Milestones*, p. 91.

> Included among these is the communist society, first because it denies the existence of Allah Most High and believes that the universe was created by 'matter' or by 'nature', while all man's activities and his history has been created by 'economics' or 'the means of production'; second, because the way of life it adopts is based on submission to the Communist Party and not to Allah Almighty.[55]

We also find practically all non-abrahamitic-religion-based societies or those societies where legislation is assumed as a human affair:

> All idolatrous societies are also among the *Jahili* societies. Such societies are found in India, Japan, the Philippines and Africa. Their *Jahili* character consists first of the fact that they believe in other gods besides Allah Almighty, in addition to Him or without Him; second, they have constructed an elaborate system of devotional acts to propitiate these deities. Similarly, the laws and regulations which they follow are derived from sources other than Allah and His Law, whether these sources be priests or astrologers or magicians, the elders of the nation, or the secular institutions which formulate laws without regard to the Law of Allah, and which attain absolute authority in the name of the nation or a party or on some other basis.[56]

Jewish and Christian societies:

> All Jewish and Christian societies today are also *Jahili* societies. They have distorted the original beliefs and ascribe certain attributes of Allah to other beings. This association with Allah Almighty has taken many forms, such as the Allah Almighty having a son or the Trinity; sometimes it is expressed in a concept of Allah which is remote from the true reality of Allah Almighty.[57]

Indeed, we saw that Qutb's normative vision includes Christians, Jews and the broader category of *dhimmi* under the domain of *dar al-Islam*. Now that Qutb is assuming a descriptive register, these same Jewish and Christian societies are irremediably subsumed within the omnipresent realm of *jahiliyyah*. This is a sign of Qutb's adoption of an extreme position when assessing the compatibility to Islam of existent human societies.

---

[55] Ibid.
[56] Ibid.
[57] Ibid., p. 92.

Even more symptomatic of this position, however, is the ultimate inclusion of Muslim societies themselves within the all-embracing realm of *jahiliyyah*:

> Lastly, all the existing so-called '*Muslim*' societies are also *Jahili* societies. We classify them among *Jahili* societies not because they believe in other deities besides Allah or because they worship anyone other than Allah, but because their way of life is not based on submission to Allah alone. Although they believe *Tawhid* (monotheism), still they have relegated the legislative attribute of Allah Almighty to others and submit to this authority, and from this authority they derive their systems, their traditions and customs, their laws, their values and standards, and almost every practice of life.[58]

Although connected, the descriptive register enacts a structural transformation of normative register, altering its inclusive system. On a broad perspective, such a transformation is informed by a *logic of replacement*, as the *dar al-Islam* is now *replaced* by an all-encompassing '*jahiliyyah*' in the plane of contingency. This entails that the Islamic community disappears as a partial and contingent manifestation, becoming an absolute *absence*. So, while the distinction between a necessary and a contingent level is maintained, the inclusive and universalistic contiguity connecting the two levels is interrupted. On the one hand, the omnipresence of *jahiliyyah* stands as a totality at the level of contingency. *Dar al-Islam* is thereby relegated to the plane of necessity alone, resulting in the loss of its quality as a fundamental connecting point between the two levels. The absolute universality of *jahiliyyah* in the state of contingency now opposes the universality of the Islamic society in the state of necessity. On the other hand, the fact that *dar al-Islam* in the subjective form of the Islamic society (as Qutb puts it: 'Muslim community in *Dar ul-Islam*') stops appearing as a concrete historical manifestation means that it can now only be thought of as a promise to be realised. A *virtualisation* of the Islamic *ummah* – its figuring both as an ideal and a potentiality – accompanies the *universalisation* of the *jahiliyyah* (see Figure 5.2).

---

[58] Ibid., p. 93.

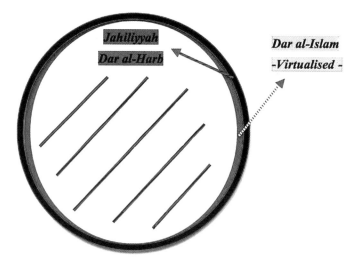

Figure 5.2   Qutb's descriptive vision

In the figure above, the inclusive pan-Islamic model of the Möbius strip that connected necessity and contingency is replaced by the overlapping of two circles expressing two closed totalities. On the one hand *jahiliyyah*, which is universalised thereby occupying the whole spectrum of contingency. On the other hand, the Islamic community, which disappears as a partial manifestation at the level of contingency, and stands as a virtual universality, i.e., a pure potentiality in the state of necessity. The overlapping of the two circles reflects the disjunction between the planes of necessity and contingency, which is established as an effect of the all-encompassing presence of *jahiliyyah* in the state of contingency. In figurative terms, the emergence of two overlapping circles marks the organisation of a strongly polarised spatial model, somehow aligned to the sort of binary structure that informs political discourses like nationalism, though some crucial difference will be highlighted in the next pages. The structural relation between the descriptive and the normative registers finds expression in its figurative representations. The return to a Euclidian plane characterised by the emergence of two circles resonates with the kind of geometric alteration that is enacted when the Möbius strip is cut down in the middle. The result here is that the strip is transformed into a single loop with very different qualities as it now has two sides instead of one. Metaphorically, the passage from the normative to the descriptive register should be seen as a *discontinuous transformation* of the topological model informing the former.

Before considering the antagonistic effects that the descriptive register enacts, it is useful to point out that the *virtualisation* of Islamic society is by Qutb made explicit:

> According to our unvarying definition of civilization, the Islamic society is not just an entity of the past, to be studied in history, but it is a demand of the present and a hope of the future. Mankind can be dignified, today or tomorrow, by striving toward this noble civilization, by pulling itself out of the abyss of *Jahiliyyah* into which it is falling. This is true not only for the industrially and economically developed nations but also for the backward nations. The values to which we referred above as human values were never attained by mankind except in the period of Islamic civilization.[59]

'Except for the period of Islamic civilisation', the society of Islam in which human values are expressed has been substantially absent from the contingent plane of history. In the face of the 'the abyss of *Jahiliyyah*', the Islamic society stands as an absent object of desire, 'a *demand* of the present and a *hope* of the future' [emphasis added]. With this assertion in mind, if history has testified to the gradual *universalisation* of *jahiliyyah* and the consequent *virtualisation* of the Islamic society, creating the risk of an irreconcilable difference between a necessary conception of humanity and a contingent reality, which kind of antagonistic relations can be traced for Muslims?

Two differing attitudes stem from this scenario. First, to strive on behalf of the Islamic society could mean to re-establish *dar al-Islam* in the plane of contingency, to assert its presence vis-à-vis its living absence, to promote its actuality vis-à-vis the ultimate virtuality in which the Muslim community has been confined (actualising the potential of such an ideal), and, finally, to re-establish Islam as an inclusive universality. This would mean recovering the connecting function of *dar al-Islam* ensuring its simultaneous presence in the state of contingency and in the state of necessity. The osmotic relation between necessity and contingency would thereby be re-ensured, and the Islamic universalism of Qutb's normative vision re-affirmed. Secondly, to strive on behalf of the Islamic society could implicate assuming the polarisation between Islam and *jahiliyyah* as definitive, so cementing the dualism between necessity and contingency. Should this happen, the antagonism of Qutb's descriptive vision would thus have been crystallised, and its normative universalism renounced. A radical antagonism would survive only, with the effect that resistance to

---

[59] Ibid., p. 117.

jahiliyyah would no longer aim at re-establishing the presence of Islam in the contingent dimension of history, in 'the here' where concrete political interests can be posited and some form of compromise can always been found; rather, it would endeavour to gain salvation and purification in 'the hereafter', where the ideal of the Islamic society can only be realised. Hence, the Muslim community in the form of a virtual object of desire based on a millenarist and puritanical vision in a number of contemporary religious movements.

Differences, thus, occur in regard to the conceptualisation of Islamic revival as a manner in which life is to be transformed for some, and access to the hereafter is to be attained for others. As far as Qutb's position is concerned, a militant and *assertive* request for *revival* takes precedence in his texts over the apocalyptic nuances that very often also appear. This means that the normative vision of Qutb overcomes the descriptive one. Despite the apocalyptic dimension surrounding contemporary life, for the true believer the irreducible task remains to assert the normative ideal of Islam, the need to recover the harmonious and inclusive universality of *dar al-Islam*. Hence the opening utterance at the beginning of his book: 'At this crucial and bewildering juncture, the turn of Islam and the Muslim community has arrived'.[60] It is here that Qutb's notion of *jihad*, the 'effort' or 'struggle' in the path of Islam, emerges as a central tenet, standing as the duty to revive Islamic society in history. That is, to fight in the way of God, calling for the soul of men 'so that there may not remain any wall between Islam and individual human beings' and fighting those 'institutions and traditions which limit man's freedom of choice.'[61] Although a spiritual aspect accompanies the military notion of *jihad*, Qutb's emphasis on the latter has been crucial in the revitalisation of this concept in the following decades, especially when associated to his notion of *jahiliyyah*. In this direction, he certainly contributed to promote the interpretation of the obligatory character of *jihad*, even though he has been also adamant in specifying that Islam 'does not attack individuals nor does it force them to accept its beliefs; it attacks institutions and traditions to release human beings from their poisonous influences, which distort human nature and which curtail human freedom'.[62]

A last point to be discussed concerns the way Qutb conceptualises the relation between the all-embracing environment of *jahiliyyah* and those believers who strive to restore Islamic society. The disappearance of the Muslim community from the contingent plane of history, its virtualisation in the face of

---

[60] Ibid., p. 24.
[61] Ibid., respectively pp. 83 and 85.
[62] Ibid., p. 85.

an all-encompassing *jahiliyyah* puts Qutb in the difficult position of asserting the difference between those who strive to revive Islamic society and the great majority of Muslims living and promoting *jahiliyyah*. It is here that Qutb establishes a fundamental disjunction between 'believers' and 'true believers'.

Such a distinction, in itself, is not a new one, for a common discursive practice among Islamist movements has been to conceive of Islam as a dormant force within Muslim societies to be revived. Hence we observe the *revivalist* definition of all Islamist discourses aimed at transforming Islam into the cornerstone of political and social order, and the idea of Islamic movements as political organisations composed of militant and zealous members calling the rest of society to revive the Islamic message. The upshot of this is a differentiation. On the one side, we find the 'partial Muslims'. That is, the majority of Muslims confining religion to a private affair or to a spiritual, cultural and ritual dimension. Thereby living Islam 'merely as a part of a section of their whole life' and drawing on other sources for the remaining aspects of their life.[63] On the other hand, we find 'true Muslims', those who live the Islamic message as an all-encompassing dimension affecting any aspect of everyday life, and who deploy activism and mobilisation to expand the Islamic movement, and to revive the social function of Islam.

Qutb makes this distinction more extreme. In spite of traditional views where all 'Muslims', whether partial and true believers, share the common destiny of being part of an existent Muslim community, in Qutb's descriptive vision Muslim societies themselves are relegated to *jahiliyyah* whilst *dar al-Islam* disappears from the contingency of history. This certainly means that 'partial Muslims' – regular believers who, for Qutb, disregard the integral and exclusive dimension of Islam in life – are included in the omnipresent domain of *jahiliyyah*. But would the 'all-encompassing' character of *jahiliyyah* also mean that 'true Muslims', those who follow Qutb's message to fight to restore Islamic universalism, are themselves a *jahili* manifestation as long as they live in the *jahili* contingency of history? This is a crucial point, for it compels Qutb to formulate some notion of Muslim community in the state of contingency of his descriptive vision. The problem could be formulated as follows: if the *ummah* is absent from the plane of contingency, if it stands only as a demand, how should true believers be thought of considering that they all are living parts of the universal realm of unbelief? How should their dispersed and 'fragmented' position as individuals in the 'ocean of *jahiliyyah*' be accounted?

---

[63] Sayyid Abul 'Ala Mawdudi, *Let Us Be Muslim* (Leicester: Islamic Foundation, 1985), pp. 116–17.

In answering this question, it would seem that true believers *anticipate* the Muslim community to come, realising a virtual illusion of presence of the *ummah* in life. The 'community' of the true believers does not eradicate the general assessment of the state of contingency being a universal expression of *jahiliyyah*, for it stands as a simulacrum; that is, a phenomenal apparition, a virtual anticipation of the Muslim community to come. Although Muslim society remains a hope to be realised, it is the community of 'true believers' that allows Muslims striving in the path of Islam to keep identifying with that promise, establishing some form of connection with that very object of desire in the state of contingency. Hence the logic of replacement found in Qutb's descriptive model. While the *dar al-harb* in his normative vision figured as a simulacrum at the level of contingency, ultimately expressing Islamic universality as a potentiality, the position of simulacrum at the level of contingency is now covered by the community of true believers. This community appears as the virtual anticipation of a promise, the potentiality of the *ummah*, the Muslim community to come. To refer to the ensemble of dispersed true believers in the ocean of *jahiliyyah*, Qutb deploys the notion of 'vanguard', which parallels the idea of a 'virtuality' of the *ummah*:

> How is it possible to start the task of reviving Islam? It is necessary that there should be a vanguard which sets out with this determination and then keeps walking on the path, marching through the vast ocean of *Jahiliyyahh* which has encompassed the entire world. During its course, it should keep itself somewhat aloof from this all-encompassing *Jahiliyyah* and should also keep some ties with it ... I have written '*Milestones*' for this vanguard, which I consider to be a waiting reality about to be materialized.[64]

It is through a 'vanguard' to be 'somewhat aloof' from an 'all-encompassing *Jahiliyyah*' that Qutb manages to articulate the anticipation of the community to come. For such a community, this requires a paradoxical status as best evidenced by the interesting expression 'somewhat aloof'. The vanguard is both immersed in *jahiliyyah*, the contingency of history, yet beyond it. By way of a virtual anticipation, such a community represents its very opposite: the Islamic community to come. It is necessary to assume the position of a single true believer as a highly dispersed and fragmented one, for he/she is surrounded by an 'all-encompassing' *jahili* environment and only connected with other true believers in the virtual conception of the vanguard. This dispersed position

---

[64] Qutb, *Milestones*, pp. 27–8.

needs furthermore to be maintained even in intimate relations such as familial ties, as 'Islam' requires exclusive loyalty. In case of the believer's parents declaring 'their alliance with the enemies of Islam', in fact, Qutb's does not hesitate to state that 'all the filial relationships of a Muslim are cut off and he is not bound to be kind and considerate to them'.[65]

This overall scenario illustrates the most radical traits of Qutb's vision, unravelling in *Milestones*' descriptive register a hypertrophic organisation of space and antagonism. In contrast to the inclusive logic of his universalistic ideal, Qutb sets here a rigid spatial and subjective configuration, one in which the universalisation of *jahiliyyah* and the virtualisation of the *ummah* seclude the very possibility of an encounter with the outside, allowing for the emergence of a vanguardist conception of resistance so central to Western radical traditions of political activism as well as to new radical trends across contemporary Islamist groups.

Final Remarks

In examining the eschatological and political vision of Sayyid Qutb, this chapter has uncovered a major topological and spatial intersection in his seminal text *Milestones*, distinguishing between a normative and a descriptive register. On a normative level, we traced the enactment of a dynamic antagonism with *dar al-harb*, which is nonetheless tempered by the inclusive and universalistic nature of Islam. *Dar al-harb* stands here as a contingent phenomenon whose existence does not compromise the concept of Islamic universality, its necessary status as an *immediate presence*. In the universalistic logic that Qutb strives to revitalise, *dar al-Islam* is in fact marked by a twofold nature, figuring as both the necessary condition of Islamic universality and a contingent historical manifestation. This double dimension plays a crucial role in terms of political antagonism. To acknowledge that *dar al-Islam* exists in the contingency of history, might entail recognising that it also expresses specific political and social interests. In the long term, concrete historical needs can lead *dar al-Islam* to promote peaceful and cooperative relations or some form of compromise with non-Muslim countries, rather than a continuous war and a permanent jihad. That compromise is possible is shown by the history of Islamic societies, where the potential antagonism between *dar al-Islam* and *dar al-harb* has been tempered through practical devices such as the *dar al-'ahd*.

---

[65] Ibid., p. 133.

At the descriptive level, on the other hand, an absolute polarisation marks Qutb's political vision. Although Qutb rejects unequivocally the binary constructions that lie behind national signifiers and celebrates the universalism of *dar al-Islam*, his analysis of his social reality risks assuming a rigid antagonism to be a definitive and intrinsic logic in the elaboration of political projects. This entails freezing the dynamism between necessity and contingency, social reality and the ideal of Islamicity, life and the hereafter. The perception that life is an expression of *jahiliyyah* and that the Muslim community can only be thought of as an ideal in the state of necessity entails, on a contingent level, the absence of concrete political interests to defend or to claim. Political compromise becomes much harder to achieve, for antagonism is not based on practical needs. No matter what the individual strives to do, if *dar al-Islam* will only be achieved in the hereafter, the contemporary world will never be able to materialise the ideal of the Islamic society and to escape its condition of *jahiliyyah*. The risk is that to die on behalf of Islam could mean to perform a ritual act: the aim would be to purify the true believer's soul, rather than to achieve concrete political results. The tension between Qutb's normative and descriptive vision entails, therefore, opposing utopian, apocalyptic and millenarist nuances of the descriptive register to a militant and universal assertiveness in the normative.

Although Qutb is clearly devoted to striving for his normative vision, this tension gives us important clues when assessing potential developments of contemporary Islamist discourses. In the Conclusion of this book, we shall point to a remarkable resonance between the more radical and apocalyptic aspects of Qutb's discursive trajectory and the vision of contemporary groups such as *Hizb ut-Tahrir* and *al-Muhajiroun* (an upshot of *Hizb ut-Tahrir*). We will see here all the influence that Qutb's descriptive vision has continued to exert over the years, sustaining a degree of pessimism in its attitude towards a world reality that these groups consider to be *jahili* in its totality, so resorting to an ideal of vanguardism.[66]

An overall assessment of Qutb's discursive articulation illustrates, therefore, Qutb's impingement on the symbolic scenario of tradition, which served the major counter-hegemonic task of challenging the dominant position of nationalist discourses, whether in their European, Nasserist or pan-Arab variants. In this respect, Qutb's discourse figured as a fundamental 'transitional' trajectory, marking a major turning point in the discursive development of

---

[66] Mary R. Habeck, *Knowing the Enemy: Jihadist Ideology and the War on Terror* (New Haven, CT: Yale University Press, 2006); Quintan Wiktorowicz, *Radical Islam Rising: Muslim Extremism in the West* (Lanham, MD: Rowman & Littlefield, 2005).

Islamism and the subsequent reactivation of the pan-Islamic ideal. Beyond the Islamist realm, however, Qutb's analysis of his post-colonial times anticipated a transmodern criticism of modernity, pointing to the declining position of its political configurations. If anything, Qutb's revitalisation of universalism resonates with those transmodern discourses that endorse forms of universalistic space in a global context where the role and sometimes the very survival of national sovereignty have been questioned.

Whether in the delineation of an inclusive universal space or in the more confrontational aspects of his antagonism, the widespread reception and potential of his work testify to the multilayer dimension and the many nuances of his eschatological and political reflection. It is these variations in Sayyid Qutb's political theology that this chapter has aimed to reveal, highlighting the complexity and richness of a controversial as much as an influential thinker.

Chapter 6

The Discourse of Osama bin Laden: A Transterritorial Trajectory

> Oh you horses (soldiers) of Allah ride and march on. This is the time of hardship so be tough. And know that your gathering and co-operation in order to liberate the sanctities of Islam is the right step toward unifying the word of the Ummah under the banner of 'No God but Allah'.[1]

Osama bin Laden (1957–2011) is probably the most famous wanted terrorist the world has known, and allegedly the most divisive Muslim figure of the last century: the man who brought the unsettling apparition of a Conradian 'horror' right to the heart of Western 'civilisation'; the incarnation of the sinister prophecy of a clash of civilisations; the figure who disrupted the notion of the alluring post-ideological future of Euphoria and prosperity that had been promised to the citizens of the liberal world in the aftermath of the Cold War, who invaded the safe space of the private home through the TV screen and dashed that promise with the alarming *breaking* news: 'America under Attack'. Viewed in the West as the epitome of all the evil on this earth, and as a shameful preacher by Muslim 'moderate' masses now compelled to 'confess' publicly their disapproval of al-Qaeda and provide clear evidence of their true democratic spirit, he was also celebrated as a legendary Islamic knight by 'radical' believers (and world 'subalterns') who saw in his jihad a revenge against the hypocrisy and the violence of an imperialist West. Controversial, phantasmal and undesirable as he might be, bin Laden contributes to the kind of discursive and speculative analysis pursued in this book. His global jihadist discourse effectively embodies a minor but extremely relevant current of Islamist political thought today, bearing testimony to a new type of engagement with the symbolic scenarios of Islamism, and showing a fundamental alignment between transmodernity and tradition in what we are calling here a *transterritorial trajectory*.

---

[1] Osama bin Laden, 'Declaration of War: Against the Americans Occupying the Land of the Two Holy Places', 23 August 1996; translation at: http://web.archive.org/web/20011106100207/http://www.kimsoft.com/2001/binladenwar.htm.

We are using this term to refer to bin Laden's attempt to fully 'invest' in the imaginary ideal of Islamic universalism that Qutb had contributed to re-activating. His re-elaboration of a pan-Islamic vision, however, shows an innovative recasting of traditional perspectives, aligning his discourse with the distinctive features of the global context, and thereby creating the possibility for strategic dialogue with transmodernity. Bin Laden's articulation of this new discursive formation, which is functional to the desedimenting and 'deterritorialising' effects of globalisation and the emergence of globalist views, is significant for the purposes of this book as it presents a further differentiation of Islamism, representing a new discursive stream and historical phase of this broader discursive universe.

An Historical Framework

When discussing Sayyid Qutb's transitional trajectory, we indicated that this was an intermediate level in the evolution of Islamism, which marked the transition from al-Banna's opening discourse in the Egyptian colonial context of the first half of the twentieth century to a revitalisation of Islamism in the 1970s. We mentioned also that this third phase followed a long period of Nasserite hegemony in Egypt during which, with a few exceptions mentioned in Chapter 5, Islamist militancy became largely enfeebled under the repressive action of Arab regimes. Expressions such as the 'rejuvenation', the 'revival' or the 'return' of political Islam have since been used to account for this renovated visibility of Islamist discourses in the political arena of the last few decades.[2] As Mandaville points out: 'the appropriateness of the term "revival" to describe this phenomenon has been much debated. It is certainly the case that segments of Middle Eastern and other Muslim-majority societies not previously interested in religious alternatives to the secular national state did indeed begin gathering behind Islamist causes during this period.'[3]

Several contingent factors help to explain the reasons behind the intensification of the Islamist appeal in this historical conjuncture. A first important element was the severe setback for Arab nationalism that occurred as a result of the Arab defeat in the Six-Day War (1967).[4] This contributed to a shifting of power from pan-Arab socialist countries such as Egypt and Syria,

---

[2] Bernard Lewis, 'The Return of Islam', *Commentary*, 61/1 (1976): 39–49.
[3] Peter Mandaville, *Global Political Islam* (New York: Routledge, 2007), p. 89.
[4] Cf. Fouad Ajami, 'The End of Pan-Arabism', *Foreign Affairs*, 57/2 (1978/9).

which had united in the United Arab Republic between 1958 and 1961 under the presidency of Nasser, towards the conservative monarchies of the Gulf and the growing influence of Saudi Arabia.[5] As we mentioned previously when discussing the discourse of the nation state in Chapter 2, the project of achieving the unity of the Arab countries encountered a growing obstacle in the emerging national interest of respective states. These developments ultimately determined the institutional fluctuation of pan-Arabism itself when conceived in terms of unity or in terms of cooperation between Arab states.[6] A major upshot in the long term was a progressive movement towards fragmentation and particularism.[7] When Anwar al-Sadat (1918–1981) became Egyptian President upon Nasser's death in 1970, however, a new path in for international relations of the Middle East was designed.

Two major moves helped Sadat to strengthen his grip on power, though they proved to be fatal for him in the long term. First, his decision to engage in conflict with Israel in the 1973 October War. This led Egypt and Israel to start a negotiating process that culminated in the Camp David Accords (1978), allowing Egypt, on the one hand, to regain some of the lands that had been lost during the Six-Day War, and Israel, on the other, to be formally recognised by an Arab neighbour. The stability promised by the Camp David Accords reduced even further the ability of pan-Arab discourses to mobilise populations in an anti-Israeli front. Second, Sadat isolated Nasser's single party, the Arab Socialist Union (ASU), liberating the vast majority of Islamist militants who had been imprisoned by Nasser and using them as a domestic counterweight. This contributed to decreasing the political role of pan-Arabism in internal affairs, while helping Islamism to re-activate its ideological appeal in the Middle East.

Although nationalism gained increasing ground at an institutional and policy level in those years, with post-colonial elites more and more inclined to defend the crucial convergence between their corporatist interests and national interests, rather than opting for broader forms of pan-Arab solidarity, over the years a general process of de-legitimation gradually began to involve these same elites. Throughout the post-colonial world the sensation that these elites

---

[5] See Roger Owen, *State, Power and Politics in the Making of the Modern Middle East* (London: Routledge, 1992).

[6] A fluctuation which is best testified to by the diversity of perspectives concerning the role of the Arab League, with crucial differences, since its foundation, between those who advocated institutional cooperation among Arab governments on the one hand, and supporters of integration and unity of policy, on the model of the European Union, on the other.

[7] Larbi Sadiki, *The Search for Arab Democracy* (London: Hurst & Company, 2004).

had been unable to deliver the wealth, prosperity and substantial economic and political independence they had promised to populations in the previous decades created, with Arab nationalism now cast aside, the premises for closer competition between lay nationalist and Islamist discourses. With the masses blaming nationalist elites for economic backwardness and political corruption following independence, a new process of desedimentation of social space across Muslim societies was enacted, not dissimilar to the one that had followed the irruption of colonisation. This offered Islamism an open terrain on which once again to posit its counter-hegemonic call.

On the one hand, Islamist movements or parties began to capitalise on their regained freedom, acting more assertively in politics, elaborating new forms of protest against corruption and immorality, and holding governments to account for failing to fulfil their promises. On the other, 'Islam' began to be ever more frequently invoked by domestic regimes themselves to justify government policy and to obtain the legitimacy necessary to maintain the status quo. A common tendency in the 1970s, for instance, was the decision of a large number of Muslim states to modify their internal constitutions so as to include articles referring to Islam or to the *shar'iah* as the fundamental source of law, or to adopt Friday as the day for their weekly festivity. Naturally these moves did not necessarily entail a substantial Islamisation of the state or the elites, which very often remained linked to nationalist and secularist attitudes, but what can be seen in action here is an instrumental function of the Islamisation from above.

A crucial connection at an institutional level came to be fully valorised in this period with Saudi Arabia's increasing sponsorship of Wahhabism, the religious doctrine traditionally legitimising the Saudi family's hold on power. The alliance between the Saud family and the reformer Muhammad Ibn Abd al-Wahhab in the eighteenth century had been at the root of a long-standing association in the Arab peninsula. While this alliance permitted the Sauds to find religious legitimacy for their political power so as to unite the vast majority of Arab tribes under their command in the Hejaz (the region on the west side on the Arab peninsula, touched by the Red Sea and including the holy cities of Mecca and Medina), it also meant that the Wahhabis could count on institutional backing to satisfy their demands for religious purification. Inherent to this was an official defence of *tawhid*, the uniqueness of God (entailing the repudiation of religious practices that worshipped anything other than God. Sufism, Shi'ism, or other movements commemorating saints were therefore declared to be heretical). It also implied a return to emulating the example provided by the Prophet and his 'companions', which justified the purification of Islam by means of purging it of all the negative 'innovations' (*bid'a*) that centuries of interpretations had brought about (in what was a conservative and puritan interpretation of salafism); and the promotion of a rigorous and literalist approach to the holy texts based on the juridical school of Hanbalism. Since the late 1970s, the increasing Saudi promotion of Wahhabism has served not only as a means to demonstrate the religious credentials of the monarchy to its internal constituencies, but also to compete on religious ground with other regimes in the region.

But the rising importance of Islam in these years can also be seen in Shia settings, with the overthrowing of the lay and nationalist regime of Shah Mohammad Reza Pahlavi in Persia. This revolution led to the creation of the Islamic Republic of Iran in 1979, which soon began to compete with Arab and Sunni states for power in the region. Finally, this historical juncture should be thought of in association with massive changes occurring on a global scale as an effect of globalisation. As we discussed in Chapter 3, globalisation and informatisation had been growing in relevance since the 1960s, promoting the consolidation of transmodernity as a broad symbolic reservoir alongside modernity and tradition. Naturally, global transformations became even more evident in the following decades, especially in the 1990s, when, despite all theoretical criticisms, globalisation became widely accepted as a sort of self-evident process, and transmodern categories such as virtuality, transnationalism, world market, etc., began to be increasingly used in everyday language.

It is against this historical backdrop that a further diversification of Islamist discourses took place, and that new strategic visions came to be devised. On the one hand, decades of prison and torture for Islamist leaders had led to harsh radicalisation, so that new extremist groups appeared. On the other, a new perspective on global politics gradually began to grow in influence with the appearance of a 'global *jihadi* movement', and the articulation of what we define as a *transterritorial* trajectory.[8]

This new perspective is best epitomised by the discourse of Osama bin Laden. In order to appreciate fully the specific nature of this relatively recent discursive formation and to remind us of the general framework we have been outlining here, let us return briefly to the immediate post-Qutb period in the 1970s, and consider what was happening in Egypt. We mentioned that the overall process of Islamic rejuvenation in the 1970s appeared with particular clarity in the Egyptian arena, where the release from prison of thousands of militants in the initial

---

[8] Cf. Patrick Sookhdeo, *Global Jihad: The Future in the Face of Militant Islam* (McLean, VA: Isaac Publishing, 2007); Devin R. Springer, James L. Regens and David N. Edger, *Islamic Radicalism and Global Jihad* (Washington, DC: Georgetown University Press, 2008); Jarret M. Brachman, *Global Jihadism: Theory and Practice* (Abingdon: Routledge, 2009); Rajeev Sharma, *Global Jihad: Current Patterns and Future Trends* (New Delhi: Kaveri Books, 2006).

period of Sadat's Egyptian presidency gave Islamist discourses new visibility. In the attempt to counter the action of former president Nasser's supporters, Sadat conceived Islamists as potential allies, promoting a period of relative freedom for militants who reorganised themselves and developed new strategic lines. Despite Sadat's expectations, however, a common feature of these groups (e.g., *Islamic Jihad*, *Takfir w-al-Hijra* and *Muhammad's Youth*) was their deep dissatisfaction with the gradualist and moderate approach to the Islamisation of society that the Muslim Brotherhood's leadership had traditionally chosen since al-Banna's times. This dissatisfaction evolved into growing aspiration to engage in a radical confrontation with the Egyptian regime, which, in their view, did not offer sufficient Islamic credentials. Crucially, while years of prison and torture had contributed to radicalising the mindset of thousands of Islamist militants in the previous decades, Qutb's descriptive approach and his extreme position towards *jahiliyyah* provided more radical militants in the 1970s with the theoretical platform upon which to establish their political agenda.

From this perspective, Sadat's decision to begin peaceful negotiations with Israel in order to recognise its right to exist and subsequently sign the Camp David Accords in 1978 marked a turning point in the relations between radical Islamists and the Egyptian government. The assassination of Sadat in 1981 by associates of *Islamic Jihad* represented the most significant action undertaken by Islamist militants against a domestic regime in that period, highlighting the emergence of a new uncompromising position by some organisations.[9]

Mohammed Abd al-Salam Faraj, who coordinated that action and was an ideologue of the movement, became well known for his 1982 pamphlet, *al-Faridah al-Ghaibah* (The Neglected Duty), which became a sort of manifesto for all the jihadist groups that emerged in the following years. In this pamphlet Faraj drew on Qutb's valorisation of jihad conceived of as the means to revive the Islamic society, stressing its militarist interpretation and its social value as an obligatory duty.

When explaining how to resist the descriptive state of *jahiliyyah*, Qutb had maintained both the spiritual and military conceptualisation of jihad, calling for a general effort to revive Muslim society in the contingency of history. For Qutb, the aim of this 'effort' was to establish a social system based on the transcendental power of *shari'ah* rather than an Islamic state tending towards immanent sovereignty. Faraj, on the other hand, celebrated and operationalised only the military dimension of jihad, highlighting its strategic function in the

---

[9] Gilles Kepel, *Muslim Extremism in Egypt: The Prophet and Pharaoh* (Berkeley, CA: University of California Press, 1985).

establishment of an Islamic state. Jihad was now defined as an individual duty, no longer subjected to official sanction by religious authorities. Its function was to contribute directly to the revolutionary eradication of jahili regimes and to the Islamisation of the modern nation state. During the 1980s and the 1990s, groups sharing a common jihadist perspective emerged in major Islamic settings, e.g. *Islamic Salvation Front* and the *Armed Islamic Group* in Algeria, the *Egyptian Islamic Jihad* and the *Gamaat Islamiya* in Egypt, the *Abu Sayyaf Group* in the Philippines, the *Jemaah Islamiyah* in Indonesia, etc. Although these groups acknowledged the role of foreign powers in affecting regional politics, their strategic priority remained insurrection against local rulers – i.e., 'the near enemy', in Faraj's terminology. Naturally, their focus on local politics and their attempt to Islamise the structures of the nation state via establishment of an 'Islamic state' reflected some resonance with al-Banna's territorial trajectory. However, they also drew from Qutb in assuming a pessimistic stance towards the lack of Islamicity of the contemporary world, re-reinterpreting Qutb's notion of jihad in more pessimistic and radical terms.

In this scenario, a first important step in the transition to *global* jihadism occurred with the Soviet invasion of Afghanistan in 1979. Thousands of Islamist militants devoted to local jihad arrived in Afghanistan throughout the 1980s to fight alongside Afghan resistance forces: the *mujahideen*. Afghanistan was seen by non-Afghan militants as a good opportunity to acquire military training and war experience which could be used back home against local rulers. Ayman al-Zawahiri (1951–), al-Qaeda's main spokesman and leader of the Egyptian group *Islamic Jihad*, recalled that Afghanistan was seen by Arabs fighting alongside Afghan resistance (the so-called Arab-Afghans) as an open battlefield where volunteers could receive training unbeknownst to the Arab security service:

> I saw [being in Afghanistan] as an opportunity to get to know one of the arenas of jihad that might be a tributary and a base for jihad in Egypt and the Arab region ... The problem to find a secure base for jihad activity in Egypt used to occupy me a lot, in view of the pursuit to which we were subjected by the security forces.[10]

In this context, while American proxies (intelligence, advisers, and economic agencies) and Saudi Arabia 'invested heavily in Afghanistan' in an anti-Soviet strategy, Pakistan's Inter-service Intelligence (ISI) and the CIA provided

---

[10] Ayman Zawahiri, 'Knights under the Prophet's Banner', in *His Own Words: Translation and Analysis of the Writings of Dr. Ayman Al Zawahiri* (Old Tappan, NJ: TLG Publications, 2006), p. 28.

technical and military capacity to the mujahideen, facilitating the upcoming creation of a first transnational network of Muslim militants and groups.[11] As David Cook argued: 'The battlefield of Afghanistan was the religious and social incubator for global radical Islam in that it established contacts among a wide variety of radicals from Muslim antigovernmental and resistance movements and fused them together.'[12]

In the aftermath of the Afghan War in the late 1980s, jihadist veterans returned from Afghanistan bringing, together with their war experience, a new self-confidence stemming from the substantial defeat of the great Soviet superpower. If a large faction of veterans reorganised jihad activities on local and territorial bases, others found new opportunities to develop their *transterritorial* mindset in the war of Bosnia in the early 1990s. New systems of recruitment were devised on a global scale as a spontaneous consequence of the network that had been created during the Afghan war. At the same time, a global jihadist perspective began to be increasingly promoted by Islamist militant Osama bin Laden and his associates, encouraging the consolidation and institutionalisation of this global Islamist network. Although transnational perspectives were already permeating Islamism in the 1970s, it was at this stage, in the mid 1990s, that global targets began to be increasingly assumed as 'prime' objectives fostering the internationalisation of jihad.

This transition occurred as result of a long historical process marked by massive structural changes in the world, most of which have been examined in Chapter 3. The surfacing of the United States as the only superpower in the post-Cold War, and the presence of American troops in the Arabian peninsula following the 1990 Iraqi invasion of Kuwait, also contributed to this gradual shift towards the internationalisation of jihad. Moreover, the persistent US support of Israel, and the protracted indifference of Europe towards the massacres in Bosnia in the early 1990s came to be assumed by jihadists as an unequivocal sign of Western indifference to the plight of their co-religionists in general. When related to the transnational experience and the creation of a global network articulated during the Afghan war, all of these factors proved significant in promoting the growth of a new global jihadist perspective. These were also the years when informatisation and globalisation began to be consolidated as major filters in the interpretation of reality, with new communication systems – i.e.,

---

[11] Fawaz A. Gerges, *The Far Enemy: Why Jihad Went Global* (Cambridge: Cambridge University Press, 2005), p. 77: Peter G. Mandaville, *Global Political Islam* (London: Routledge, 2007), p. 243.

[12] David Cook, *Understanding Jihad* (Berkeley, CA: University of California Press, 2005), p. 128.

email, chat rooms, mobile phones – contributing to a reshuffling of common perceptions of space and time.

In his work on global jihad, Fawaz A. Gerges locates the shift to globalism 'long after the end of the Afghan war around the mid-1990s', and considers the 9/11 attacks to represent the peak of this transition.[13] It was during this crucial period that bin Laden's articulation of a transterritorial trajectory began to emerge as one of the most appealing Islamist visions at the beginning of the millennium, challenging dominant Islamist discourses, which had either adopted a moderate and mainstream approach to political life or were keen to proceed with a localist conception of jihad, revealing, in both case, the influence of a territorial perspective.

Osama bin Laden's Articulatory Practice: A Discursive Inquiry[14]

Internationally known as al-Qaeda's leader and the main instigator of the 9/11 attacks, bin Laden committed to jihad in the early 1980s when, still very young, he left his lucrative family empire to join Arab volunteers in the Afghan war.[15] Here, bin Laden became one of the prominent associates of Abdullah Azzam (1941–1989), a Palestinian Islamic scholar, charismatic leader and major coordinator of jihad volunteering in Afghanistan. As bin Laden put it, it is probably thanks to Azzam's influence that most volunteers began to develop their transterritorial perspective: 'When the Sheikh [Azzam] started out, the atmosphere among the Islamists and sheikhs was limited, location-specific, and regional, each dealing with their own particular locale, but he inspired the Islamic movement and motivated Muslims to the broader jihad.'[16]

In the early years of work in the Afghan-Pakistani Frontier, bin Laden helped organise a training camp, the *Sijil al-Qaeda* (the 'Register of the Base'), simply known as al-Qaeda (the Base), for the Arab volunteers that arrived from the Middle East to join the mujahideen. Within 18 years, the early al-Qaeda's embryonic network had become a formal organisation striving to connect a

---

[13] Gerges, *The Far Enemy*, p. 14.
[14] Bruce Lawrence's *Messages to the World: The Statements of Osama Bin Laden* (London and New York: Verso, 2005) is one of the first collections of bin Laden's statements in a Western language, i.e., English. Most quotes by bin Laden in this section will conveniently be referring to Lawrence's anthology.
[15] Michael Scheuer, *Osama Bin Laden* (Oxford: Oxford University Press, 2011).
[16] Osama bin Laden, 'A Muslim Bomb, December 1998', in Lawrence, *Messages to the World*, p. 77.

wide range of radical groups under the banner of what, in 1998, bin Laden called the 'World Islamic Front'.[17]

When considering bin Laden's overall trajectory, the celebration of a traditional pan-Islamic ideal appears in clear terms. As bin Laden put it during an interview with *al-Jazeera*'s reporter Tayseer Allouni just two weeks after the beginning of American military operations in Afghanistan:

> our concern is that this nation (*ummah*) unites either under the Words of the Book of Allah (*subhannahu wa ta'aala*) or His Prophet (*sallallahu 'alayhi wasallam*) ... the righteous Khilafah will return with the permission of Allah (*sallallahu 'alayhi wasallam*), and the nation (*ummah*) is asked to unite itself under this Crusaders' campaign.[18]

Since his early public statements in 1994, specific geographical locations, e.g., Sudan, Saudi Arabia, Afghanistan, Palestine, were immediately signified as Islamic constituencies in the spatial domain of *dar al-Islam*:

> The legal duty regarding Palestine and our brothers there – the poor men, women, and children who have nowhere to go – is to wage jihad for the sake of God, and to motivate our umma to jihad so that Palestine may be completely liberated and returned to Islamic sovereignty.[19]

In the above statement, Palestine stands as an Islamic land, requiring the whole Muslim ummah to 'wage jihad' so as to return this land to 'Islamic sovereignty'. Despite the strategic importance of specific geo-political settings, e.g., the US military presence in Saudi Arabia or the Israeli occupation of Palestine, a strong universalistic conception of territoriality marks bin Laden's trajectory from the start, allowing *dar al-Islam* in its global dimension to preserve a privileged position. This can be seen, for instance, in a 1996 statement centring on the illegal presence of US military bases on Arabian soil, 'Declaration of Jihad', where an opening quote from the Sunna focusing on the Arabian peninsula: 'Expel the Polytheists from the Arabian peninsula', is immediately followed by the assumption of a wider global perspective:

---

[17] Osama bin Laden, 'World Islamic Front Statement, 23 February 1998: Jihad against Jews and Crusaders', translation at http://fas.org/irp/world/para/docs/980223-fatwa.htm.

[18] Osama bin Laden, 'Osama Bin Ladin, Interview by Tayseer Allouni, 21 October 2001', translation at: http://www.religioscope.com/info/doc/jihad/ubl_int_3.htm.

[19] Osama bin Laden, 'The Betrayal of Palestine, 29 December 1994', in Lawrence, *Messages to the World*, p. 9.

> Their [Muslim] blood was spilled in Palestine and Iraq. The horrifying pictures of the massacre of Qana, in Lebanon are still fresh in our memory. Massacres in Tajakestan, Burma, Cashmere, Assam, Philippine, Fatani, Ogadin, Somalia, Erithria, Chechnia and in Bosnia-Herzegovina took place, massacres that send shivers in the body and shake the conscience.[20]

All these areas are conceived of as single parts of the 'Islamic world' reflecting the existence of a whole 'unified umma' that believers, regardless of their geographical origin, ought to defend by jihad:

> You know, we are linked to all of the Islamic world, whether that be Yemen, Pakistan, or wherever. We are part of one unified umma, and by the grace of God the number of those who have conviction and have set out to wage jihad are increasing every day.[21]

Drawing on the traditional appeal of Islamic universalism, bin Laden articulates an inclusive representation of space and subjectivity, celebrating the ideal of a unified reality which 'neither recognizes race nor colour; nor does it pay any heed to borders and walls'.[22] This impinging upon tradition, however, is fuelled by the combination and inclusion of what has been described as a globalist transmodern perspective in Chapter 3. This allows for the assumption of an antagonistic perspective defining the enemy as a 'global' presence, rather than a local and domestic one:

---

[20] Osama bin Laden, Osama bin Laden, 'Declaration of War: Against the Americans Occupying the Land of the Two Holy Places', 23 August 1996; translation at: http://web.archive.org/web/20011106100207/http://www.kimsoft.com/2001/binladenwar.htm; the Qur'anic verse at the incipit of the statement refers to al-Bukhari's hadith collection, no. 2.932. A hadith is an oral tradition reporting the sayings and the deeds of the Prophet Muhammad. The collection of such narrations in the early centuries of Islam constituted the Sunna, which represents the religious source of Islam after the Qur'an. In the statement above, the reference to the massacre of Qana refers to the killing of 102 civilians and the wounding of over 300 by an Israeli shell accidentally launched on a UN compound next to the Southern Lebanon village of Qana in 1996. All the other regions mentioned above, constituted major war theatres involving non-Muslim powers.

[21] Osama bin Laden, 'A Muslim Bomb, December 1998', in Lawrence, *Messages to the World*, p. 88.

[22] Osama bin Laden, 'Under Mullah Omar, 9 April 2001', in Lawrence, *Messages to the World*, p. 96.

> I write these lines to you at a time when the blood of children and innocents has been deemed fair game, when the holy places of Islam have been violated in more than one place, under the supervision of the new world order and under the auspices of the United Nations, which has clearly become a tool with which the plans of global unbelief against Muslims are implemented. This is an organization that is overseeing with all its capabilities the annihilation and blockade of millions of Muslims under the sanctions, and yet still is not ashamed to talk about human rights![23]

This passage is particularly telling, for it shows the kind of alignment that bin Laden instantiates between a pan-Islamic imaginary and the specific historical and political conditions informing the international scene in the late 1990s, when the idea of a 'new world order' was just consolidating and circulating across emerging transmodern formations. Bin Laden's criticism of the enfeebled role of the United Nations parallels a number of transmodern discourses on empire and universalism, which assume the United Nations to have become a mere intermediate 'tool' of the new global order (in lay and critical terms, 'global unbelief' reads here as 'global capital'), endorsing an instrumental and rhetorical use of human rights.

This statement testifies to bin Laden's perception of globalisation as a worldwide structural context, requiring Muslims to renounce their local perspective in a new transterritorial effort against 'global unbelief', here standing as the 'far enemy' in Faraj's terminology, the 'greatest external enemy' or 'the crusaders-Jewish alliance' in bin Laden's language.[24] As he puts it when describing the activity of fellow jihadists: 'The people and the young men are concentrating their efforts on the sponsor and not on the sponsored. The concentration at this point of *Jihad* is against the American occupiers'.[25]

From these early statements, it is possible to notice that 'jihad' plays a central role in bin Laden's discourse, being celebrated, as we saw above, as the most important 'legal duty' that Muslims are called on to perform today. 'Jihad' is, however, largely connoted by a defensive and military tone. Hence, an important difference from a foundational thinker like al-Banna, who, while acknowledging the importance of defensive and military jihad, also emphasised the spiritual dimension of the term, and valorised *da'wa* (Islamic call), education, and charity.

---

[23] Ibid.

[24] bin Laden, 'A Muslim Bomb, December 1998', in Lawrence, *Messages to the World*, p. 80.

[25] Osama bin Laden, 'Osama Bin Ladin, Interview by Peter Arnett, 20 March 1997', translation at: http://www.anusha.com/osamaint.htm.

In this sense, these two figures are clearly the products of different backgrounds, with al-Banna remaining a teacher and thinker vis-à-vis bin Laden's militant role as an actual fighter in the Afghan land. This is best evidenced by bin Laden's almost exclusive focus on politics, and the little emphasis he put on religious and doctrinal issues or on the broader ethical and socio-economic dimension of Islam.

If examined through the lens of Qutb's discourse, bin Laden's position reveals some affinity to Qutb's 'normative' vision, though he turned Qutb's invitation to restore Islamic society into concrete jihadist militancy. While acknowledging bin Laden's lack of direct references to Qutb, wide consensus among scholars has tended to stress some kind of influence of the Egyptian thinker over the leader of al-Qaeda.[26] Recent criticism, however, has been made in this regard by Michael Scheuer in his insightful work on Osama bin Laden.

Doctrinal and personal differences, for Scheuer, make immediate and direct links between the two highly problematic. Apart from minor considerations challenging the assumption of Qutb's authoritative appeal for bin Laden (e.g., Qutb was not 'in any formal sense a trained religious scholar' and followed 'the teachings of the Sunni scholar Abu al-Hasan al-Ash'ari, who championed a non-literalist approach to the Koran'), the latter would hardly 'embrace Qutb's Hobbes-like doctrine of a religious war of everyone against everyone else', or 'Qutb's call for an offensive jihad'.[27]

Although we agree that a degree of caution is necessary here, we found much richer and more complex thought in the Egyptian thinker, evidencing the way in which the inclusive dimension of his normative vision affected his understanding of jihad. This makes Scheuer's image of Qutb as a theorist of offensive jihad feel unlikely. What is important to stress here is, rather, the discursive alignment between the two as far as the endorsement of a universalistic tradition is concerned. According to Scheuer, a proof of bin Laden's disinterest towards Qutb can also be seen in the al-Qaeda leader's familiarity with all the traditional sources that Qutb himself had re-articulated in his pan-Islamic call, including the political thought of classic Islamic scholar Ibn Taymiyyah (1263–1328). This would make Qutb's ideas less original and appealing for bin Laden than is usually claimed. Although it is impossible to prove the impact of the former on the latter or to demonstrate the type and quality of engagement

---

[26] In indirect terms, for instance, bin Laden is said to have achieved familiarity with elements of Qutb's discourse during his years at the King Abdul Aziz University in Jeddah, when he allegedly met Qutb's brother, Muhammad Qutb, who was teaching in Saudi universities in the 1970s.

[27] Scheuer, *Osama Bin Laden*, p. 44.

with traditional texts that bin Laden had established in his early years (especially when considering the scant attention he gave to doctrinal issues in his overall statements), we would still stress, however, the influence that Qutb's writings had continued to exert after his death well beyond the Egyptian scene. It is likely that the political value of Qutb's activism and militancy, up to the point of his martyrdom for the restoration of an Islamic society, would have been taken into consideration by bin Laden in his years of fighting, reducing the impact of doctrinal differences. Bin Laden's ability to create networks with Muslims of different doctrinal orientations, and to fight alongside militants from Egypt who were familiar with and even devoted to the political vicissitude of Qutb, are indicative of this.[28] This is not, however, to dismiss important distinctions between the two. We shall see soon that differences immediately emerge as we consider Qutb's descriptive vision, and his inclusion of Muslim societies within *jahiliyyah*, something that bin Laden, like al-Banna and others, would reject.

In terms of the role that jihad fulfils in relation to bin Laden's pan-Islamic call, we saw earlier that a major feature of his universalistic vision is the idea that the Muslim ummah stands as a universal community whose territorial dimension does not recognise national differentiations. At the same time, bin Laden acknowledges the historical presence of non-Muslim countries, which figure as *dar al-harb* any time they directly wage war against Islam. Hence, bin Laden's advocacy of jihad as an *individual duty* for all Muslims aiming to *defend* and restore Islamic sovereignty in *dar al-Islam*:

> The ruling to kill the Americans and their allies – civilians and military – is an individual duty for every Muslim who can do it in any country in which it is possible to do it, in order to liberate the al-Aqsa Mosque and the holy mosque

---

[28] Bruce Lawrence, in this regard, while endorsing the claim that elements of Qutb's vision such as *jahiliyya* 'substantially informs bin Laden's discourse' (Lawrence, 2005, p. 16), highlights the close relationship between bin Laden's closest associate, the Egyptian Ayman al-Zawahiri, and Sayyid Qutb (confirmed by Zawahiri's explicit and long tribute to Qutb in his 'Knights under the Prophet's Banner', where al-Qaeda's militant relates 'the beginning of the formation of the nucleus of the modern Islamic jihad movement in Egypt' to Qutb's ideas; Zawahiri, 'Knights under the Prophet's Banner', p. 50). According to Lawrence, Zawahiri became acquainted with Qutb when he joined the Muslim Brotherhood at the early age of 14, becoming 'a student and follower' of the Egyptian theorist (it would be correct to specify that Zawahiri's interest in Qutb originated under the influence of his uncle, Mafouz Azzam, who was Qutb's student and pupil).

(Mecca) from their grip, and in order for their armies to move out of all the lands of Islam, defeated and unable to threaten any Muslim.[29]

A few caveats are needed from the passage above. First, as we have already mentioned, bin Laden was keen to sustain the idea of a non-offensive war:

> We ourselves are the victims of murder and massacres. We are only defending ourselves against the United States. This is a defensive jihad to protect our land and our people. That's why I have said that if we don't have security, neither will the Americans. It's a very simple equation that any American child could understand: live and let others live.[30]

Crucially, the interpretation of jihad as a defensive act is persistently accompanied by a notion of *reciprocity*: 'live and let others live'. This can also be seen in the very articulation of the signifier 'terror'. By sharing a common criticism in the West of the political use of the term 'terrorist', bin Laden questions the US's unclear deployment of this term, which encompasses, by way of its fluidity, any form of rebellion against Western power:

> The US today as a result of the arrogant attitude has set a double standard, calling whoever goes against its injustice a terrorist ... With a simple look at the US behaviors, we find that it judges the behavior of the poor Palestinian children whose country was occupied: if they throw stones against the Israeli occupation, it says they are terrorists whereas when the Israeli pilots bombed the United Nations building in Qana, Lebanon while was full of children and women, the US stopped any plan to condemn Israel.[31]

At the same time, bin Laden is fully aware of the counter-hegemonic potential that the signifier 'terrorism' might play in a global context marked by the increasing circulation of transmodern signifiers. Hence, his rearticulation and ultimate endorsement of the term 'terror' now defined as a reactive force to the new world order:

---

[29] Osama bin Laden, 'World Islamic Front Statement, 23 February 1998: Jihad against Jews and Crusaders'. The al-Aqsa mosque in Jerusalem and the Holy mosque in Mecca are among the most important sanctuaries of Islam and are here used to indicate, respectively and metaphorically, both Palestine and Arabia.

[30] Osama bin Laden, 'The Example of Vietnam, 12 November 2001', interview published in *Al-Quds Al-Arabi*, in Lawrence, *Messages to the World*, p. 141.

[31] bin Laden, 'Osama Bin Ladin, Interview by Peter Arnett, 20 March 1997'.

> These young men, whom Allah has cleared the way for, they have shifted the battle to the heart of the United States and they have destroyed its most outstanding (*abraz*) landmarks, their economic landmarks and their military landmarks, that being with the grace of Allah (*dhalika fadlu allah*). And they have done this from what we understand, and we have incited and roused for this (*harradna*) before, and it is in self-defense, defense of our brothers and sons in Palestine and for freeing our holy sites. And if inciting (*tahrid*) for this is terrorism, and if killing the ones that kill our sons is terrorism, then let history witness that we are terrorists.[32]

The defensive nature of jihad promotes, therefore, the counter-hegemonic rearticulation of 'terror', which is aimed at re-establishing a sense of 'balance' between the occupiers and the occupied:

> So, as they kill us, without a doubt we have to kill them, until we obtain a balance of terror (*tawaazun fil ru'b*). This is the first time that the scale of terror has evened out between the Muslims and the Americans in these recent times; in the past, the Americans did to us whatever they pleased, and the victim wasn't even allowed to cry.[33]

What is interesting to stress, however, is that the presence of *dar al-harb* in the contingency of history (in the contemporary world) is not conceived of as a universal and all-encompassing dimension replacing *dar al-Islam* integrally. As we mentioned above, from this point of view bin Laden remains faithful to a classic or 'normative' pan-Islamic conception, without ceding to the kind of pessimism that marks Qutb's analysis when he moves to a descriptive level. Bin Laden, in fact, is eager to assert the immediate *presence* of Islamic society in the contingency of history and its historical coexistence with non-Muslim countries:

> We are a nation [*ummah*] and have a long history, with the grace of God, Praise and Glory be to Him ... If we look back at our history, we will find there were many types of dealings between the Muslim nation and the other nations in time of peace and in time of war, including treaties and matters to do with commerce. So it is not a new thing that we need to come up with. Rather, it already, by the grace of God, exists.[34]

---

[32] bin Laden, 'Osama Bin Ladin, Interview by Tayseer Allouni, 21 October 2001'.
[33] Ibid.
[34] bin Laden, 'Osama Bin Ladin, Interview by Peter Arnett, 20 March 1997'.

It is true that bin Laden defines *dar al-harb* as 'global unbelief', but 'global' means for bin Laden the worldwide '*hegemony* of the infidels over us' [emphasis added].[35] Hegemony implies the survival of something that can be hegemonised, rather than the total replacement of something with something else. The recurrence of the expression 'global unbelief' reflects the acknowledgment of an *interconnected* global context 'dominated' or 'hegemonised' by a specific power structure, the *world order*, a term bin Laden explicitly borrows from the West: 'the US started to look at itself as a Master of this world and established what it calls the new world order'.[36] This illustrates the integration of a transmodern tone in bin Laden's re-elaboration of tradition, rather than the descriptive and pessimistic Qutbian assumption that 'the whole world is steeped in *Jahiliyyah*'.[37]

It is in this context that jihad plays a central strategic function in bin Laden's discourse, providing the means to oppose the assimilation of *dar al-Islam* by *dar al-harb*, and therefore hampering the realisation of Qutb's descriptive universalisation of *jahiliyyah*:

> Had the believers not fought the infidels, the latter would have defeated the believers and the earth would have been corrupted by their ill deeds. So, pay attention to the importance of conflict.[38]

Naturally the assumption of a universalistic perspective does not entail abandoning forms of polarisation. In traditional pan-Islamic terms, the very idea of Islamic universality entails the potential integration of *dar al-harb* by *dar al-Islam*. If this holds true in principle, the historical context that bin Laden is facing points to the opposite; that is, the risk is for *dar al-Islam* to be assimilated by global unbelief. When accounting for al-Banna's territorial trajectory, we mentioned that al-Banna warned against the increasing infiltration of colonial political and cultural forces *into* the Islamic land. Bin Laden's vision in the historical climate at the turn of the millennium expresses, instead, the sensation of secularisation and Western political power being part of the cultural and political life of Islamic land, working *within* Muslim states, even though he acknowledges the presence of entire sections of societies that resist cultural assimilation and occupation. In this sense, bin Laden expresses a common feature among religious communities

---

[35] bin Laden, 'Among a Band of Knights, 14 February 2003', p. 196.
[36] bin Laden, 'Osama Bin Ladin, Interview by Peter Arnett, 20 March 1997'.
[37] Sayyid Qutb, *Milestones*, special edition by A.B. al-Mehri (Birmingham: Maktabah Booksellers and Publishers, 2006), p. 26.
[38] Osama bin Laden, 'Resist the New Rome, 4 January 2004', in Lawrence, *Messages to the World*, p. 217.

in the global context: that of conceiving the religious community in terms of a 'minority' in the face of global-westernised cultural patterns (or 'hegemony' as he put it) marked by strong secular tendencies.

The risk of global unbelief pervading *dar al-Islam* in its entirety configures the articulation of an antagonistic relation marked by transnational contours, and defining two opposite *globalised* poles: the Muslim societies on the one hand, and Western powers on the other: 'One the one side is the global Crusader alliance with the Zionist Jews, led by America, Britain, and Israel, and the other side is the Islamic world'.[39] Needless to say, such a perspective shares the language of the 'Clash of Civilizations'; that is, Huntington's thesis that modern ideological conflicts would be replaced in the new world order by new forms of antagonism between major civilisations.[40] In an interview in October 2001, bin Laden explicitly endorses the Western notion of the 'Clash of Civilizations', re-articulating it along traditional lines, and defining it as a 'very clear matter, proven in the Book and the Sunna.'[41]

Bin Laden's polarised impingement upon ideas of 'global unbelief', 'terror' and 'clash of civilizations' mirrors the central use of similar terms in the Western arena, where transmodern belligerent signifiers have been heavily used to account for a global context marked by spatial dislocation and de-territorialisation. Hence a central category like 'global war on terror', which functioned as a 'signature rhetorical legacy' of George W. Bush's presidency.[42] This expression conveyed the idea – together with minor variants like 'global struggle against violent extremism' (preferred by then-Defense Secretary Donald H. Rumsfeld) – of an indeterminate, indefinite and boundless war against what Bush first described, paralleling bin Laden's notion of global unbelief, as the 'axis of evil'. Described by Bush in 2001 as a war that 'will not end until every terrorist group of global reach has been found, stopped and defeated', the same language has been reproduced by president Obama.[43] A new 'decaffeinated' expression for war, 'overseas contingency operations' (OCO), has thus been adopted in US official documents since 2009, accounting for a new transmodern world

---

[39] bin Laden, 'A Muslim Bomb, December 1998', p. 73.
[40] Samuel Huntington, *The Clash of Civilizations and the Remaking of World Order* (New York: Usborne Books, 1996).
[41] bin Laden, 'Osama Bin Ladin, Interview by Tayseer Allouni, 21 October 2001' .
[42] Scott Wilson and Al Kamen, '"Global War on Terror" Is Given New Name', *Washington Post*, 25 March 2009, http://www.washingtonpost.com/wp-dyn/content/article/2009/03/24/AR2009032402818.html.
[43] George W. Bush, 'Address to a Joint Session of Congress and the American People', 20 September 2001, http://georgewbush-whitehouse.archives.gov/news/releases/2001/09/20010920-8.html.

where 'disorderly regions, failed states, diffuse enemies' replace the 'great power conflicts and clear lines of division that defined the 20th century', requiring a continual war for the preservation of 'global security'.[44] By resorting to the same rhetorical strategy of the Bush administration, the assumption of this globalist perspective has been recently intensified following the new challenges presented by the ISIS in the summer of 2014, against which 'a steady, relentless effort' has to be counterposed so as to 'hunt down terrorists who threaten our country, wherever they are', and oppose their 'acts of barbarism' and every 'trace of evil from the world'.[45]

On a broad perspective, we saw that while adopting a globalist antagonistic outlook, which fully mobilises the language of the clash of civilisations, bin Laden is eager to maintain a strict reference to what, in Qutbian terms, could be identified as a normative universalistic framework. That is, the competition for survival with global unbelief (*dar al-harb*) does not compromise the idea of the Muslim society as a concrete reality in the contingency of history. This entails a further element of differentiation from Qutb as far as the notion of a vanguard is concerned. In Chapter 5, we argued that the assessment of an all-encompassing *jahiliyyah* led Qutb to consider vanguardism as the virtual anticipation of the Muslim community to come. By re-articulating traditional radical perspectives on the vanguard, Qutb distinguished between 'believers' – self-proclaiming Muslims acting non-Islamically – and 'true believers', the expression of the vanguard of God.

Although, on several occasions, bin Laden defines jihadist militants as a vanguard, the term is used more traditionally here to indicate that part of the broader ummah committed to jihad in defence of Islam, rather than a distinct group of true believers immersed in *jahiliyyah* (this one including self-professing Muslims):

> Our nation (the Islamic world) has been tasting this humiliation and this degradation for more than 80 years. Its sons are killed, its blood is shed, its sanctuaries are attacked, and no one hears and no one heeds. When God blessed one of the groups of Islam, vanguards of Islam, they destroyed America.[46]

---

[44] Barack Obama, 'Remarks by the President in Address to the Nation on the Way Forward in Afghanistan and Pakistan', 1 December 2009, http://www.whitehouse.gov/the-press-office/remarks-president-address-nation-way-forward-afghanistan-and-pakistan.

[45] Barack Obama, 'Statement by the President on ISIL', 10 September 2014, http://www.whitehouse.gov/the-press-office/2014/09/10/statement-president-isil-1.

[46] Osama bin Laden, 'Bin Laden's Statement, 7 October 2001', translation at http://www.theguardian.com/world/2001/oct/07/afghanistan.terrorism15.

So defined, the vanguard groups bin Laden is talking about are an integral part of the existing ummah. This can be seen, for instance, in bin Laden's description of al-Qaeda as an organisation that cannot be 'separated from this nation (*ummah*). We are the children of a nation, and we are an unseparable part of it, and from those public demonstrations which spread from the far east, from the Philippines, to Indonesia, to Malaysia, to India, to Pakistan, reaching Mauritania ... and so we discuss the conscience of this nation (*ummah*).'[47] Moreover, bin Laden is aware of the risk of dissociating the true believers from believers as Qutb's descriptive analysis tended to do, especially in a time when the war on terror requires extensive degrees of solidarity between Muslims.

It is true that, despite bin Laden's personal position, actors within the global jihadist movement often tend to share Qutb's notion of vanguardism, looking at regular Muslims as sinful manifestations of *jahiliyyah*. Several biographical accounts of al-Qaeda sympathisers, including some of the twin towers hijackers, have described the increasing dissociation of these jihadist members from the rest of the Muslim community.[48] In an article describing the true meaning of salafism, the *Qur'an and Sunnah Society of Canada* defines the true salafi as he/she who 'revives the Sunnah of the Prophet in his worship and behavior. This makes him a stranger among people.'[49] The same approach applies to some of the groups directly or indirectly affiliated to al-Qaeda.

Aware of such possibilities, and loyal to a normative vision which considered the presence of the ummah in the contingency of history as a constitutive feature of Islamic universalism, bin Laden explicitly warns against the inclusion of Muslims into the domain of *jahiliyyah* or the potential virtualisation of the Islamic community:

> We think that the Muslims are Muslims, and we don't call any Muslims disbelievers unless they specifically commit one of the well-known big wrongdoings (*naaqitha*) of Islam, while having full knowledge that this is one of the actions of wrongdoings in religion.[50]

In another statement this position is expressed in even stronger terms, for bin Laden publicly clarified that no sin forces a believer 'outside his faith', and the

---

[47] bin Laden, 'Osama Bin Ladin, Interview by Tayseer Allouni, 21 October 2001'.

[48] See, for instance, Olivier Roy, *Globalized Islam: Fundamentalism, Deterritorialization and the Search for a New Ummah* (London: Hurst & Company, 2004).

[49] The Qur'an and Sunnah Society of Canada, *An Introduction to the Salafi Da'wah*, http://www.qss.org/articles/salafi/text.html.

[50] bin Laden, 'Osama Bin Ladin, Interview by Tayseer Allouni, 21 October 2001'

killing of Muslims during al-Qaeda activities does not occur as a consequence of conceiving regular Muslims to be sinful or jahili. It is, rather, the result of an 'accidental manslaughter', for which jihadist groups take 'responsibility':

> We believe that no sin besides that of unbelief makes a believer step outside his faith, even if it is a serious sin, like murder or drinking alcohol … We do not anathematize people in general, nor do we permit the shedding of Muslim blood. If some Muslims have been killed during the operations of the mujahidin then we pray to God to take mercy on them; this is a case of accidental manslaughter, and we beg God's forgiveness for it and we take responsibility for it.[51]

Although bin Laden's speeches have been very often described by Western media as irrational and fanatical, a closer scrutiny of his statements demonstrates a highly coherent and practical position, very often led by a patent, though tragic sense of realpolitik. We agree with Scheuer that:

> Those who claim that bin Laden is somewhat or totally mad, that his allies are not only few in number but are illiterate homicidal maniacs disconnected from 'real' Islam, and that he wants to kill all non-Muslims are much like those contemporary scholars who believe that classical Athens was populated by democratic, lifestyle-tolerant, and arts-loving Athenians, and that Sparta, by contrast, was run by totalitarian and unsophisticated citizens.[52]

Bin Laden's discourse, in this respect, is infused with a pragmatic and realistic tone, constantly pointing to concrete economic interests and political objectives in his references to matters of international politics:

> We must take into consideration that this war brings billions of dollars in profit to the major companies, whether it be those that produce weapons or those that contribute to reconstruction, such as the Halliburton Company, its sisters and daughters. Based on this, it is very clear who is the one benefiting from igniting this war and from the shedding of blood. It is the warlords, the bloodsuckers, who are steering the world policy from behind a curtain.[53]

---

[51] Osama bin Laden, 'Depose the Tyrants, 16 December 2004', in Lawrence, *Messages to the World*, p. 262.
[52] Scheuer, *Osama bin Laden*, p. ix.
[53] Osama bin Laden, 'Bin Laden Tape, 15 April 2004', translation at http://news.bbc.co.uk/2/hi/middle_east/3628069.stm.

Naturally his emphasis on the financial benefits that the Iraqi war has brought to some of the biggest multinational corporations associated with the White House is also likely to serve the related effect of sharing or provoking anti-war feelings in the West. Bin Laden's attention to the possibility of addressing issues of particular relevance for a more critical audience in the West remains a constant in his talks. In one of his later statements in 29 January 2010, for instance, bin Laden criticises the US's reluctance to promote climate change, calling for a global boycott of American goods and companies. In line with the most fancy non-global language, he stated that to 'talk about climate change is not an ideological luxury but a reality', adding that 'all of the industrialized countries, especially the big ones, bear responsibility for the global warming crisis'.[54]

More generally, cost-benefit analysis is very often deployed by bin Laden to rate the efficacy of jihadist operations, for instance when he estimates the financial loss that the US experienced as a consequence of the 9/11 attacks or the political consequences of the Riyadh attacks of 1995.[55] More sadly, strategic and logical thinking and a reference to a principle of reciprocity are used to sanction the killing of civilians by jihadists, rather than a merely fanatical allusion to the fact that the victims are non-Muslim, or to the need to pursue the purification of souls:

> Who is the one that said that our blood isn't blood and their blood is blood? Who is the one that declared this? What about the people that have been killed in our lands for decades? More than 1,000,000 children died in Iraq and are still dying, so why don't we hear people that cry or protest or anyone who reassures or anyone who gives condolences? ... How do these people move when civilians die in the America, when we are killed every day? Every day in Palestine, children are killed.[56]

In the same vein, the strategic relevance of the 9/11 attacks has to be understood for bin Laden in relation to the symbolic role of its location. The killing of non-Muslim civilians here is not motivated by religious or dogmatic concerns, but finds a reason in the alleged material support on the part of the victims for the political and economic agenda of Western powers:

---

[54] http://www.nytimes.com/2010/01/30/world/middleeast/30binladen.html?_r=0.
[55] For estimations about the costs of the 9/11 attack, see Osama bin Laden, 'Osama Bin Ladin, Interview by Tayseer Allouni, 21 October 2001'; for a reference to the Riyadh attack, see Osama bin Laden, 'The Saudi Regime, November 1996', in Lawrence, *Messages to the World*, p. 36.
[56] bin Laden, 'Osama Bin Ladin, Interview by Tayseer Allouni, 21 October 2001'.

> Those young men, that Allah has cleared the way for, didn't intend to kill children, but instead, they attacked the biggest center of military power in the world, the Pentagon ... As for the World Trade Center, the ones who were attacked and who died in it were a financial power. It wasn't a children's school! And it wasn't a residence. And the general consensus is that most of the people who were in there were men that backed the biggest financial force in the world that spreads worldwide mischief.[57]

A practical justification for the killing of civilians is found in the very democratic logic that Western powers celebrate:

> The American people should remember that they pay taxes to their government and that they voted for their president. Their government makes weapons and provides them to Israel, which they use to kill Palestinian Muslims. Given that the American Congress is a committee that represents the people, the fact that it agrees with the actions of the American government proves that America in its entirety is responsible for the atrocities that it is committing against Muslims.[58]

Throughout his statements, bin Laden retains a persistent focus on the political and pragmatic motivations of his actions, downplaying dogmatic or doctrinal concerns vis-à-vis declared enemies. This is an important factor that should not be neglected, especially in consideration of his impingement on Islamic universalism.

As we saw, although bin Laden maintains a dynamic antagonistic position towards *dar al-harb*, this antagonism is often justified, whether genuinely or instrumentally, on the basis of a defensive relation. The strong pragmatism he displays, with the implicit unavailability to forms of irreducible antagonism when non-motivated by concrete offence (along the above-mentioned principle 'live and let others live'), suggests a potential alignment of bin Laden with the principle of mediation often informing the history of pan-Islamic discourse, where the material existence of *dar al-Islam* in the contingency of history and the preservation of concrete interests to be defended led to forms of compromise or agreements with *dar al-harb*, in the form, for instance, of *dar al-'ahd* or other devices. In this sense, bin Laden's position seems to remain, at least in principle, open to negotiation. This is suggested, for instance, on the occasion of a peace proposal he offered to Europe on 15 April, 2004:

---

[57] Ibid.
[58] bin Laden, 'The Example of Vietnam, 12 November 2001', pp. 140–41.

> I also offer a reconciliation initiative to them, whose essence is our commitment to stopping operations against every country that commits itself to not attacking Muslims or interfering in their affairs – including the US conspiracy on the greater Muslim world. This reconciliation can be renewed once the period signed by the first government expires and a second government is formed with the consent of both parties. The reconciliation will start with the departure of its last soldier from our country. The door of reconciliation is open for three months of the date of announcing this statement. For those who reject reconciliation and want war, we are ready. As for those who want reconciliation, we have given them a chance.[59]

It should be noted that a preliminary step for these proposals to be implemented is Western acceptance of bin Laden's requests (mainly, Western renunciation of intervention into Muslim affairs both politically and militarily).[60] In bin Laden's later statements, a few years later, this condition was explicitly formulated as a request to European countries to pull out of Afghanistan (29 November, 2007).[61] On 25 September, 2009, this claim was connected, as a matter of strategic convenience, to the recent financial crisis in Europe:

> When Europe suffers from an economic crisis today, when its center is no longer topping the list of the world's export nations, and the United States has started to weaken because of the bloodletting caused by a pricey war, then what will it be like for you after the withdrawal of the Americans – God willing – when we decide to revenge ourselves for the oppression?[62]

The statement concludes with a reiterated offer of conciliation if his requests are met: 'And if they incline to peace, then incline to it and trust in Allah'. On 27 October, 2010 and 21 January, 2011, the conditional dimension of his offer was again emphasised, as bin Laden engaged in a direct confrontation with France, conditioning the liberation of some French hostages kidnapped in Kabul to her

---

[59] bin Laden, 'Bin Laden Tape, 15 April 2004'.
[60] See, for instance, another example of bin Laden's opening, in bin Laden, 'Osama Bin Ladin', Interview by Peter Arnett, 20 March 1997.
[61] Osama bin Laden, 'Purported bin Laden Message to Europe: Leave Afghanistan, 29 November 2007', available at http://edition.cnn.com/2007/WORLD/meast/11/29/bin.laden.message/index.html#cnnSTCText.
[62] Osama bin Laden, 'Bin Laden Message to Europe: Withdraw from Afghanistan, 25 September 2009', translation at http://www.juancole.com/2009/09/bin-laden-message-to-europe-withdraw.html.

withdrawal from Afghan soil.[63] In this general context, bin Laden's conditional offer for reconciliation appears more as a diktat, than a sincere opening to negotiation. Rhetorical or instrumental as it might be, a peace proposal, however, expresses a less uncompromising position than a reluctance to speak with 'infidels' at all – although in this respect the European and US mantra 'no negotiation with [Muslim] terrorists' appears no less uncompromising. Of course, bin Laden's overtures also stand as rhetorical or strategic moves aimed at slowing down the tension with the American coalition. Although the sincerity of his intention will remain unknown – as well as the dubious circumstances of his death in a shootout with American Special Forces in Pakistan on 2 May, 2011 – his endorsement of a normative framework is, in principle, in line with universalistic historical experiences of mediation.

Conclusion

By introducing the reader to Osama bin Laden's transterritorial trajectory, the aim of this chapter has been to demonstrate that tradition is a central factor in the articulation of bin Laden's discourse, and the manner in which a pan-Islamic ideal is here creatively revitalised, resonating with transmodern representations of the world. While rejecting any possible conceptualisation of the Muslim community based on national, linguistic or ethnic affiliations and therefore refusing to prioritise national loyalty, which was so central to al-Banna's territorial trajectory, bin Laden's promotion of a pan-Islamic ideal in fact went beyond the universalistic framework that Sayyid Qutb had outlined in his normative vision. We have attempted to show that bin Laden's universalistic conception of the ummah is accompanied by a strong emphasis on the defensive and military aspects of *jihad* in the articulation of a 'global jihadist' discourse. The recovery of this central signifier plays a crucial role in the strategic opposition to the 'American-Jewish alliance', which functions here as a stand-in for *dar al-harb*. In depicting this antagonistic space, however, bin Laden shows a fundamental shift in terms of hegemonic relations, pointing to a new interconnected space dominated by a Westernising global power. This means that the traditional discourse of Islamic universalism has been recast to combine it with a transmodern perspective, reflecting new structural changes in the global context. Hence, the strategic importance of signifiers such as 'global

[63] http://nypost.com/2011/01/21/france-defiant-after-bin-laden-links-fate-of-hostages-to-afghanistan-pullout/.

governance', 'world market', 'world order', 'interconnected space', 'global terror', 'clash of civilisation' and so forth – all so central to transmodern configurations.

In a major counter-position between *dar al-Islam* and *dal al-harb*, the latter is assumed as a hegemonic space that does not dissolve, however, the reality of *dar al-Islam* in the contingency of history. In this respect, we have shown that the inclusion of all Muslims within the ummah is assumed by bin Laden as something that no Islamic vanguard ought to question, while the contingent status ascribed to *dar al-Islam*, with its practical needs and interests to be defended, allows bin Laden to open himself, in principle as well as on a discursive level, to forms of pragmatism and potential negotiation.

Conclusion

The aim of this book has been to examine the role of tradition, modernity and transmodernity as 'symbolic scenarios' of Islamism. By adopting a discourse theory perspective, a case has been made for including within contemporary analyses of Political Islam both a *semiotic* differentiation of Islamist discourses and a *speculative* assessment of their spatial representations and subjectivity formations, thereby preserving a 'sense' of singularity of Islamist phenomena, while at the same time accounting for the multiple characterisations of this complex discursive universe.

While Chapter 1 introduced the reader to the general framework of this study, Chapters 2 and 3 described tradition, modernity and transmodernity as *convenient indicators* or *indexes* in the organisation of discourses, which sustain the imaginary potential and internal discursive composition of Islamist formations. Two political discourses, which establish the genealogical terrain of Islamism, influencing its ongoing variants, have been given particular attention: nationalism and pan-Islamism – while a third discourse, 'globalism', has also been considered as a minor transmodern formation in the development of later Islamist articulations. The aim of this examination has been to reveal the organisational function of two speculative paradigms presiding over the construction of Islamist representations of space and subjectivity: *dualism* and *universalism*.

Within this framework, a textual examination and speculative analysis of the discourse of three leading Islamist figures was carried out, differentiating between a 'territorial' trajectory of Islamism (Hasan al-Banna) in Chapter 4; a 'transitional' trajectory (Sayyid Qutb) in Chapter 5; and a 'transterritorial' trajectory (Osama bin Laden) in Chapter 6. The ensemble of these trajectories shows the internal dynamism of Islamism and the imaginary appeal that tradition, modernity and transmodernity respectively play within each of these discourses.

This conceptualisation of modernity, tradition and transmodernity presupposes, therefore, the presence of a complex discursive space marked by the symbolic competition among these scenarios. While coexisting as broader discursive constellations, political, economic or cultural factors in different settings or simple contingent experiences in the personal life of a subject contribute to either reinforcing or challenging their respective symbolic functions in different times. In this book, attention has been given to the desedimenting effects produced by both colonialism and globalisation, which have contributed to a shifting of the discursive terrain upon which the discourses of al-Banna, Qutb and bin Laden were articulated, producing different kinds of response and engagement with these scenarios. Accordingly, we identified a colonial terrain for al-Banna, a globalised terrain for bin Laden, and a kind of middle-ground terrain for Qutb, who wrote in the immediate post-colonial era. These three different 'terrains' also reflected three distinct phases in the historical development of Islamism: the foundation of the first Islamist movement by Hasan al-Banna in 1928; a period of quasi dormancy of Islamism between the 1950s and the 1960s, with Qutb's vigorous attempt to recover a universalistic ethos; and bin Laden's recent incarnation of a transnational trajectory, very much reflective of a global context.

Each of the authors examined in the book reveals the historical complexity of Islamism, reflecting a different phase of its evolution. Their discursive trajectories, however, reach far beyond their immediate historical and geopolitical contexts. Just as tradition, modernity and transmodernity coexist in the complex contemporary world, these Islamist trajectories, which emerged in different times and contexts, do not replace one another diachronically. They continue to function alongside each other, exemplifying different ways of engaging with symbolic reservoirs. Resonances can be found between the political imaginary articulated by these figures, and the vision that a number of Islamist actors have been promoting in recent decades.

Enduring Resonances

One 'mainstream' tendency among Islamist groups in recent years has been to prioritise a national political agenda, participating in domestic politics and enacting what might be called a political 'normalisation' of Islamism, resonating with the territorial trajectory that al-Banna first envisioned in his times.[1] A case in point is the current discourse of the Muslim Brotherhood in Egypt, where the territorial trajectory of al-Banna remains a vital source of inspiration. An interesting document written in 2007 by Mohamed Morsi, a leading member

---

[1] Cf. Gilles Kepel, *Jihad: The Trail of Political Islam* (London: I.B. Tauris, 2002); Olivier Roy, *The Failure of Political Islam* (London: I.B. Tauris, 1994); Malise Ruthven, *Fundamentalism: The Search for Meaning* (Oxford: Oxford University Press, 2004); Peter G. Mandaville, *Global Political Islam* (New York: Routledge, 2007).

of the Brotherhood and former president of Egypt between June 2012 and July 2013, reinstates the value al-Banna gave to national signifiers, emphasising the importance of establishing *Islamic state* and gradually progressing along the path towards the Islamisation of the whole 'nation':

> Carrying out its main role of guiding the society and its components, the MB targets forming the Muslim individual, the Muslim family and the Muslim nation. It stresses that the truly Muslim individual is a true foundation of a good citizen. The MB realizes that the truly Muslim family is the main foundation of a truly virtuous society, and knows that the truly Muslim nation, when formed, can, God willing, establish justice in rule so as not to get astray and does not suffer ... Hence, the group is carrying out its duty and shows the nation the Islamic moderate method so that it achieves these targets and purposes and forms the Islamic state that applies Islam in all its affairs and in all aspects of life.[2]

It should be pointed out that the notion of Islamic state is left undefined in this document. The only specification concerns the statement that the aim of the Brotherhood is the 'founding of an Islamic state for Muslims, not a theocratic state', which resonates with al-Banna's aspiration to Islamise the nation state rather than to establish some traditional form of Islamic government.[3] In common with al-Banna, therefore, the Brotherhood's aim would appear to be to preserve the existing structures of the state model, allowing the religious agenda of the movement to be implemented without rejecting the immanent foundations of modern state power. This point is best highlighted by another document published on the international website of the Brotherhood in 2007, *The Legal Concept of an Islamic State According to the MB*.[4] This document analyses a draft constitution written by the Brotherhood in 1952, which is considered to be 'one of the illuminating documents that determines the legal viewpoint on the notion of an Islamically-ruled state'. In the *General Principle* section, it states that:

> The **MB draft constitution puts forth the notion of a civil state based on citizenship and loyalty with the state** [bold in the original]. This means that

---

[2] Mohamed Morsi, 'Muslim Brotherhood, Contemporary Islamic Parties', posted on 5 August 2007; available at http://www.ikhwanweb.com/article.php?id=13748.
[3] Ibid.
[4] The Brotherhood's official English website, 'The Legal Concept of an Islamic State According to The MB', posted on 13 June 2007; available at http://www.ikhwanweb.com/article.php?id=810.

the articles of the draft excluded the divisions set up by ancient scholars. For example, the **draft did not determine religion when recording rights. It only mentioned the word 'individual', a clear expunction of the notion of dthimmah (custody of non-Muslims).** In this respect, Dr. Ibrahim Zahmoul, Professor of Law, indicates that the draft constitution proposed by the **MB put forward the idea of one state embracing Muslims and non-Muslims under the umbrella of loyalty with the nation.** It never stipulated for parliamentary membership affiliation with a particular religion or cult. Rather, as obvious in article 4, the draft stipulates that the member be an Egyptian.[5]

In this passage, an unequivocal reference to 'nationhood' as the basis for citizenship ('the member be an Egyptian') reflects a clear attempt to re-articulate Western constitutional procedures in defence of civil rights; for instance by mentioning the expunction of the traditional notion of *dhimmi* (custody of non-Muslims) advocated by 'ancient scholars', and the equality of all citizen regardless of their racial or religious differences. The focus here is on 'loyalty with the nation', which resonates strongly with al-Banna's emphasis on the conceptualisation of the Islamic government, 'as a servant to the nation in the interest of the people'.[6]

This is not to deny the many shortcomings that have marked the history of the Brotherhood in its lengthy attempt to implement its 'Islamic moderate method'. Despite its vital role as the main political opponent of the authoritarian regimes that followed the 1952 Egyptian Revolution, recent political practice dramatically falls short of more favourable expectations, questioning the democratic credentials of its leadership. With the Brotherhood's coming to power in the wake of the 2011 uprising against former President Hosni Mubarak, which led Mohamed Morsi to become the first democratically elected president of Egypt, the Brotherhood failed to heed the urgent call for social justice and democracy of the 2011 January Revolution. What was seen instead was the emergence of autocratic tendencies, particularly the occupation of key positions in the institutions of the state and the approval of a controversial constitution. The reaction to this, and the apparent inability or unwillingness to seriously address a shared need for the kind of economic and political reform able to secure social justice, guarantee civil rights and fight widespread corruption, led to the formation of a vast popular front against Morsi. A grass-root campaign

---

[5] Ibid. MB stands for Muslim Brothers.
[6] Hasan al-Banna, *The Message of the Teachings* (Cairo, n.d.; appeared in the early 1940s), available from: http://thequranblog.files.wordpress.com/2008/06/_3_-the-message-of-the-teachings.pdf.

in 2013 (Tamarod movement) called for his resignation, ultimately allowing the military to play on the widespread dissent and terminate Morsi's 13 months in power with a coup. This was followed by Morsi's imprisonment, together with hundreds of other Muslim Brothers and political opponents, in a repetition of history that oscillates between tragedy and farce. While acknowledging the genuine democratic ethos of many Egyptian Islamists, Teti and Gervasio pointed out the 'unmitigated disaster' of the Brotherhood's experience in power: 'Morsi's not-so-creeping authoritarianism was in your face, and alienated virtually every political counterpart in Egypt. He handpicked a prosecutor-general in an attempt to neutralise the judiciary, rammed through a partisan (and poorly written) Constitution, played with the fire of sectarianism, and passed a constitutional decree conferring on himself powers so vast they probably made Mubarak blush'.[7]

Notwithstanding the democratic deficiencies manifested by the Brotherhood's recent hold on power, which contradicted its long asserted principles of moderate method, this experience not only shows that the adaptation of the movement to the autocratic potential of Egyptian state apparatus is highly problematic, but also demonstrates its fundamental alignment with the modern binary foundations of national space. Beyond its inability to fully meet democratic expectations, Morsi's 2012 Constitutional project openly aligned itself with the multilayer approach to subjectivity devised by al-Banna in his vision of 'Islamic order', which coalesced national loyalty with broader Arab and Islamic forms of belonging. This can be seen, for instance, in the crucial passage in Article 1 of the Constitution stating that 'The Egyptian people are part of the Arab and Islamic nations', or in the central link connecting the orienting force of Islam, 'Islam is the religion of the state' (Art. 2), with a modern conceptualisation of power along immanent and national lines, 'Sovereignty belongs to the people. The people exercise and protect sovereignty, and safeguard their national unity. The people are the source of power. This is as provided in this Constitution' (Art. 5).[8]

---

[7] Andrea Teti and Gennaro Gervasio, 'The Army's Coup in Egypt: For the People or against the People?', *openDemocracy*, 23 July 2013, available at https://www.opendemocracy.net/andrea-teti-gennaro-gervasio/army%E2%80%99s-coup-in-egypt-for-people-or-against-people.

[8] *2012 Drafted Constitution of the Arab Republic of Egypt*, unofficial translation prepared by The International Institute for Democracy and Electoral Assistance (IDEA), available at aceproject.org/ero-en/regions/mideast/EG/egypt-draft-constitution-english-version/at_download/file; the Constitution was approved by the Constituent Assembly on 30 November 2012 in the version here provided. It was then passed in a constitutional referendum on December 2012, with a 32.9 per cent turnout rate of which 63.8 per cent voted in favour of the charter. It was finally signed into law by President Mohamed Morsi on

Other historical experiences in this direction have revealed interesting resonances with al-Banna's territorial discourse and his immanent approach to sovereignty. Emblematic of this process is the assertion made by Sayyid Ruhollah Khomeini (1902–1989) that the interest of the Islamic state takes pre-eminence over *shari'a*. A religious authority and one of the key figures of the movement leading the 1979 Iranian Revolution and the downfall of the constitutional monarchy of Shah Mohammad Reza Pahlavi, Khomeini played a crucial role in the ultimate formation of an Islamic republic in Iran, becoming the Supreme Leader (*al-Waliy al-Faqih*) of the new republic in 1979, and marking the 'zenith of modern Islamic revival'.[9]

In 1987, a conflict over a number of laws on property rights arose between the Iranian Parliament, the legislative body of the Islamic Republic of Iran, and the Council of Guardians, a body composed of religious scholars whose role was to evaluate the conformity of state legislation to *shari'ah*. Although Khomeini recognised that the Council of Guardians was right to assert that these laws contradicted *shari'ah*, he intervened on behalf of the parliament, maintaining that the principle of *Wilayat al-Faqih* (the mandate of the jurist) allowed the Supreme Leader to override *shari'ah* when 'public interest' required it. When the president of Iran, Ali Khamanei, explained Khomeini's action as the right to override specific *shari'ah* provisions, provided that the overall spirit of the Islamic law and its fundamental imperatives were respected, Khomeini intervened once again disavowing him.[10] In a letter on January 1988, Khomeini argued that the Islamic government was the most important of all divine ordinances and that the interest of the Islamic state coincided with the interest of Islam itself. This meant that the Islamic state was superior to all religious obligations including the 'pillars of Islam' such as praying, fasting, or performing the pilgrimage. This was conceptualised as the principle of the 'Absolute Mandate of the Jurist' (*Wilayat al-Faqih al-Mutlaqa*). As El-Affendi put it: 'what the judgment effectively

---

26 December 2012, before being suspended by the Egyptian army on July 2013, and replaced by a new Constitution on January 2014.

[9] Peter Mandaville, *Global Political Islam* (New York: Routledge, 2007), p. 179.

[10] While the constitution of the Islamic Republic of Iran ascribes to the 'President' of the republic most of the functions of the executive – e.g., signing international treaties, appointing ministers, supervising national planning, the budget and state employment affairs – the most significant powers associated with the executive (such as the control of foreign policy, the armed forces, or the nuclear policy) are delegated to the figure of the 'Supreme Leader', a role covered by Khomeini from 1979 up to his death in 1989, and by the former President Khamenei from 1989 up to the present.

said was that the state could accept subjection to no norms outside it'.[11] This principle was soon assimilated by the 1989 amended constitution, and enforced by the creation of the Expediency Council with the aim of defining the 'interest of the regime' (*Maslahat al-Nizam*). By emerging as the supreme value to which all political and religious deliberations were subjected, this principle reflected the ultimate adaptation of the Islamic state to the nation state model examined in Chapter 2. It marked the affirmation of a modern doctrinal approach to state sovereignty as a unique, absolute, exclusive and unrestricted source of legitimacy of state control, which does not recognise any superior principle of power *outside* itself (*summa potestas*).

Another example in this development includes the discursive trajectory of the Islamic Resistance Movement, i.e., Hamas. Despite persistent international criticism against this organisation, which is accused of remaining a religious movement aimed at establishing an Islamic state and 'obliterating' Israel, Hamas has demonstrated its increasing valorisation of 'national' signifiers and some kind of political 'normalisation'.[12] Since its emergence in 1987, Hamas, whose roots are to be found in the Palestinian branch of the Muslim Brotherhood, has revealed the great influence played by al-Banna's territorial approach to the Islamic message: 'The Islamic Resistance Movement is a distinguished Palestinian movement, whose allegiance is to Allah, and whose way of life is Islam. It strives to raise the banner of Allah over every inch of Palestine'.[13] The national characterisation of Palestine is thus infused with Islamic traits, with Islamic tradition used as a moderating principle in the appropriation of modernity. This can be seen in the 1988 Covenant's deployment of the traditional notion of *waqf*, which, in line with its discursive re-articulation described in Chapter 4, is here used to re-connote the national concept of the 'territory' along Islamic lines: 'The Islamic Resistance Movement believes that the land of Palestine is an Islamic Waqf consecrated for future Moslem generations until Judgement Day. It, or any part of it, should not be squandered: it, or any part of it, should not be given up.'[14]

An explicit reference to al-Banna's conceptualisation of identity as a complex overlapping of growing concentric circles is also devised in Article 14 of the

---

[11] Abdelwahab El-Affendi, *Who Needs an Islamic State?* (London: Grey Seal, 1991), p. 154.
[12] A reference to the obliteration of Israel can be found in the incipit of 1988 Hamas Covenant: *The Covenant of the Islamic Resistance Movement*, available at http://avalon.law.yale.edu/20th_century/hamas.asp.
[13] Ibid., article 6.
[14] Ibid., article 11.

Covenant: 'The question of the liberation of Palestine is bound to three circles: the Palestinian circle, the Arab circle and the Islamic circle. Each of these circles has its role in the struggle against Zionism.'[15] In line with the binary and nationalising logic informing al-Banna's territorial space, each of these circles achieves full ontological consistency in opposition to a 'Zionist' space playing here the organising function of a constitutive outside in the face of which internal differences among Palestinians can be erased and a unified internal space can be re-compacted: 'Our homeland is one, our situation is one, our fate is one and the enemy is a joint enemy to all of us.' Hence, the open attitude towards the Palestinian Liberation Organisation (PLO), which, notwithstanding its 'secular' ideology, the Covenant describes as being 'closest to the heart of the Islamic Resistance Movement' in the common fight in 'the Arab-Israeli conflict'.[16]

Paralleling al-Banna's increasing valorisation of nation signifiers, Hamas's early acknowledgment and integration of national discourse has achieved growing recognition in recent years. Hamas's decision to participate in the Palestinian Legislative Council elections (PLC) on January 2006, which led to the formation of the first Hamas government, marks the implicit acceptance of the 'national' and 'parliamentary' framework that was outlined in the Oslo Accords, and the subsequent adjustment of its Islamic ideological platform. Finalised in Oslo on 20 August, 1993, the Oslo Agreements were the first direct accords signed by Israeli and Palestinian representatives. Besides acknowledging the principle of a 'two-state solution', the Oslo Accords drafted the framework for the future relations between the two parties. While promoting the creation of a Palestinian Authority responsible for the administration of the territory under its control, the Oslo Accords also entailed 'self-government arrangements' in the West Bank and Gaza to be organised through democratic elections 'under agreed supervision and international observation'.[17] From this viewpoint, Hamas's participation in the elections was a direct and unequivocal consequence of the accords signed with Israel, implying not only the inherent acceptance of the accords themselves, but also the recognition of the 'parties' that signed them, Israel included.

But the increasing value given to national signifiers by Hamas can also be seen in its 2006 Electoral Campaign Platform, *List for Change and Reform* (C&R), where references to the Islamic state are omitted and the Islamic articulation of

---

[15] Ibid., article 14.
[16] Ibid., article 27.
[17] Section: 'Declaration of Principles on Interim Self-Government Arrangements', *The Oslo Accords: And Related Agreements*; available from http://almashriq.hiof.no/general/300/320/327/oslo.html.

national signifiers is fully devised, with 'National Unity' assumed as 'one of the priorities of the Palestinian national work':

> 1. The true religion of Islam and its civilization achievements are our reference and a way of life in all its aspects: politically, economically, socially and legally.
>
> 2. Historical Palestine is a part of the Arab and Islamic land; It is a right for the Palestinian people that does not made ineffective by prescription. Any other military or allegedly legal procedures cannot change such a fact.
>
> 3. The Palestinian people are one unit, wherever they exist; they are part and parcel of the Arab and Islamic nation. Allah Says in the holy Qur'an 'Truly! This, your Ummah [Sharia or religion (Islamic Monotheism)] is one religion, and I am your Lord, therefore worship Me (Alone)'.
>
> 4. Our Palestinian people are still living a stage of national liberation; they have the right to work for regaining their rights as well as ending the occupation by using all available means including armed resistance. We have to exploit all our energy to support the resistance of our people and to provide all abilities to end occupation and establishing the Palestinian state whose Jerusalem is its capital.
>
> 5. The right of all Palestinians who are expatriated and refugees to return to their home and properties; the right of self-determination and all our national rights are not negotiable; such rights are also fixed and they can not be diminished by any political concessions.
>
> 6. Full adherence to our people's fixed and original rights in land, Jerusalem, holy places, water, borders and a Palestinian state of complete sovereignty with Jerusalem as a capital.
>
> 7. Support and protection of Palestinian national unity is one of the priorities of the Palestinian national work.
>
> 8. The prisoners and detainees issue is at the head of the priorities of the Palestinian work.[18]

---

[18] Hamas – 2006 Electoral Campaign Platform 'List for Change and Reform', available in the English website of the Brotherhood http://www.ikhwanweb.com/article.php?id=4921.

The passage above clearly configures the upholding of a nationalist perspective. While a central and all-embracing 'reference' to Islam supports the multilayer definition of Palestine as 'part of the Arab and Islamic land', national signifiers trace here the discursive contours of Hamas's political imaginary: hence, the 'Palestinian people' figuring as 'one unit, wherever they exist', the 'National Liberation' process, the right of self-determination, and the other inalienable, 'fixed and original rights' of Palestinians accompanying the general effort of Hamas for the 'support and protection of Palestinian national unity'.

Besides these enduring resonances with the territorial trajectory that al-Banna first embodied, and his surviving influence as an exemplary way of engaging with modernity and tradition, other discursive routes have been elaborated in recent times, which draw on the type of social and political imaginary that Sayyid Qutb traced in his descriptive vision. This is the case with groups such as *al-Muhajiroun* and *Hizb ut-Tahrir*. While these organisations share with both Qutb and bin Laden the celebration of a pan-Islamic ideal and the rejection of national signifiers, their analysis of the contemporary world very much resonates with Qutb's uncompromising critique of present-day societies. Resounding with Qutb's descriptive considerations examined in Chapter 5, *Hizb ut-Tahrir* (the same applies to *al-Muhajiroun*, which is an upshot of *Hizb ut-Tahrir*) assumes *jahiliyyah* as a universal reality in the contingency of history, including within its domain both Muslim and non-Muslim lands. At the same time, the ummah is transposed to an ideal and necessary plane, with its full realisation figuring as a demand for the future rather than a present reality to be defended. As the official website of *Hizb ut-Tahrir* puts it:

> Hizb ut-Tahrir is a political party whose ideology is Islam. Its objective is to resume the Islamic way of life by establishing an Islamic State that executes the systems of Islam and carries its call to the world ... As for the resumption of the Islamic way of life, the reality of all the Islamic lands is currently a Kufr [infidel] household, for Islam is no longer implemented over them; thus Hizb ut-Tahrir adopted the transformation of this household into a household of Islam.[19]

In line with Qutb's notion of jahiliyyah, self-professing Muslims reside in the domain of *kufr* (here standing for *jahiliyyah*), for Islam is not lived as an integral and exclusive dimension of life. Moreover, the laws that regular Muslims respect

---

[19] Official website of *Hizb ut-Tahrir*, 'About Us', available at http://english.hizbuttahrir.org/index.php/about-us?format=pdf, last accessed 20 March 2015.

and abide by are the expression of the immanent power of the people, rather than a direct emanation of the transcendent sovereignty of God:

> With regard to deeming the household as being Islamic does not depend on whether its inhabitants are Muslims or not, but rather in what is implemented in terms of rules and in whether the security of the household is in the hands of the Muslims, not the Kuffar. These two conditions determine whether the household is a household of Islam, even if most of its inhabitants were non Muslims. The fact that the current existing states in the Islamic world are states of Kufr is evident and does not require explanation, for all of their constitutions do not consider the sins as crimes that entail punishment, and they adopt the systems and the rules of the capitalist democratic system and they effectively implement them in economy, education and all the aspects of life. These constitutions deem the sovereignty to belong to the people, not to Allah (swt), they recognise the international treaties that totally contradict Islam.[20]

In this context, *Hizb ut-Tahrir* is an emblematic case. Unlike jihadist organisations, *Hizb ut-Tahrir* does not figure as a movement essentially devoted to violent strategies. Where al-Qaeda, in the words of Osama bin Laden, is mainly concerned with the penetration of Western military and political forces into Islamic lands, *Hizb* reflects a widespread range of conservative perspectives in that it focuses on the very lack of 'Islamicity' of the surrounding environment, whose ethical and social qualities it questions.

It is fair to say, however, that 'jihad' still reflects an important demand in the discursive articulation of this group. While acknowledging that Hizb ut-Tahrir remains a 'non-violent' organisation, pursuing its idea of radical change by 'acting within the legal system of the countries in which it operates', a 2008 report by the US Committee on Homeland Security and Governmental Affairs defines it as 'a *de facto* conveyor belt for terrorists'.[21] In this direction, it has been argued that some of the militants involved in violent operations of recent years have been heavily influenced by organisations such as *Hizb ut-Tahrir* and *al-Muhajiroun*.[22] Despite the ambiguous position of these groups towards global

---

[20] Ibid.

[21] Zeyno Baran, 'The Roots of Violent Islamist Extremism and Efforts to Counter It', US Committee on Homeland Security and Governmental Affairs, 10 July 2008, www.investigativeproject.org/documents/testimony/354.pdf#page=5.

[22] Gabriel Weimann, *Terror on the Internet: The New Arena, the new Challenges* (Washington, DC: United States Institute of Peace Press, 2006), and Quintan Wiktorowicz, *Radical Islam Rising: Muslim Extremism in the West* (Oxford: Rowman & Littlefield, 2005).

jihad, however, it is important to highlight those traits that differentiate, at least in principle, bin Laden's platform from *Hizb ut-Tahrir*'s, especially when considering the latter's alignment with Qutb's descriptive vision.

We saw that, unlike bin Laden's emphasis on the 'existing' quality of the ummah and his unwillingness to include Muslims within the space of jahiliyyah, *Hizb ut-Tahrir* and *al-Muhajiroun* share Qutb's puritanical and pessimistic vision, which views the ummah as a promise to be realised, rather than a good to be defended. In this context, even a superior aspiration, as is the restoration of caliphate that radical groups such as *al-Muhajiroun* and *Hizb* advocate, functions as an impossible ideal rather than a practical goal, for sin and damnation cannot be eliminated from the contingency of life. This is the reason why, despite provocative statements by Anjem Choudary, a controversial figure of the disbanded *al-Muhajiroun*, whose ambiguous position towards jihad and ISIS led to him being taken into custody 'on suspicion of encouraging terrorism' in September 2014, leading members of Hizb ut-Tahrir have rejected a recent declaration of caliphate by the Islamic State of Iraq and Syria (ISIS).[23]

The latter is an Islamist group that has gained international reputation as an effect of its recent military success and ferocious beheading of enemies, included a number of Western hostages. The organisation stemmed from a regrouping of the Islamic State of Iraq (ISI), which, in turn, amalgamated several groups that had been operating in Iraq since 2004, including the former al-Qaeda in the Land of Two Rivers (al-Qaeda in Iraq) and the Army of the Sunni People Group (*Jamaat Jaysh Ahl al-Sunnah wa-l-Jamaah*). Following its entrance and involvement in the Syrian Civil War, ISIS was able to develop a robust army, which, according to CIA intelligence assessments, numbered between 20,000 and 31,500 fighters in September 2014, including about 2,000 Western militants.[24] Led by Abu Bakr al-Baghdadi, a Sunni preacher claiming a hereditary blood line with the Prophet Muhammad, the movement seized a vast portion of lands from northern Syria to central and northern Iraq, declaring the inclusion of these regions within the structure of the new 'Islamic State of Iraq and Syria', and demanding allegiance from other Islamist groups and Arab tribes. The Arabic denomination for the movement, together with its unilateral declaration of statehood, is *Al-Dawla*

---

[23] http://www.theguardian.com/uk-news/2014/sep/26/anjem-choudary-released-on-bail; http://www.breitbart.com/Breitbart-London/2014/08/14/Anjem-admits-ISIS-demonstrators-are-his-students.

[24] http://www.dailymail.co.uk/news/article-2753004/CIA-believes-ranks-ISIS-fighters-swollen-TRIPLE-number-previously-thought-31-500-fighters-2-000-Westerners.html.

Al-Islamiya fi al-Iraq wa al-Sham (DAIISH is therefore the Arab acronym of the group).

In Chapter 2, we described *al-dawla* as a political arrangement denoting the administration of a specific province of *dar al-Islam* by a ruling elite. Although often associated with the concept of nation state, we located a crucial difference between the two in the open character of the *dawla*, whose complex system of loyalty blurs the fundamental distinction between the inside and the outside of the nation, challenging the exclusive and immanent character of national sovereignty. While the ruler of the *dawla* – whether an emir, an executive officer or an imam – was accountable internally towards its domestic constituencies (the 'subjects' of the *dawla*), an outward accountability was also established externally with the caliph, who represented the whole Muslim community on a global scale, thereby indicating the subjection of the *dawla* to the wider ummah. As Barghuti notes:

> because the Dawla referred to any authoritative arrangement, it was used to refer to different levels of political authority, some of which had legal priority over others but none of which were sovereign. During the longer part of Islamic history there were many Dawlas within one Dawla. For example, the Abbasid and Ottoman empires, were referred to respectively as al-*Dawla al-Abbasiyya* and *al-Dawla al-Uthmaniyya*, both of which were headed by an Imam who claimed to be the successor of the Prophet (only in his executive capacity) and therefore the representative and guide of the Umma.[25]

In its fundamental link with the global dimension of both *dar al-Islam* and the *ummah*, the *dawla* expresses therefore the pre-eminence of a universalistic paradigm. In the case of *Al-Dawla Al-Islamiya fi al-Iraq wa al-Sham*, the establishment of an Islamic *dawla* comprehends the land extending over the current national territories of Iraq and Syria, though it has also been noted that the term 'al-Sham' could refer to the medieval Arab Caliphate province of *Bilad al-Sham* (the old 'Levant'), encompassing the Eastern Mediterranean and Western Mesopotamia. A previous English acronym of the group, combining national and traditional denominators, was in fact 'Islamic State of Iraq and the Levant' (ISIL).[26] Despite the little information still available, strategic moves

---

[25] Tamim Barghuthi, *The Umma and the Dawla: The Nation State and the Arab Middle East* (London and Ann Arbor, MI: Pluto Press, 2008), p. 57.
[26] Ishaan Tharoor, 'ISIS or ISIL? The Debate over What to Call Iraq's Terror Group', *Washington Post*, 18 June 2014, available at http://www.washingtonpost.com/blogs/worldviews/wp/2014/06/18/isis-or-isil-the-debate-over-what-to-call-iraqs-terror-group.

from the group have so far included the attempt to combine the provision of social services with harsh judicial punishments, the establishment of some form of institutional platform sustaining the idea of a material statehood in progress, military operations directed towards strategic locations (for instance control of some oil fields), and the implacable execution of enemies and rival tribes. Symbolic targets have also played a fundamental role in sustaining the victorious image of the movement, whilst also denoting the extraordinary reliance on tradition as a primary symbolic scenario in the articulation of this group's discourse.

From a broad perspective, the strong pan-Islamic appeal of the movement seems to be accompanied by the rejection of national signifiers. One of the major symbolic gestures in this sense has been the deployment by ISIS fighters of a bulldozer to crash through the sand berm used as part of the boundary dividing between Syria and Iraq, accompanying this gesture with chants, prayers and pictures, which were successfully disseminated via social networks all over the world, together with the announcement that they were in fact destroying the 'Sykes-Picot' border. As insightfully noted by Malise Ruthven, the reference to a 1916 Franco-British agreement on the Middle East served the major objective: to smash the symbolic representation of national territory as it has been devised by European powers, destroying the borders that had been imposed in colonial times on the inclusive space of *dar al-Islam*, and therefore reconnecting with the idea of pre-colonial territoriality and the pan-Islamic imaginary of the caliphate.[27] Even more radical as a gesture – but also novel and controversial in the history of Islamist movements – was the decision of the group, through its Shura Council, to supplement the declaration of the Islamic *dawla* with the proclaimed 'restoration of caliphate' on 29 June, 2014. While renouncing the reference to Iraq and Syria, with 'Islamic State' (IS) now remaining the only denomination for the new entity, the celebration of a universalistic ideal has thus been fully realised, with the decision to declare Abu Bakr al-Baghdadi, born Ibrahim ibn Awwad ibn Ibrahim ibn Ali ibn Muhammad al-Badri al-Samarrai, the Caliph of all Muslims and the Prince of the Believers (*Amir al-Mu'minin*). Although future developments might point to the need for alternative directions and strategies by ISIS, this gesture seems currently to differentiate its experience of the Islamic Dawla from the Iranian experience of Islamic State, which we associated with a territorial approach of Islamisation ultimately resounding with the national model.

---

[27] Malise Ruthven, 'The Map ISIS Hates', *The New York Review of Books*, 25 June 2014, available at http://www.nybooks.com/blogs/nyrblog/2014/jun/25/map-isis-hates.

For the time being, it is interesting to note that the restoration of the caliphate by ISIS has not failed to attract harsh criticism within the Islamist galaxy as well. Not only have prominent Muslim leaders and scholars across the Sunni Islamic spectrum, including Al-Azhar graduates, rejected the Islamic State group's self-proclaimed caliphate as 'null' and 'deviant',[28] but in addition, Islamist figures, such as the Qatar-based Egyptian religious leader, Yusuf al-Qaradawi, the founder of the al-Nahda Party, Rachid Ghannuchi, and Assem Barqawi, a supporter of the al-Qaeda-affiliated Nusra Front, have questioned the legitimacy of this operation, rebuking ISIS for their initiative.[29] Likewise, we observed that although the restoration of the caliphate constitutes a primary objective in the pan-Islamic discursive articulation of Hizb ut-Tahrir, this group has added their voice to the criticism, dismissing ISIS's declaration of caliphate. While Mamdooh Qatishaat, the Head of the Media Office of Hizb ut-Tahrir in Jordon, declared that the claim 'is nothing more than empty speech that does not add anything to the reality of ISIS', Reza Pankhurst, who spent four years in an Egyptian prison for his affiliation with Hizb ut-Tahrir, also rejected ISIS's proclamation of a caliphate, adding that 'these announcements appear to have little relationship to ground realities, and are more to do with internal politics and competition between various militant factions'.[30] An official document posted on the international website of the group on July 2014 explains that a declaration of caliphate should follow the formation of a self-sufficient state capable of defending itself and establishing its full authority, while also securing an oath of allegiance (*bay'a*) by religious leaders, and guaranteeing vast consensus among Muslim masses on a world scale. When considering ISIS's unconsolidated force and the acrimonious context in which it operates, 'the announcement of the organisation of the establishment of the Khilafah holds no value and has no effect'.[31]

Besides rivalries, and doctrinarian and ethical concerns, we suggested that *Hizb*'s rejection of ISIS's initiative could also be interpreted in the light of the group's alignment with the kind of pessimistic attitude informing Qutb's

---

[28] http://www.al-monitor.com/pulse/politics/2014/07/syria-iraq-isis-caliphate-egypt-azhar-reaction.html#.

[29] Shafik Mandhai, 'Muslim Leaders Reject Baghdadi's Caliphate', *al-Jazeera*, 7 July 2014, available at http://www.aljazeera.com/news/middleeast/2014/07/muslim-leaders-reject-baghdadi-caliphate-20147744058773906.html.

[30] http://www.khilafah.com/index.php/news-watch/middle-east/19152-leading-members-of-hizb-ut-tahrir-reject-isis-declaration-of-khilafah.

[31] http://www.hizb.org.uk/current-affairs/media-statement-regarding-isiss-declaration-in-iraq.

descriptive vision, with the caliphate working as an impossible ideal in the face of a generalised jahili society. As an ex-member of *Hizb ut-Tahrir* declared in 2007 with some sort of prophetic vision: 'If the Muslim Brotherhood were to seize power in Egypt – a situation not wholly inconceivable – then *Hizb ut-Tahrir* would condemn the "Islamic state" for not being sufficiently Islamic, as they do today with Iran and Saudi Arabia. The perfect Islamic state is a cherished myth.'[32]

The resonance between *Hizb ut-Tahrir* and Qutb's descriptive approach, entailing the *universalisation* of *jahiliyyah* and a propensity to envision a *virtualisation* of the ummah, is reflected in the articulation of the signifier 'vanguardism' that *Hizb* and *al-Muhajiroun* tend to promote by presenting themselves as 'the elite vanguard of the coming *khilafat*'.[33] French scholar Olivier Roy rightly asserts that the vanguard community of true believers, manifest in neo-fundamentalist groups such as *al-Muhajiroun* and *Hizb ut-Tahrir*, embody a mental attitude, an immaterial 'virtual' or 'potential' presence rather than a physical entity:

> If I am fighting in Afghanistan or Bosnia to protect the *ummah* against the encroachment of unbelievers, it means that there is something worth protecting on one side of the battle line. But glancing over his shoulder the *mujahid* sees nothing but *kafir* in the lands that he is supposed to protect … They fight not to protect a territory but to re-create a community. They are besieged in a fortress they do not inhabit.[34]

This emphasis on 'vanguardism' and '*jahiliyyah*' testifies to the influence that Qutb's descriptive vision continues to exert upon recent articulations, combining millenarian outlooks with the utopian idea of a community still to be founded. As Roy puts it: 'This imagined *ummah* can be expressed in historical paradigms (the Ottoman Empire), in political myth (the Caliphate), in legal Muslim categories (*Dar-ul-Harb* and *Dar-ul-Islam*) or in modern anti-US rhetoric (anti-imperialism), but it has never fitted with a given territory.'[35] According

---

[32] Ed Husain, *The Islamist: Why I Joined Radical Islam in Britain, What I Saw and Why I Left* (London: Penguin, 2007), p. 255.

[33] Ian G. Williams, 'Relics and Baraka: Devotion to the Prophet Muhammad among Sufis in Nottingham, UK', in Elisabeth Arweck and Peter Collina (eds), *Reading Religion in Text and Context: Reflections of Faith and Practice in Religious Materials* (Aldershot: Ashgate, 2006), p. 80; Mary R. Habeck, *Knowing the Enemy: Jihadist Ideology and the War on Terror* (New Haven, CT: Yale University Press, 2006), p. 144.

[34] Oliver Roy, *Globalized Islam: Fundamentalism, Deterritorialization and the Search for a New Ummah* (London: Hurst and Company, 2004), pp. 288–9.

[35] Ibid.

to Roy, this tendency reveals the 'deterritorialised' trait of contemporary neo-orthodox groups, which for Roy also explains the kind of de-culturised vision of religion that very often informs vanguardist movements. In Chapter 3 we argued that in the face of a global context marked by spatial displacement and fragmentation, sectarian and vanguardist attitudes are often accompanied by the rejection of religious and ethnic identity. This can lead to the 'objectification of Islam', by which a system (*minhaj*) of pure religious beliefs and practices come to be identified, objectified and codified, disembodying them from surrounding cultural and secular components.[36] This is a trend particularly visible among second- and third- generation Muslims in the West, who may feel a strong need to reinvent a location and a sense of belonging beyond both the pristine cultural environment of their family, which remains remote and often alien to them, and the public secular environment of Western societies. In this sense, a common strategy for dealing with the instability produced by spatial displacement and fragmentation might be to recast religion in purely *normative* terms. The attempt to distinguish a 'true Islam' from its cultural components leads to the translation and objectification of Islam into a set of mere procedures and codes of behaviour based on religious tenets and holy texts only. Such codes are thereby decoupled from any given culture and, consequently, from the values which are embodied in specific social contexts. The reference to original normative 'sources' offers, therefore, an invaluable opportunity to recast the relation with a social outside, bypassing the mediation of both cultural and secular patterns. New forms of collective ties are thus established among fellow Muslims all around the world, which adopt the same scriptural approach to holy texts disregarding the relation with their social and cultural context.

The concrete expression of this trend can be found in the enormous production of material in the form of books, pamphlets, websites, collections of *fatwas* and speeches of preachers which aim to specify in detail the norms of conduct for the believer in every single aspect of life – including desired manners for eating, drinking, sleeping and sitting. The result is that a new formulation of selfhood is enacted, constructing a sort of *homo juridicus* whose *habitus* – 'habit' as 'standardised' and fragmented mode of behaviour but also as a 'performative' way of 'dressing' and constructing selfhood – is constituted by *norms* and precepts which transcend the immediate social and cultural environment. In a highly emblematic pamphlet, *the Six Points of Tabligh*, the Tablighi movement, a quietist and revivalist organisation of missionaries whose presence has become

---

[36] Dale F. Eickelman and James Piscatori, *Muslim Politics* (London: Princeton University Press, 2nd edn, 2004), p. 42.

increasingly significant in Western societies, lists a well-detailed range of norms of conduct objectifying Islam as a set of procedures and codes:

> 1. Wash your hands before and after meals, and wash your mouth also; 2. Begin to take meals by saying; 'Bismillaah wa'alaa barkatillaah'; 3. Take your meals with your right hand … 6. Do not eat from the centre of the utensil, for the blessing of Allah descends at that point; 7. Finish all the food in the utensil, and do not spare anything for the Shaytaan [Satan] … 8. Lick your fingers before washing your hands, it is mentioned in a hadith, 'One does not know in which particle of the food is the blessing of Allah'; 9. Take your meals with three fingers of the right hand; 10. If a morsel falls on the table cloth, pick it up and eat it, and do not spare it for Shaytaan; 11. One should not lean on a cushion or arrogantly recline whilst eating; 12. Do not object to the quality of food …[37]

In this trend we can detect the elaboration of an efficient response to the desedimenting effects of spatial displacement and fragmentation produced by globalisation, with selfhood here reduced to a homogeneous kit of norms that, being deculturised and based on the tenets of Islam alone, can be deployed in any geographical environment in a similar way, offering a consistent mode of conduct and self-representation in the face of a highly volatile and mobile context. At the same time, new forms of collective ties are established. Whether in the case of a dispersed Islamist vanguard or the case of single believers participating in spiritual movements such as the Tablighi, the *codification* or *normativisation* of subjectivity and the *objectification of Islam* allow new definitions of space and community, which are well-suited to a deterritorialised and indistinct outside, ultimately eroding the modern private/public divide.

Apart from the conservative and millenarist approaches examined above, however, other trends have translated the mobilisation of a universalistic imaginary in less pessimistic or conventional terms, seeing it as a more fluid and globalist process which renounces any normative construction of subjectivity, drawing on the more open-minded aspects of both tradition and transmodernity. Cleansed of any jihadist ethos, a wide range of cultural and social phenomena in recent years have thus testified to the attempt to recover a pan-Islamic ideal, re-interpreting it in the light of a transmodern virtualist vocabulary that bears

---

[37] *The Six Points of Tabligh, Lesson 9*, http://www.scribd.com/doc/5551200/Six-Fundamentals?autodown=pdf, last accessed June 2009; see also, 'Manners of Eating and Drinking', http://www.inter-islam.org/Actions/manners.htm, last accessed June 2009; and 'Etiquette of Eating', http://www.islamicacademy.org/html/Articles/Anwar-ul-Hadees/English/Etiquette_of_Eating.htm, last accessed June 2009.

little relation with the militant and jihadist outlook informing bin Laden's transterritorial trajectory, or its resonances across groups such as ISI and the like.

A case in point is the widespread emphasis on the idea of a new *virtual ummah* that a number of believers have been promoting on a global scale in recent years. A new age of worldwide unity of the Muslim community, which transcends geographical, political and cultural references, has thus been celebrated and encouraged, with a complex network of websites, chat forums, newsletters, blogs, bulletin boards giving voice to an extraordinary exchange of opinions and information about every aspect of a Muslim's life, and paving the way for the establishment of new forms of community ties.[38] Here, the 'desirability' and 'visibility' of a new 'virtual' infrastructural space overcome the practical obstacles posed by the territorial displacement of globalisation that we described in Chapter 3, working as an immediate plan of action.

It is within this context that a virtual phenomenon called *Muxlim* was experimented with for a few years following its creation in 2006. *Muxlim* – an Islamic world made of digital towns, cities, buildings, mosques, parks, etc. – provided an Islamic alternative to secular British or US virtual-world developers (e.g., Second Life) allowing Muslim 'virtual citizens' to create a new community, communicating through movable avatars. As *Muxlim*'s developers put it when presenting their social networking website before it was eventually shut down due to financial problems, 'Muxlim is focused on the Muslim lifestyle as part of a diverse, all-inclusive world which recognizes and welcomes people of all faiths and backgrounds who want to share, learn and have fun'.[39] Similarly, blogs, forums and social networks have contributed to developing innovative cultural movements, such as Islamic hip hop and Islamic punk.[40] Spreading beyond its original African-American context, Muslim rappers, from Mos Def to JT the Bigga Figga, have been central to the evolution of hip hop, giving voice to the needs and grievances of a marginalised subculture in an attempt to bridge the gaps between Muslim communities, and encourage the formation of 'transglobal hip hop *ummah*'.[41] The Internet's ability to popularise Muslim rappers' lyrics has

[38] Gary Bunt, *iMuslims: Rewiring the House of Islam* (New Delhi: Cambridge University Press, 2009).

[39] Muxlim, 'Welcome to Muxlim', available from http://muxlim.com/about, last accessed 1 May 2010.

[40] Andrea Teti and Andrea Mura, 'Sunni Islam and Politics', in Jeff Haynes (ed.), *Routledge Handbook of Religion and Politics* (London: Routledge, 2010).

[41] See the interview with Mos Def in H. Samy Alim, 'A New Research Agenda: Exploring the Transglobal Hip Hop Umma', in Miriam Cooke and Bruce B. Lawrence (eds), *Muslim Networks from Hajj to Hip Hop* (Chapel Hill, NC: University of North Carolina Press, 2005), pp. 264–74.

been crucial in bringing it to a wider audience, in turn providing an Islamo-hip hop melting pot, with Islam being celebrated by new rappers like Vinnie Paz (an Italian-American convert), the European Muslims Aki Nawaz (Fun-Da-Mental, UK), Natacha Atlas (Transglobal Underground, UK), and Akhenaton (IAM, France), as well as the Egyptian MBS and Arabian Knightz, the Algerian Intik, Hamma and Le Micro Brise Le Silenc, etc. This phenomenon has not gone unnoticed by conservatives: www.muslimhiphop.com, for example, criticised the rebellious attitude prevalent among Muslim rappers, offering a counter-selection of morally conservative artists and '100% Halal Lyrics' [*halal* means religiously permitted].[42]

'Islamopunk' is another trend encompassing punk, hard rock, and hip hop influences. Initially spreading particularly among American Asian Muslims, its popularity grew after the publication of Michael Muhammad Knight's 2004 novel, *The Taqwacores*.[43] The author, an American of Irish-Catholic descent who converted to Islam, proposes the adaptation of *taqwa*, an Islamic concept of love and fear of Allah, to Hardcore, a punk subgenre. In his view, what relates Islam to punk is that both 'smash idols' such as materialism and dogmatism, thereby also contesting conservative establishments. A wide range of intellectual activities and music groups inspired by Islamic punk and, partly, by this novel, gave rise to several forums and blogs. Among the most popular groups – with Facebook profiles – are *Vote Hezbollah*, *Al-Thawra*, and above all, *The Kominas*, whose provocative song, 'Rumi Was a Homo, (but Wahhaj is a Fag)', controversially attacked Siraj Wahhaj, a prominent Brooklyn imam accused of homophobia.

By drawing on the imaginary of *virtualism* and *globalism*, two discourses we briefly mentioned in Chapter 3, these examples illustrate the attempt to combine the traditional ideal of the universal *ummah* with Muxlim's transmodern project of a 'diverse, all-inclusive world' that a new global and virtual community should embody. Central here is the articulation of the transmodern signifier 'virtuality', aimed at dealing with the desedimenting effects of globalisation by overcoming, as Žižek suggests, the divide 'between "true life" and its mechanical simulation: between objective reality and our false (illusory) perception of it; between my fleeting affects, feelings, attitudes, and so on, and the remaining hard core of my Self'.[44]

---

[42] http://www.muslimhiphop.com.
[43] Michael Muhammad Knight, *The Taqwacores* (New York: Autonomedia, 2004).
[44] Slavoj Žižek, *The Plague of Fantasies* (London: Verso, 1997), p. 133.

Concluding Remarks

In the attempt to uncover the discursive complexity and vitality informing Islamism, and to avoid most of the clichés and essentialisms that continue to pervade public and academic debates over Islam, this book has focused on the creative engagements that Islamist discourses enact with modernity, tradition and transmodernity in their specific contexts, mobilising rich and diverse discursive strategies to deal with the particular challenges that they face. In discursive terms, we have highlighted the degree of mobility that characterises fundamental political concepts, revealing their crucial connection to forms of subjugation or counter-hegemonic appropriation. This was done by tracing the way in which different signifiers such as 'people', 'caliphate', 'terrorism', etc., migrate from one discourse to another across different symbolic scenarios – examining, for example, how the notion of 'territory' travelled from the European discourse of the 'nation' to al-Banna's discourse of 'Islam', merging with the traditional pan-Islamic notion of 'territoriality' and producing al-Banna's concept of the 'concentric circles'. We have shown how the original relations of power that the discourse of the nation sustained in the hands of colonial forces was used in counter-hegemonic and anti-imperialist ways against those same forces once it was integrated and re-signified in the negative dialectic operationalised by al-Banna in a kind of anti-colonial realisation of Caliban's famous injunction to Prospero: 'You taught me language, and my profit on't / Is I know how to curse. The red plague rid you / For learning me your language!'[45]

From a broad perspective, Islamist discourses creatively produce imaginaries and visions that resonate with, complement, innovate or challenge similar elaborations in the West, and that could, therefore, engage in a fruitful intellectual dialogue with them, producing new, unexpected discursive outcomes. Together, they contribute to altering, consolidating or questioning the morphology as well as the symbolic appeal of modernity, tradition and transmodernity, allowing for new solutions to the challenges of our times. A case in point is the central mobilisation of a universalistic paradigm in both settings.

In continental philosophy, the question of universalism – for all its attendant complexities and ambiguities – is on the intellectual agenda again. One should acknowledge, for instance, Žižek's defence of universalism against globalisation; that is, the universalistic endorsement of a space for political litigation against the multicultural ideology of a peaceful *global order* 'with

---

[45] William Shakespeare, *The Tempest*, I. ii. 362–4.

each part in its allocated place'.[46] Similarly, Badiou's engagement with St. Paul's universalism has been central to philosophical debate.[47] Religious universalism has been instrumental for rethinking lay forms of political action in what has been called a 'communist appropriation of Christianity'.[48] Although this revived interest in the notion of universalism has brought the concept to the centre of academic debate in Europe, examination of non-Western traditions has been seriously lacking, leaving the similarities and differences among speculative notions of 'universal' space and community substantially unexplored, which brings the risk of falling once again into 'Eurocentrism of the field of political theory'.[49] This can perhaps be explained by the feeling of unintelligibility that characterises the tension/relation between Western and non-Western forms of knowledge. The differences between the universalistic perspectives of Qutb and those of continental thinkers, for example, cannot be underestimated. We showed in Chapter 4 that *Milestones*' universalism reveals an eschatological idea of world order, where Islamic territoriality, *dar al-Islam*, (ideally) absorbs its non-Muslim outside (*dar al-harb*), creating a new form of human association which transcends closed, exclusive communities based on soil, nationhood, blood, culture and so on. But while *dar al-Islam* upsets and broadens previous groupings, it might require a commitment to a new set of substantive rules and norms: a commitment to a shared ethical form of life. Conversely, universality in the Pauline tradition reveals a universal space set against this kind of ethical grouping. The contemporary interest in Paul seems to lie precisely in the replacement (or destruction) of law with love; that is, Pauline universality appears as an empty or content-less form of association. Hence, for instance, Badiou's and Žižek's respective emphasis on the empty set and negativity.

The analysis provided here has given emphasis instead to the crucial symbolic function that God plays in the articulation of Qutb's discourse. The attempt to re-interpret modern sovereignty in divine terms, allowing for an upward re-directing of it from humankind to God, and the ethical and normative appeal pervading his conception of humanity, are indicative of the crucial mobilising

---

[46] Slavoj Žižek, *The Ticklish Subject: The Absent Centre of Political Ontology* (London: Verso, 1999), p. 200.

[47] Alain Badiou, *Saint Paul: The Foundation of Universalism* (Stanford, CA: Stanford University Press, 2003).

[48] Nathan Coombs, 'Christian Communists, Islamic Anarchists?: Part 1', *International Journal of Žižek Studies*, 3/1 (2009): 1; available at http://zizekstudies.org/index.php/ijzs/article/view/153/269, last accessed 1 May 2010. Cf. Badiou, *Saint Paul*.

[49] Megan C. Thomas, 'Orientalism and Comparative Political Theory', *The Review of Politics*, 72/4 (2010): 653.

power that an imaginative symbolism predicated upon the discourse of prophecy assumes in his vision. From a broad perspective, this mobilising function is completely in line with what Muhammad Azadpur has recently described as a traditional objective in Islamic philosophy aimed at the 'realization of a human exemplar as the standard of wisdom'.[50] According to Azadpur, this objective 'is constitutive of the philosophical activity as such – the transformation of the self for the sake of knowledge', and informs the specific project that the Greeks reserved for philosophy, notwithstanding common interpretations of Greek philosophy as a system of rational knowledge. What stands as unique in Islamic philosophy is, for Azadpur, the appropriation of this tradition 'into a legacy of Islamic prophetology'.[51] In the light of this interpretation, therefore, Qutb's vision can be seen as a philosophical project aimed at the transformation of the self in accordance with the precepts expressed in the religious discourse of prophecy. This is fundamental for our understanding of the crucial role that *jihad* plays for Qutb as an *effort* and a fight in the *way of God*, allowing for the moulding of a new kind of believer devoted to the restoration of the Islamic society. By pursuing the cultivation of the soul through a prophetic imaginative symbolism leading to the liberation from the mundane and culminating in an experience of the divine, Qutb's hermeneutics fully adheres here to the Islamic philosophical legacy that Azadpur discusses. What needs to be emphasised, however, is that Qutb sees religious faith as the immediate and necessary condition to interpret and access the fundamental link between prophecy and philosophy. This link is also constitutive of both the descriptive critique that Qutb poses of his historical era, and the substantial judgement that he ascribes to any possible conceptualisation of power and authority. Hence the symbolic power that the discourse of revelation covers in Qutb's rejection of immanentist accounts of sovereignty. Hence also the fundamental anti-hegemonic tone of Qutb's political theology, a tone that both reflects and mobilises the influence that theological-political questions have traditionally exerted upon ideas of power, sovereignty, the worldly and the spiritual and the relationship between political and religious authority – an influence that current debates on political theology in its Christian and European variants have similarly contributed to highlight.

In accounting for the differences at work between Islamic universalism and other ways of engaging with ideas of political universalism, immediate emphasis

---

[50] Muhammad Azadpur, *Reason Unbound: On Spiritual Practice in Islamic Peripatetic Philosophy* (New York: SUNY Press, 2011), p. 4.

[51] Ibid., p. 7.

is given therefore to those forms of incommensurability that mark the relation between knowledges. This should not hinder, however, the possibility of cultural translation between these traditions, dismissing any potential for creative and productive exchange. If anything, this book aims to demonstrate that Islamist post-colonial re-elaborations of universalistic ideals parallel attempts in the critical humanities to endorse forms of universalistic space marked by an anti-national and inclusive dynamics or dealing with a globalised context expressing a certain crisis of the national model. If considered beyond Qutb's eschatological implications, for instance, inverting the emancipatory focus of his inclusive structure – with the domain of Islam becoming the universalistic space of the common, the multitude, or a global citizenship, and the non-Islamic outside epitomising the *ever-emerging* and *positivised* realm of the excluded, those 'who have no voice' – the topological representation of *dar al-Islam* that we have outlined in this book could be assumed as a useful geographical model for imagining the kind of spatial configuration that content-less forms of association instantiate.[52] As Boaventura de Sousa Santos insightfully recalls: 'incommensurability does not necessarily impede communication and may even lead to unsuspected forms of complementarity'.[53]

---

[52] Jacques Rancière, *Disagreement* (Minneapolis, MN: The University of Minnesota Press, 1999), p. 208.
[53] Boaventura de Sousa Santos, 'Beyond Abyssal Thinking: From Global Lines to Ecologies of Knowledges', *Review*, 30/1 (2007): 75.

Bibliography

Abdel-Malek, Anour. *La pensée politique arabe contemporaine* (Paris: Éditions du Seuil, 1970).

Abdelnasser, Walid Mahmoud. *The Islamic Movement in Egypt: Perceptions of International Relations 1967–1981* (London: Kegan Paul International, 1994).

AbuKhalil, As'ad. 'A New Arab Ideology? The Rejuvenation of Arab Nationalism', *Middle East Journal*, 46/1 (1992): 22–36.

Abu-Rabi, Ibrahim M. *Intellectual Origins of Islamic Resurgence in the Modern Arab World* (Albany, NY: State University of New York Press, 1996).

Abu-Rabi', Ibrahim M. *The Contemporary Arab Reader on Political Islam* (Edmonton, AB: University of Alberta Press, 2010).

Abu-Sahlieh, Sami A. Aldeeb. 'The Islamic Conception of Migration', *International Migration Review, Special Issue: Ethics, Migration, and Global Stewardship*, 30/1 (1996): 37–57.

Adorno, Theodor W. and Max Horkheimer. *Dialectic of Enlightenment* (1st edn, 1947; London: Verso, 1997).

Ajami, Fouad. 'The End of Pan-Arabism', *Foreign Affairs*, 57/2 (1978/9): 355–73.

al-Ahsan, Abdullah. *Ummah or Nation: Identity Crisis in Contemporary Muslim Society* (Leicester: Islamic Foundation, 1992).

al-Banna, Hasan. 'Da'wa ilā Allāh', *Majallat al-Fath*, no.100, 1346/1928.

al-Banna, Hasan. 'Aghrad al-Ikhwan al-Muslimin', *Jaridat al-Ikhwan al-Muslimin*, no.7, 1352/1933.

al-Banna, Hasan. *To What Do We Invite Humanity?* (Cairo, 1934); Also appeared as a pamphlet in 1936; translated by http://thequranblog.wordpress.com, available at https://thequranblog.files.wordpress.com/2008/06/_2_-to-what-do-we-invite-humanity.pdf, last accessed 20 March 2015.

al-Banna, Hasan. 'Da'watuna' (Our Message), in *Jaridat al-Ikhwan al-Muslimin* (1353/1935); also appeared as a pamphlet in 1937; translated by http://thequranblog.wordpress.com, available at http://thequranblog.files.wordpress.com/2008/06/_6_-our-message.pdf, last accessed 20 March 2015.

al-Banna, Hasan. *Towards the Light* (Cairo: Dar al-Kitab al-Arabi, 1936); translated by http://thequranblog.wordpress.com, available at https://

- al-Banna, Hasan. thequranblog.files.wordpress.com/2008/06/_1_-toward-the-light.pdf, last accessed 20 March 2015.
- al-Banna, Hasan. *Oh Youth* (pamphlet, 1939); translated by http://thequranblog.wordpress.com, available at https://thequranblog.files.wordpress.com/2008/06/_9_-oh-youth.pdf, last accessed 20 March 2015.
- al-Banna, Hasan. *Between Yesterday & Today* (pamphlet, 1939); translated by http://thequranblog.wordpress.com, available at https://thequranblog.files.wordpress.com/2008/06/_7_-between-yesterday-today.pdf, last accessed 20 March 2015.
- al-Banna, Hasan. *Al-Jihad* (Cairo, n.d.; appeared in the late 1930s), translated by http://thequranblog.wordpress.com, available at http://thequranblog.files.wordpress.com/2008/06/_10_-al-jihad.pdf, last accessed 20 March 2015.
- al-Banna, Hasan. *Memoirs of the Call and the Preacher* (*Mudhakkirāt Al-Daʻwah Wa-Al-Dāʻiyah*) (Cairo: 1947), [first parts published in instalments in 1942].
- al-Banna, Hasan. *The Message of the Teachings* (Cairo, n.d.; appeared in the early 1940s), translated by http://thequranblog.wordpress.com, available at https://thequranblog.files.wordpress.com/2008/06/_3_-the-message-of-the-teachings.pdf, last accessed 20 March 2015.
- al-Banna, Hasan. *Our Message in a New Phase* (Cairo, n.d.; appeared in the 1940s), translated by http://thequranblog.wordpress.com, available at https://thequranblog.files.wordpress.com/2008/06/_5_-our-message-in-a-new-phase.pdf, last accessed 20 March 2015.
- al-Banna, Hasan. *Peace in Islam* (Cairo, 1948), translated by http://thequranblog.wordpress.com, available at https://thequranblog.files.wordpress.com/2008/06/_4_-peace-in-islam.pdf, last accessed 20 March 2015.
- al-Banna, Hasan. *Al-Aqaa'id* (*Islamic Creed*) (Cairo, 1949), translated by http://thequranblog.wordpress.com, available at https://thequranblog.files.wordpress.com/2008/06/_8_-al-aqaaid.pdf, last accessed 20 March 2015.
- al-Banna, Hasan. *Majmūʻat Rasāʼil Al-Imām Al-Shahīd Hasan Al-Bannā* (Bayrūt: al-Muʼassasah al-Islāmīyah lil-Tibāʻah wa-al-Sihāfah wa-al-Nashr, 1981).
- al-Banna, Hasan. *Five Tracts of Hasan Al-Bannāʼ (1906–1949): A Selection from the Majmūʻat Rasāʼil Al-Imām Al-Shahīd Hasan Al-Bannā*, trans. Charles Wendell (Berkeley, CA: University of California Press, 1978).
- al-Ghazali, Muhammad. *al-Islam al-muftara ʻalayh bayn al-shuyuʻiyin waʼl-raʼsmaliyin* (Cairo: Society of the Muslim Brothers, 3rd edn, 1953).
- al-Husayni, Ishaq Musa. *The Moslem Brethren: The Greatest of Modern Islamic Movements* (Beirut: Khayat's College Book Cooperative, 1956).
- Alim, H. Samy. 'A New Research Agenda: Exploring the Transglobal Hip Hop Umma', in Miriam Cooke and Bruce B. Lawrence (eds), *Muslim Networks*

from Hajj to Hip Hop (Chapel Hill, NC: University of North Carolina Press, 2005), pp. 264–74.
al-Jabri, Mohammed Abed. *Arab-Islamic Philosophy: A Contemporary Critique* (Austin, TX: University of Texas Press, 1999).
Allievi, Stefano. *Musulmani d'Occidente: Tendenze dell'Islam Europeo* (Rome: Carocci, 2002).
Almond, Gabriel A. *Political Development: Essays in Heuristic Theory* (Boston, MA: Little, Brown, 1970).
Almond, Ian. *The New Orientalists: Postmodern Representations of Islam from Foucault to Baudrillard* (London: I.B. Tauris, 2007).
Amin, Ash (ed.). *Post-Fordism: A Reader* (Oxford: Blackwell, 1994).
Anderson, Perry. *Lineages of the Absolutist State* (London: N.L.B, 1974).
Anderson, Perry. *The Origins of Postmodernity* (London: Verso, 1998).
Anderson, Benedict. *Imagined Communities: Reflection on the Origin of the Spread of Nationalism* (London: Verso, 1983).
Anzaldúa, Gloria E. *Borderlands/La Frontera: The New Mestiza* (San Francisco, CA: Aunt Lute Books, 1999).
Apter, David. *The Politics of Modernization* (Chicago, IL, and London: University of Chicago Press, 1965).
Arendt, Hannah. *The Human Condition* (New York: Doubleday, 1959).
Arjomand, Said Amir. 'Social Change and Movements of Revitalization in Contemporary Islam', in James A. Beckford (ed.), *New Religious Movements and Rapid Social Change* (London: SAGE; Paris: UNESCO, 1986), pp. 87–112.
Arkoun, Mohammed. *Islam: To Reform or to Subvert?* (London: Saqi Essentials, 2006).
Asad, Talal. 'The Idea of an Anthropology of Islam', *Qui Parle*, 17/2 (2009): 1–30.
Asad, Talal. *Formations of the Secular: Christianity, Islam, Modernity* (Stanford, CA: Stanford University Press, 2003).
Augé, Marc. *Non-Places: Introduction to an Anthropology of Supermodernity* (1st edn, 1992; London: Verso, 1995).
Azadpur, Muhammad. *Reason Unbound: On Spiritual Practice in Islamic Peripatetic Philosophy* (New York: SUNY Press, 2011).
Badiou, Alain. *Saint Paul: The Foundation of Universalism* (Stanford, CA: Stanford University Press, 2003).
Badiou, Alain. *Infinite Thought: Truth and the Return of Philosophy* (London: Continuum, 2003).
Badiou, Alain. *Logiques des mondes* (Paris: Éditions du Seuil, 2006).

Balibar, Etienne and Immanuel Wallerstein. *Race, Nation and Class* (London: Verso, 1991).
Balibar, Etienne. *We, the People of Europe?: Reflections on Transnational Citizenship* (Princeton, NJ, and Oxford: Princeton University Press, 2004).
Baran, Zeyno. 'The Roots of Violent Islamist Extremism and Efforts to Counter It', US Committee on Homeland Security and Governmental Affairs, 10 July 2008.
Barghuthi, Tamim. *The Umma and the Dawla: The Nation State and the Arab Middle East* (London and Ann Arbor, MI: Pluto Press, 2008).
Baudrillard, Jean. *The Ecstasy of Communication* (New York: Semiotext(e), 1988).
Baudrillard, Jean. *The Transparency of Evil* (New York: Verso, 1993).
Baudrillard, Jean. *Simulacra and Simulation* (Ann Arbor, MI: University of Michigan Press, 1994).
Baudrillard, Jean. *The Conspiracy of Art: Manifestos, Interviews, Essays* (New York: Semiotext(e), 2005).
Bauman, Zygmunt. *Liquid Modernity* (Cambridge: Polity Press, 2000).
Beck, Ulrich. *Risk Society: Towards a New Modernity* (London: SAGE, 1992).
Becker, Carl Heinrich. 'Panislamismus', *Islamstudien* (Leipzig, 1932).
Berger, Peter. *The Social Reality of Religion* (London: Faber, 1969).
Bertier, Francis. 'L'idéologie politique des frères musulmans', *Orient*, 8 (1958): 43–57.
Bhabha, Homi. *The Location of Culture* (London: Routledge, 1994).
bin Laden, Osama. 'The Betrayal of Palestine, 29 December 1994', in Bruce Lawrence (ed.), *Messages to the World: The Statements of Osama Bin Laden* (London and New York: Verso, 2005), pp. 3–14.
bin Laden, Osama. 'Declaration of War: Against the Americans Occupying the Land of the Two Holy Places', 23 August 1996; translation at http://web.archive.org/web/20011106100207/http://www.kimsoft.com/2001/binladenwar.htm, last accessed 20 March 2015.
bin Laden, Osama. 'The Saudi Regime, November 1996', in Bruce Lawrence (ed.), *Messages to the World: The Statements of Osama Bin Laden* (London and New York: Verso, 2005), pp. 31–43.
bin Laden, Osama. 'Osama Bin Ladin, Interview by Peter Arnett, 20 March 1997', translation at http://www.anusha.com/osamaint.htm, last accessed 20 March 2015.
bin Laden, Osama. 'World Islamic Front Statement, 23 February 1998: Jihad against Jews and Crusaders', translation at http://fas.org/irp/world/para/docs/980223-fatwa.htm, last accessed 20 March 2015.

bin Laden, Osama. 'A Muslim Bomb, December 1998', in Bruce Lawrence (ed.), *Messages to the World: The Statements of Osama Bin Laden* (London and New York: Verso, 2005), pp. 65–94.

bin Laden, Osama. 'Under Mullah Omar, 9 April 2001', in Bruce Lawrence (ed.), *Messages to the World: The Statements of Osama Bin Laden* (London and New York: Verso, 2005), pp. 95–9.

bin Laden, Osama. 'Bin Laden's Statement, 7 October 2001', translation at http://www.theguardian.com/world/2001/oct/07/afghanistan.terrorism15, last accessed 20 March 2015.

bin Laden, Osama. 'Osama Bin Ladin, Interview by Tayseer Allouni, 21 October 2001', translation at http://www.religioscope.com/info/doc/jihad/ubl_int_3.htm, last accessed 20 March 2015.

bin Laden, Osama. 'The Example of Vietnam, 12 November 2001', interview published in *Al-Quds Al-Arabi*, in Bruce Lawrence (ed.), *Messages to the World: The Statements of Osama Bin Laden* (London and New York: Verso, 2005), pp. 139–44.

bin Laden, Osama. 'Among a Band of Knights, 14 February 2003', in Bruce Lawrence (ed.), *Messages to the World: The Statements of Osama Bin Laden* (London and New York: Verso, 2005), pp. 186–206.

bin Laden, Osama. 'Resist the New Rome, 4 January 2004', in Bruce Lawrence (ed.), *Messages to the World: The Statements of Osama Bin Laden* (London and New York: Verso, 2005), pp. 212–32.

bin Laden, Osama. 'Bin Laden Tape, 15 April 2004', translation at http://news.bbc.co.uk/2/hi/middle_east/3628069.stm, last accessed 20 March 2015.

bin Laden, Osama. 'Depose the Tyrants, 16 December 2004', in Bruce Lawrence (ed.), *Messages to the World: The Statements of Osama Bin Laden* (London and New York: Verso, 2005), pp. 245–75.

bin Laden, Osama. 'Purported bin Laden Message to Europe: Leave Afghanistan, 29 November 2007', available at http://edition.cnn.com/2007/WORLD/meast/11/29/bin.laden.message/index.html#cnnSTCText, last accessed 20 March 2015.

bin Laden, Osama. 'Bin Laden Message to Europe: Withdraw from Afghanistan, 25 September 2009', translation at http://www.juancole.com/2009/09/bin-laden-message-to-europe-withdraw.html, last accessed 20 March 2015.

Bodin, Jean. *On Sovereignty: Four Chapters from the Six Books of the Commonwealth* (1st edn, 1576; Cambridge: Cambridge University Press, 1992).

Bonner, Michael David. *Jihad in Islamic History: Doctrines and Practice* (Princeton, NJ: Princeton University Press, 2006).

Bouagache, Chafika Kahina. 'The Algerian Law on Associations within Its Historical Context', *The International Journal of Not-for-Profit Law*, 9/2 (2007): 37–55.

Boullata, Issa J. 'Sayyid Qutb's Literary Appreciation of the Qur'an', in Issa J. Boullata (ed.), *Literary Structures of Religious Meaning in the Qur'ān* (Richmond: Curzon, 2000), pp. 354–71.

Brachman, Jarret M. *Global Jihadism: Theory and Practice* (Abingdon: Routledge, 2009).

Brah, Avtar. *Cartographies of Diaspora: Contesting Identities* (London: Routledge, 1996).

Brah, Avtar and Annie E. Coombes (eds). *Hybridity and its Discontents: Politics, Science, Culture* (London: Routledge, 2000).

Breisinger, Clemens, Olivier Ecker and Perrihan Al-Riffai. 'Economics of the Arab Awakening: From Revolution to Transformation and Food Security', *IFPRI Policy Brief*, 18 (2011).

Brown, Wendy. *Walled States, Waning Sovereignty* (Brooklyn, NY: Zone Books, 2010).

Bruno, Etienne. *L'islamisme radical* (Paris: Hachette, 1987).

Brykczynski, Paul. 'Radical Islam and the Nation: The Relationship between Religion and Nationalism in the Political Thought of Hassan Al-Banna and Sayyid Qutb', *History of Intellectual Culture*, 5/1 (2005): 1–19.

Bunt, Gary. *iMuslims: Rewiring the House of Islam* (New Delhi: Cambridge University Press, 2009).

Burdeau, Georges. *L'État* (Paris: Éditions du Seuil, 1980).

Burgat, Francois. *Face to Face with Political Islam* (London and NewYork: I.B. Tauris, 2003).

Burns, Robert Ignatius and Paul E. Chevedden. *Negotiating Cultures: Bilingual Surrender Treaties in Muslim-Crusader Spain* (Leiden: Brill, 1999).

Bush, George W. 'Address to a Joint Session of Congress and the American People', 20 September 2001, http://georgewbush-whitehouse.archives.gov/news/releases/2001/09/20010920-8.html, last accessed 20 March 2015.

Calvert, John. *Sayyid Qutb and the Origins of Radical Islamism* (New York: Columbia University Press, 2010).

Campbell, David. *National Deconstruction* (Minneapolis, MN: University of Minnesota Press, 1998).

Carpenter, Joel A. *Revive Us Again: The Reawakening of American Fundamentalism* (Oxford: Oxford University Press, 1997).

Carré, Olivier and Michel Seurat. *Les frères musulmans (1928–1982)* (Paris: L'Harmattan, 1983).

Casanova, José. *Public Religions in the Modern World* (Chicago, IL: University of Chicago Press, 1994).

Castells, Manuel. *The Information Age: Economy, Society and Culture. Vol. 1: The Rise of the Network Society* (Cambridge, MA: Blackwell Publishers, 1996).

Chiurazzi, Gaetano. *Il postmoderno* (Milan: Bruno Mondatori, 2002).

Christiansen, Thomas, Knud Erik Jorgensen and Antje Wiener (eds). *The Social Construction of Europe* (London and Thousand Oaks, CA: SAGE, 2001).

Cohen, Roger. 'When Fear Breaks', *New York Times*, 9 June 2011, available at http://www.nytimes.com/2011/06/10/opinion/10iht-edcohen10.html?_r=1.

Colombe, Marcel. *L'Évolution de l'Égypte: 1924–1950* (Paris: G.P. Maisonneuve et Cie, 1951).

Cook, David. *Understanding Jihad* (Berkeley, CA: University of California Press, 2005).

Coole, Diana. 'Cartographic Convulsions: Public and Private Reconsidered', *Political Theory*, 28/3 (2000): 337–54.

Coombs, Nathan. 'Christian Communists, Islamic Anarchists?: Part 1', *International Journal of Žižek Studies*, 3/1 (2009): 1–19; available at http://zizekstudies.org/index.php/ijzs/article/view/153/269 last accessed 1 May 2010.

Coombs, Nathan. 'Christian Communists, Islamic Anarchists?: Part 2', *International Journal of Žižek Studies*, 3/3 (2009): 1–24.

Constant, Benjamin. 'The Liberty of the Ancients Compared with That of the Moderns', in B. Fontana (ed.), *Political Writings* (1st edn, 1819; Cambridge, UK: Cambridge University Press, 1988), pp. 308–28.

Crone, Patricia. *God's Rule: Government and Islam* (New York: Columbia University Press, 2004).

Davis, Horace B. *Toward a Marxist Theory of Nationalism* (New York and London: Monthly Review Press, 1978).

Davis, Horace B. *National Question: Selected Writings by Rosa Luxembourg* (New York: Monthly Review Press, 1981).

Debord, Guy. *La société du spectacle* (Paris: Buchet-Chastel, 1967).

De Certeau, Michel. *The Practice of Everyday Life* (Berkeley, CA: University of California Press, 1984).

Deeb, Marius. 'Continuity in Modern Egyptian History: The Wafd and the Muslim Brothers', in AAVV, *Problems of the Modern Middle East in Historical Perspective: Essays in Honour of Albert Hourani* (London: Ithaca Press/Garnet Publishing, 1992), pp. 49–61.

Delanque, Gilbert. 'Al-Ikhwan al-Muslimun', *Encyclopaedia of Islam* (Leiden: E.J. Brill, 1960; new edn, vol. 3, 1969), pp. 1068–71.

Delanty, Gerard. *Inventing Europe: Idea, Identity, Reality* (Basingstoke: Macmillan, 1995).

Demant, Peter R. and Asghar Ali Engineer. *Islam vs. Islamism: The Dilemma of the Muslim World* (Westport, CT, and London: Praeger, 2006).

Desai, Meghnad. *Rethinking Islamism: The Ideology of the New Terror* (London and New York: I.B. Tauris, 2007).

Dieter, Melvin E. *The Holiness Revival of the Nineteenth Century* (Lanham, MD: The Scarecrow Press, 1996).

Dussel, Enrique. *The Invention of the Americas: Eclipse of 'the Other' and the Myth of Modernity* (New York: Continuum, 1995).

Ebert, Teresa. *Ludic Feminism and After: Postmodernism, Desire, and Labor in Late Capitalism* (Ann Arbor, MI: University of Michigan Press, 1996).

Eickelman, Dale F. and James Piscatori. *Muslim Politics* (London: Princeton University Press, 2nd edn, 2004).

El-Affendi, Abdelwahab. *Who Needs an Islamic State?* (London: Grey Seal, 1991).

Esposito, John. 'Islam and Civil Society', in John L. Esposito and Francois Burgat (eds), *Modernizing Islam: Religion in the Public Sphere in Europe and the Middle East* (London: Hurst & Company, 2003), pp. 69–98.

Euben, Roxanne L. *Enemy in the Mirror: Islamic Fundamentalism and the Limits of Modern Rationalism* (Princeton, NJ: Princeton University Press, 1999).

Fichte, Gottlieb. *Addresses to the German Nation* (New York and Evanston, IL: Harper & Row, 1968).

Flusser, Vilém. 'Thinking about Nomadism', in A. Finger (ed.), *The Freedom of the Migrant: Objections to Nationalism* (Urbana, IL: University of Illinois Press, 2003), pp. 38–46.

Foucault, Michel. *Surveiller et punir: Naissance de la prison* (Paris: Gallimard, 1975).

Foucault, Michel. 'What is Enlightenment?' ('Qu'est-ce que les Lumières?ì), in Paul Rabinow (ed.), *The Foucault Reader* (New York: Pantheon Books, 1984), pp. 32–50.

Foucault, Michel. *Discipline & Punish: The Birth of the Prison* (NY: Vintage Books 1995).

Foucault, Michel. *Security, Territory, Population: Lectures at the Collège de France, 1977–1978* (Basingstoke: Palgrave Macmillan, 2007).

Gabrieli, Francesco. 'Il concetto di 'asabiyya nel pensiero storico di Ibn Khaldun' in *L'Islam nella storia. Saggi di storia e storiografia musulmana* (Bari: Dedalo spa, 1966), pp. 211–53.

Gauchet, Marcel. *The Disenchantment of the World: A Political History of Religion* (Princeton, NJ: Princeton University Press, 1985, 1999).

Gause III, F. Gregory. 'Why Middle East Studies Missed the Arab Spring', *Foreign Affairs*, 90/4 (2011): 81–90.

Geary, Patrick J. *The Myths of Nations: The Medieval Origins of Europe* (Princeton, NJ, and Oxford: Princeton University Press, 2002).

Gellner, Ernest. *Nations and Nationalism* (1st edn, 1983; Malden, MA: Blackwell, 2006).

Gerges, Fawaz A. *The Far Enemy: Why Jihad Went Global* (Cambridge: Cambridge University Press, 2005).

Giddens, Anthony. *The Consequences of Modernity* (Cambridge: Polity Press, 1990).

Giddens, Anthony. *Modernity and Self Identity* (Cambridge: Polity Press, 1991).

Gilpin, Robert. *Global Political Economy* (Princeton, NJ: Princeton University Press, 2001).

Gore, Al. 'Forging a New Athenian Age of Democracy', *Intermedia*, 22/2 (1995): 4–7.

Habeck, Mary R. *Knowing the Enemy: Jihadist Ideology and the War on Terror* (New Haven, CT: Yale University Press, 2006).

Habermas, Jürgen. 'Modernity versus Postmodernity', *New German Critique*, 22 (1981): 3–14.

Habermas, Jürgen. 'Modernity: An Incomplete Project', in P. Brooker (ed.), *Modernism/Postmodernism* (Harlow: Longman, 1996), 125–38.

d'Haen, Theo and Hans Bertens (eds). *Liminal Postmodernisms: The Postmodern, the (Post-)Colonial and the (Post-)Feminist* (Amsterdam: Rodopi B.V. Editions, 1994).

Haddad, Yvonne Y. 'Sayyid Qutb: Ideologue of Islamic Revival', in John Esposito (ed.), *Voices of the Islamic Revolution* (Oxford: Oxford University Press, 1983), pp. 67–98.

Hague, Euan. 'Benedict Anderson', in P. Hubbard, R. Kitchin and G. Valentine (eds), *Key Thinkers on Space and Place* (London and New York: SAGE, 2004), pp. 18–25.

Haider, Aliya. 'The Rhetoric of Resistance: Islamism, Modernity and Globalization', *Harvard BlackLetter Law Journal*, 18 (2002): 91–128.

Haj, Samira. *Reconfiguring Islamic Tradition: Reform, Rationality, and Modernity* (Stanford, CA: Stanford University Press, 2009).

Hallaq, Wael B. *A History of Islamic Legal Theories: An Introduction to Sunni Usul al-Fiqh* (Cambridge: Cambridge University Press, 1997).

Hamas Covenant. *The Covenant of the Islamic Resistance Movement*, available at http://www.ikhwanweb.com/article.php?id=4921, last accessed 20 March 2015.
Hamas. 2006 Electoral Campaign Platform 'List for Change and Reform', available at http://www.ikhwanweb.com/article.php?id=4921.
Haraway, Donna. *Simians, Cyborgs and Women: The Reinvention of Nature* (New York: Routledge, 1991).
Hardt, Michael and Antonio Negri. *Empire* (London: Harvard University Press, 2000).
Harvey, David. *The Condition of Postmodernity: An Enquiry into the Origins of Cultural Change* (Oxford: Blackwell, 1990).
Herder, Johann Gottfried von. *Reflections on the Philosophy of the History of Mankind* (Chicago, IL, and London: University of Chicago Press, 1968).
Heyworth-Dunne, James. *Religious and Political Trends in Modern Egypt* (Washington, DC: The author, 1950).
Hizb ut-Tahrir. 'About Us', available at http://english.hizbuttahrir.org/index.php/about-us?format=pdf, last accessed 20 March 2015.
Hobbes, Thomas. *De Cive* (1st edn, 1642; Whitefish, MT: Kessinger Publishing, 2004).
Hobbes, Thomas. *Leviathan* (1st edn, 1651; Oxford: Oxford University Press, 1998).
Humboldt, Wilhelm von. *The Limits of State Action* (1st edn, 1791; London and Cambridge University Press, 1969).
Hunter, Shireen T. (ed.). *The Politics of Islamic Revivalism: Diversity and Unity* (Bloomington, IN: Indiana University Press, 1988).
Huntington, Samuel. *The Clash of Civilizations and the Remaking of World Order* (New York: Usborne Books, 1996).
Husain, Ed. *The Islamist: Why I Joined Radical Islam in Britain, What I Saw and Why I Left* (London: Penguin, 2007).
Husain, Mishal. 'How Facebook Changed the World: The Arab Spring', BBC documentary, available at http://www.bbc.co.uk/programmes/b014l2ck, last accessed 20 March 2015.
Hussain, Shahrul. *Dar Al-Islam and Dar Al-Harb: An Analytical Study of its Historical Inception, its Definition by the Classical Scholars and its Application to the Contemporary World* (Manchester: Al Hikma Publishing, 2012).
Husserl, Edmund. *The Crisis of European Sciences and Transcendental Phenomenology: An Introduction to Phenomenological Philosophy* (Evanston, IL: Northwestern University Press, 1970).

Ibrahim, Raymond. 'Tunisian Elections and the Road to the Caliphate', *Jihad Watch*, 27 October 2011, available at http://www.jihadwatch.org/2011/10/raymond-ibrahim-tunisian-elections-and-the-road-to-the-caliphate.html, last accessed 20 March 2015.

Inalcık, Halil. 'The Rise of the Ottoman Empire', in P.M. Holt, Ann K.S. Lambton and Bernard Lewis (eds), *The Cambridge History of Islam* (Cambridge: Cambridge University Press, 1970), pp. 293–323.

Inalcık, Halil. 'Introduction: Empire and Population', in Halil Inalcık and Donald Quataert (eds), *An Economic and Social History of the Ottoman Empire, 1300–1916* (Cambridge and New York: Cambridge University Press, 1994), pp. 11–43.

Isin, Engin F. *Being Political: Genealogies of Citizenship* (Minneapolis, MN: University of Minnesota Press, 2002).

Isin, Engin F. 'Citizenship after Orientalism: Ottoman Citizenship', in Fuat Keyman and Ahmet Icduygu (eds), *Citizenship in a Global World: European Questions and Turkish Experiences* (London: Routledge, 2005), pp. 31–51.

Ismail, Salwa. 'State-Society Relations in Egypt: Restructuring the Political', *Arab Studies Quarterly*, 17/3 (1995): 39–54.

Ismail, Salwa. *The Popular Movement Dimensions of Contemporary Militant Islamism: Socio-Spatial Determinants in the Cairo Urban Setting* (Cambridge: Cambridge University Press, 2000).

Ismail, Salwa. *Rethinking Islamist Politics: Culture, the State and Islamism* (London: I. B. Tauris, 2006).

Jameson, Fredric. *Postmodernism: ,or, The Cultural Logic of Late Capitalism* (London: Verso, 1991).

Jankowski, James P. *Redefining the Egyptian Nation, 1930–1945* (Cambridge: Cambridge University Press, 1995).

Jauss, Hans Robert. *Toward an Aesthetic of Reception* (Minneapolis, MN: University of Minnesota Press, 1982).

Jones, Steven G. (ed.). *CyberSociety: Computer-Mediated Communication and Community* (Thousand Oaks, CA: London: SAGE Publications, 1995).

Karpat, Kemal H. *The Politicization of Islam: Reconstructing Identity, State, Faith, and Community in the Late Ottoman State* (New York and Oxford: Oxford University Press, 2001).

Karam, Azza. *Transnational Political Islam: Religion, Ideology and Power* (London: Pluto Press, 2004).

Karpat, Kemal H. 'Millets and Nationality: The Roots of the Incongruity of Nation and State in the Post-Ottoman Era', in Benjamin Brad and Bernard

Lewis (eds), *Christians and Jews in the Ottoman Empire: The Functioning of a Plural Society* (New York: Holmes & Meier Publishers, 1980), pp. 141–70.

Karpat, Kemal H. *The Politicization of Islam: Reconstructing Identity, State, Faith, and Community in the Late Ottoman State* (New York and Oxford: Oxford University Press, 2001).

Keddie, Nikki R. *An Islamic Response to Imperialism: Political and Religious Writings of Sayyid Jamāl ad-Dīn 'al-Afghānī'* (Berkeley, CA: University of California Press, 1983).

Keddie, Nikki R. *Sayyid Jamāl ad-Dīn'al-Afghānī': A Political Biography* (Berkeley, CA, and London: University of California Press, 1972).

Kepel, Gilles. *Muslim Extremism in Egypt: The Prophet and Pharaoh* (Berkeley and Los Angeles, CA: University of California Press, 1985).

Kepel, Gilles. *Jihad: The Trail of Political Islam* and (London: I.B. Tauris, 2002).

Kepel, Gilles. 'Islamism Reconsidered: A Running Dialogue with Modernity', *Harvard International Review*, 22/2 (2000): 22–7.

Khadduri, Majid. *The Islamic Law of Nations: Shaybani's Siyar* (Baltimore, MD: Johns Hopkins Press, 1966).

Khadduri, Majid. *War and Peace in the Law of Islam* (1st edn, 1955; Clark, NJ: The Lawbook Exchange, 2006).

Khaldun, Ibn. *The Muqaddimah: An Introduction to History* (Princeton, NJ: Princeton University Press, 2005).

Khatab, Sayed. *The Power of Sovereignty: The Political and Ideological Philosophy of Sayyid Qutb* (London: Routledge, 2006).

Khatab, Sayed. 'Hakimiyyah and Jahiliyyah in the Thought of Sayyid Qutb', *Middle Eastern Studies*, 38/3 (2002): 145–70.

Khatab, Sayed. *The Political Thought of Sayyid Qutb: The Theory of Jahiliyyah* (London: Routledge, 2009).

Kirk, Gorge. *The Middle East in the War* (London: Royal Institute of International Affairs, 1952).

Korany, Bahgat. 'Alien and Besieged Yet Here to Stay: The Contradictions of the Arab Territorial State', in Ghassan Salamé (ed.), *The Foundation of the Arab State* (London: Croom Helm, 1987), pp. 47–74.

Kunstler, James Howard. *The Geography of Nowhere: The Rise and Decline of America's Man-Made Landscape* (New York: Simon & Schuster, 1993).

Krasner, Stephen D. *Sovereignty: Organized Hypocrisy* (Princeton, NJ: Princeton University Press, 1999).

Kumar, Krishan. 'The Nation-State, the European Union and the Transnational Identities', in Nezar N. AlSayyad and Manuel Castells (eds), *Muslim Europe* or *Euro-Islam: Politics, Culture, and Citizenship in the Age of Globalization* (Oxford: Lexington Books, 2002), pp. 53–68.

Kumar, Krishan. *From Post-Industrial to Post-Modern Society: New Theories of the Contemporary World* (New York: Wiley-Blackwell, 2004).

Lacan, Jacques. *The Psychoses: 1955–1956*, ed. Jacques-Alain Miller, trans. Russell Grigg (New York: W.W. Norton, 1993).

Lacan, Jacques. 'The Instance of the Letter in the Unconscious', *Écrits: The First Complete Edition in English* (1st edn, 1957; New York: W.W. Norton & Company, 2006).

Laclau, Ernesto and Chantal Mouffe. *Hegemony and Socialist Strategy* (London and New York: Verso, 1985).

Laclau, Ernesto. *New Reflections on the Revolution of Our Time* (London: Verso, 1990).

Laclau, Ernesto. 'Discourse' in Robert A. Goodin and Philip Pettit (eds), *A Companion to Contemporary Political Philosophy* (Oxford: Blackwell, 1995).

Laclau, Ernesto. 'Philosophical Roots of Discourse Theory'. Unpublished paper, Centre for Theoretical Studies in the Humanities and Social Sciences, Essex University, 2005.

Laclau, Ernesto. *On Populist Reason* (London: Verso, 2006).

Lahoud Nelly, and A.H. Johns (eds). *Islam in World Politics* (Abingdon: Routledge, 2005).

Lahoud, Nelly. *Political Thought in Islam: A Study in Intellectual Boundaries* (Abingdon: Routledge, 2012).

Lawrence, Bruce. *Messages to the World: The Statements of Osama Bin Laden* (London and New York: Verso, 2005).

Lee, Dwight E. 'The Origins of Pan-Islamism', *The American Historical Review*, 47/ 2 (1942): 278–87.

Lenin, Vladimir Ilyich. 'The Right of Nations to Self-Determination', *Collected Works*, vol. 20 (Moscow: Progress Publishers, 1972).

Lewis, Bernard. 'The Return of Islam', *Commentary*, 61/1 (1976): 39–49.

Lewis, Bernard. *The Political Language of Islam* (Chicago, IL, and London: University of Chicago Press, 1988).

Lewis, Bernard. *What Went Wrong?: The Clash between Islam and Modernity in the Middle East* (London: Weidenfeld & Nicolson, 2002).

Lia, Branjar. *The Society of the Muslim Brothers in Egypt: The Rise of an Islamic Mass Movement 1928–1942* (London: Ithaca Press/Garnet Publishing, 1998).

Licklider, J.C.R. and R.W. Taylor. 'The Computer as a Communication Device', *Science and Technology*, 76 (1968): 21–31.

Lipovetsky, Gilles and Sebastien Charles. *Hypermodern Times* (Cambridge: Polity, 2005).

Ludlow, Peter. *High Noon on the Electronic Frontier: Conceptual Issues in Cyberspace* (Cambridge, MA: MIT Press, 1996).

Lyotard, Jean-Francois. *The Postmodern Condition: A Report on Knowledge* (Manchester: Manchester University Press, 1979/1984).

McGrew, Anthony. 'Globalization and Global Politics', in John Baylis and Steve Smith (eds), *The Globalization of World Politics: An Introduction to International Relations* (Oxford: Oxford University Press, 3rd edn, 2005), pp. 19–40.

Maffesoli, Michel. *Du nomadisme: Vagabondages initiatiques* (Paris: Librairie Générale Française, 2000).

Mandaville, Peter G. *Global Political Islam* (New York: Routledge, 2007).

Mandaville, Peter G. *Transnational Muslim Politics: Reimagining the Umma* (London: Routledge, 2001).

Mandhai, Shafik. 'Muslim Leaders Reject Baghdadi's Caliphate', *al-Jazeera*, 7 July 2014, available at http://www.aljazeera.com/news/middleeast/2014/07/muslim-leaders-reject-baghdadi-caliphate-20147744058773906.html, last accessed 20 March 2015.

Mann, M. 'Has *Globalization* Ended the Rise of the *Nation-State*?', *Review of International Political Economy*, 4/3 (1997): 472–96.

March, Andrew F. 'Taking People as They Are: Islam as a "Realistic Utopia" in the Political Theory of Sayyid Qutb', *American Political Science Review*, 104/1 (2010): 189–207.

Maréchal, Brigitte. *The Muslim Brothers in Europe: Roots and Discourse* (Leiden and Boston, MA: Brill, 2008).

Marramao, Giacomo. *The Passage West: Philosophy after the Age of the Nation State* (London: Verso, 2012).

Martin, David. *A General Theory of Secularization* (New York: Harper & Row, 1979).

Mazzini, Giuseppe. *Scritti Editi e Inediti* (Imola: Galeati, 1906, vol. 83).

Mawdudi, Sayyid Abul. 'Ala, *Let Us Be Muslim* (Leicester: Islamic Foundation, 1985).

May, Samantha. 'God's Land: Blurring the National and the Sacred in Waqf Territory', *Politics, Religion & Ideology*, 16/3 (2014): 421–41.

Mitchell, Robert. *The Society of the Muslim Brothers* (London: Oxford University Press, 1969).

Moaddel, Mansoor. *Islamic Modernism, Nationalism, and Fundamentalism: Episode and Discourse* (Chicago, IL: University of Chicago Press, 2005).

Morsi, Mohamed. 'Muslim Brotherhood, Contemporary Islamic Parties', posted on 5 August 2007, www.ikhwanweb, available at http://www.ikhwanweb.com/article.php?id=13748, last accessed 20 March 2015.

Moscovici, Claudia. *Double Dialectics: Between Universalism and Relativism in Enlightenment and Postmodern Thought* (Lanham, MD: Rowman & Littlefield, 2002).

Moussalli, Ahmad S. *Radical Islamic Fundamentalism: The Ideological and Political Discourse of Sayyid Qutb* (Beirut: American University of Beirut, 1992).

Moussalli, Ahmad S. 'Hasan Al-Banna's Islamist Discourse on Constitutional Rule and Islamic State', *Journal of Islamic Studies*, 4/2 (1993): 161–74.

Muhammad Knight, Michael. *The Taqwacores* (New York: Autonomedia, 2004).

Mundy, Martha and Basim Musallam (eds). *The Transformation of Nomadic Society in the Arab East* (Cambridge: Cambridge University Press, 2000).

Muñoz, Gema Martín. *Politica y Elecciones en el Egipto Contemporaneo: 1922–1990* (Madrid: M.A.E., 1992).

Murden, Simon. *Islam, the Middle East, and the New Global Hegemony* (London: Lynne Rienner, 2002).

Musallam, Adnan A. *From Secularism to Jihad: Sayyid Qutb and the Foundations of Radical Islamism* (Westport, CT: Praeger, 2005).

Muslim Brotherhood. 'The Legal Concept of an Islamic State According to The MB', posted on 13 June 2007, www.ikhwanweb, available at http://www.ikhwanweb.com/article.php?id=810, last accessed 20 March 2015.

Muxlim. 'Welcome to Muxlim', available from http://muxlim.com/about, last accessed 1 May 2010.

Nasr, Seyyed Hossein. *Traditional Islam in the Modern World* (London: Kegan Paul International, 1987).

Negri, Antonio and Danilo Zolo. 'L'Impero e la moltitudine – Un dialogo sul nuovo ordine della globalizzazione', *Jura Gentium - Rivista di filosofia del diritto internazionale e della politica globale*, 1/1 (2005): 11–13.

Neumann, Iver B. *Uses of the Other: 'The East' in European Identity Formation* (Manchester: Manchester University Press, 1999).

Nietzsche, Friedrich Wilhelm. *On the Genealogy of Morals* (1st edn, 1887; New York: Vintage Books, 1989).

Norval, Aletta. 'Trajectories of Future Researches in Discourse Theory', in David Howarth, Aletta Norval and Yannis Stavrakakis (eds), *Discourse Theories and Political Analysis* (Manchester: Manchester University Press, 2000), pp. 219–36.

Novak, Marcus. 'Transarchitectures and Hypersurfaces: Operations of Transmodernity', in Stephen Perrella (ed.), *Hypersurface Architecture* (New York: John Wiley & Sons, 1998), pp. 85–94.

Nunes, Mark. 'Baudrillard in Cyberspace: Internet, Virtuality and Postmodernity', *Style*, 29/2 (1995): 314–27.

Obama, Barack. 'Remarks by the President in Address to the Nation on the Way Forward in Afghanistan and Pakistan', 1 December 2009, available at http://www.whitehouse.gov/the-press-office/remarks-president-address-nation-way-forward-afghanistan-and-pakistan, last accessed 20 March 2015.

Obama, Barack. 'Statement by the President on ISIL', 10 September 2014, available at http://www.whitehouse.gov/the-press-office/2014/09/10/statement-president-isil-1, last accessed 20 March 2015.

Ohmae, Kenichi. *The End of the Nation State* (New York: Free Press, 1995).

Olalquiaga, Celeste. *Megalopolis: Contemporary Cultural Sensibilities* (Minneapolis, MN: University of Minnesota Press, 1992).

Opwis, Felicitas. 'Maslaha in Contemporary Islamic Legal Theory', *Islamic Law and Society*, 12/2 (2005): 182–223.

Owen, Roger. *State, Power and Politics in the Making of the Modern Middle East* (London: Routledge, 1992).

Pascale, Ghazaleh (ed.). *Held in Trust: Waqf in the Islamic World* (Cairo: American University in Cairo Press, 2011).

Parsons, Talcott and Neil Joseph Smelser. *Economy and Society: A Study in the Integration of Economic and Social Theory* (London: Routledge, 1956).

Parvin, Manoucher and Maurie Sommer. 'Dar al-Islam: The Evolution of Muslim Territoriality and Its Implications for Conflict Resolution in the Middle East', *International Journal of Middle East Studies*, 11/1 (1980): 1–21.

Peters, Rudolph. *Jihad in Classical and Modern Islam: A Reader* (Princeton, NJ: Markus Wiener Publishers, 2005).

Phelps Harris, Christina. *Nationalism and Revolution in Egypt: The Role of the Muslim Brotherhood* (The Hague: Mouton & Co., 1964).

Pipes, Daniel. *The Hidden Hand: Middle East Fears of Conspiracy* (Basingstoke: Macmillan, 1996).

Poggi, Gianfranco. *The Development of the Modern State: A Sociological Introduction* (London: Hutchinson, 1978).

Pollock, John. 'Streetbook', *Technology Review*, September/October (2011): 72–8.

Poster, Mark. *The Second Media Age* (Cambridge: Polity Press, 1995).

Qutb, Sayyid. *Social Justice in Islam* (Oneonta, NY: Islamic Publications International, 2000).

Qutb, Sayyid. *Milestones* (Birmingham: Maktabah Booksellers and Publishers, 2006).
Ramadan, Tariq. *Aux sources du renouveau musulman: d'al-Afghani à Hasan al-Banna, un siècle de réformisme islamique* (Lyon: Tawhid, 2002).
Rancière, Jacques. *Disagreement* (Minneapolis, MN: The University of Minnesota Press, 1999).
Relph, Edward. *Place and Placelessness* (London: Pion, 1976).
Renan, Ernest. 'What Is a Nation?', in Geoff Eley and Ronald Grigor Suny (eds), *Becoming National: A Reader* (1st edn, 1882; New York and Oxford: Oxford University Press, 1996), pp. 41–55.
Rheingold, Howard. *The Virtual Community: Homesteading on the Electronic Frontier* (Cambridge, MA, and London: MIT Press, 2000).
Rodríguez Magda, Rosa María. *Transmodernidad* (Barcelona: Anthropos, 2005).
Rosenthal, Franz. 'The "Muslim Brethren" in Egypt', *Muslim World*, 38 (1947): 278–91.
Roy, Olivier. *The Failure of Political Islam* (London: I.B. Tauris, 1994).
Roy, Oliver. *Globalized Islam: Fundamentalism, Deterritorialization and the Search for a New Ummah* (London: Hurst & Company, 2004).
Ruthven, Malise. *Fundamentalism: The Search for Meaning* (Oxford: Oxford University Press, 2004).
Ruthven, Malise. 'The Map ISIS Hates', *The New York Review of Books*, 25 June 2014, available at http://www.nybooks.com/blogs/nyrblog/2014/jun/25/map-isis-hates, last accessed 20 March 2015.
Sadiki, Larbi. 'Occidentalism: The "West" and "Democracy" as Islamist Constructs', *Orient*, 39/1 (1998): 103–20.
Sadiki, Larbi. *The Search for Arab Democracy* (London: Hurst & Company, 2004).
Sadowski, Yaha. 'The New Orientalism and Democracy Debate', *Middle East Report*, 183 (1993): 14–21, 40.
Said, Edward. *Orientalism* (Harmondsworth: Penguin, 1978).
Salmi, Ralph H. *Islam and Conflict Resolution: Theories and Practices* (Lanham, MD: University Press of America, 1998).
Sardar, Ziauddin. *Postmodernism and the Other: The New Imperialism of Western Culture* (London and Chicago, Il: Pluto Press, 1997).
Sartre, Jean-Paul. 'Preface', in Frantz Fanon, *The Wretched of the Earth*, trans. Constance Farrington (New York: Grove Press, 1963), pp. 7–31.
Saussure, Ferdinand de. *Cours de linguistique générale*, trans. Wade Baskin as *Course in General Linguistics* (London: Fontana, 1974).
Sayyid, Bobby S. *A Fundamental Fear: Eurocentrism and the Emergence of Islamism* (London: Zed Books, 1997).

Scheuer, Michael. *Osama Bin Laden* (Oxford: Oxford University Press, 2011).
Scholte, Jan Aart. *Globalization: A Critical Introduction* (London: Macmillan, 2000).
Sedar, Irving and Harold J. Greenberg. *L'Egypte entre deux mondes* (Paris: Éditions aux carrefours du monde, 1956).
Shahin, Emad El-Din. 'Political Islam in Egypt', *CEPS Working Document No. 266*, May 2007.
Shakespeare, William. *The Tempest*.
Sharma, Rajeev. *Global Jihad: Current Patterns and Future Trends* (New Delhi: Kaveri Books, 2006).
Sieyès, Emmanuel Joseph. *What is the Third Estate?* (London: Pall Mall Press, 1963).
Smith, Anthony. *The Ethnic Origins of Nations* (Oxford: Blackwell, 1986).
Soage, A.B. and J.F. Fraganillo. 'The Muslim Brothers in Egypt', in B. Rubin (ed.), *The Muslim Brotherhood: The Organization and Policies of a Global Islamist Movement* (New York: Palgrave Macmillan, 2010), pp. 39–56.
Soja, Edward W. *Postmodern Geographies: The Reassertion of Space in Critical Social Theory* (London: Verso, 1989).
Sookhdeo, Patrick. *Global Jihad: The Future in the Face of Militant Islam* (McLean, VA: Isaac Publishing, 2007).
Sousa Santos, Boaventura de. 'Beyond Abyssal Thinking: From Global Lines to Ecologies of Knowledges', *Review*, 30/1 (2007): 45–89.
Spivak, Gayatri Chakravorty. *A Critique of Postcolonial Reason: Toward a History of the Vanishing Present* (Cambridge, MA: Harvard University Press, 1999).
Springer, Devin R., James L. Regens and David N. Edger. *Islamic Radicalism and Global Jihad* (Washington, DC: Georgetown University Press, 2008).
Starrett, Gregory. 'Islam after Empire: Turkey and the Arab Middle East', in R. Michael Feener (ed.), *Islam in World Cultures: Comparative Perspectives* (Oxford: ABC-CLIO, 2004), pp. 41–71.
Stavrakakis, Yannis, with Nikos Chrysoloras. '(I Can't Get No) Enjoyment: Lacanian Theory and the Analysis of Nationalism', *Psychoanalysis, Culture & Society*, 11 (2006): 144–63.
Stone, Allucquére Rosanne. 'Will the Real Body Please Stand Up: Boundary Stories about Virtual Cultures', in M. Benedikt (ed.), *Cyberspace* (Cambridge, MA: MIT Press, 1991), pp. 81–118.
Tadros, Mariz. *The Muslim Brotherhood in Contemporary Egypt: Democracy Redefined or Confined?* (London: Routledge, 2012).
Taji-Farouki, Suha and Basheer M. Nafi (eds). *Islamic Thought in the Twentieth-Century* (London: I.B. Tauris, 2004).

Tatsuo, Inoue. 'Liberal Democracy and Asian Orientalism', in Joanne R. Bauer and Daniel A. Bell (eds), *The East Asian Challenge for Human Rights* (Cambridge: Cambridge University Press, 1999), pp. 27–59.

Taylor, Charles. *The Malaise of Modernity* (Toronto, ON: Anansi, 1991).

Taylor, Charles. *Sources of the Self: Making of the Modern Identity* (Cambridge: Cambridge University Press, 1989).

Teti Andrea and Andrea Mura. 'Sunni Islam and Politics', in Jeff Haynes (ed.), *Routledge Handbook of Religion and Politics* (London: Routledge, 2010), pp. 92–110.

Teti, Andrea and Gennaro Gervasio. 'The Army's Coup in Egypt: For the People or against the People?', *Open Democracy*, 23 July 2013, available at https://www.opendemocracy.net/andrea-teti-gennaro-gervasio/army%E2%80%99s-coup-in-egypt-for-people-or-against-people, last accessed 20 March 2015.

Tharoor, Ishaan. 'ISIS or ISIL? The Debate over What to Call Iraq's Terror Group', *Washington Post*, 18 June 2014, available at http://www.washingtonpost.com/blogs/worldviews/wp/2014/06/18/isis-or-isil-the-debate-over-what-to-call-iraqs-terror-group, last accessed 20 March 2015.

The Oslo Accords: And Related Agreements; available from http://almashriq.hiof.no/general/300/320/327/oslo.html.

The Qur'an and Sunnah Society of Canada. *An Introduction to the Salafi Da'wah*, available at http://www.qss.org/articles/salafi/text.html, last accessed 20 March 2015.

The Six Points of Tabligh, Lesson 9, http://www.scribd.com/doc/5551200/Six-Fundamentals?autodown=pdf, last accessed June 2009.

Thomas, Megan C. 'Orientalism and Comparative Political Theory', *The Review of Politics*, 72/4 (2010): 653–77.

Tibi, Bassam. *Arab Nationalism: Between Islam and the Nation-State* (London: Macmillan, 1997).

Tocqueville, Alexis de. *Democracy in America* (1st edn 1835; Stilwell, KS: Digireads.com Publishing, 2007).

Tort, Michel. *La fin du dogme paternel* (Paris, France: Flammarion, 2007).

Toscano, Alberto. 'The Bourgeois and The Islamist, or, The Other Subjects of Politics', *Cosmos and History: The Journal of Natural and Social Philosophy*, 2/1–2 (2006): 15–38.

Turkle, Sherry. *Life on the Screen: Identity in the Age of the Internet* (New York: Simon & Schuster, 1995).

Turner, Bryan. 'Orientalism and the Problem of Civil Society', in Asaf Hussaini, Robert Oslon and Jamil Qureichi (eds), *Orientalism, Islam and Islamicists* (Brattleboro, VT: Amana Books, 1984), pp. 23–42.

Utvik, Bjorn Olav. 'The Modernizing Force of Islam', in John L. Esposito and Francois Burgat (eds), *Modernizing Islam: Religion in the Public Sphere in Europe and the Middle East* (London: Hurst & Company, 2003), pp. 43–67.

Vaccaro, Salvo. 'Prefazione', in Todd May, *Anarchismo e post-strutturalismo* (Milan: Eleuthera, 1998), pp. 7–17.

Vighi, Fabio and Heiko Feldner. 'Ideology Critique or Discourse Analysis? Žižek against Foucault', *European Journal of Political Theory*, 6/2 (2007): 141–59.

Virilio, Paul and Sylvere Lotringer. *Pure War* (New York: Semiotext(e), 1983).

Virilio, Paul. *The Aesthetics of Disappearance* (New York: Semiotext(e), 1991).

Virno, Paolo. 'Virtuosity and Revolution: The Political Theory of Exodus', in Paolo Virno and Michael Hardt (eds), *Radical Thought in Italy* (Minneapolis, MN: University of Minnesota Press, 1996), pp. 13–37.

Wallerstein, Immanuel. *The Modern World System* (New York: Academic Press, 1974).

Wallerstein, Immanuel Maurice. *Utopistics: or, Historical Choices of the Twenty-First Century* (New York: New Press, 1998).

Warburg, Gabriel R. *Egypt and the Sudan: Studies in History and Politics* (London: Frank Cass, 1985).

Watt, William Montgomery. *Islamic Fundamentalism and Modernity* (London: Routledge, 1988).

Weber, Max. *The Protestant Ethic and the Spirit of Capitalism* (1st edn, 1905; New York: Charles Scribner's Sons, 1958).

Weber, Max. 'Science as a Vocation', in H. Gerth and C. Wright Mills (eds), *From Max Weber: Essays in sociology* (1st edn, 1918; New York: Oxford University Press, 1946), pp. 129–56.

Weimann, Gabriel. *Terror on the Internet: The New Arena, the New Challenges* (Washington, DC: United States Institute of Peace Press, 2006).

Wickham, Carrie Rosefsky. *The Muslim Brotherhood: Evolution of an Islamist Movement* (Princeton, NJ: Princeton University Press, 2013).

Widder, Nathan. 'What's Lacking in the Lack: A Comment on the Virtual', *Angelaki: Journal of the Theoretical Humanities*, 5/3 (2000): 117–138.

Wiktorowicz, Quintan (ed.). *Islamic Activism: A Social Movement Theory Approach* (Bloomington, IN.: Indiana University Press, 2004).

Wiktorowicz, Quintan. *Radical Islam Rising: Muslim Extremism in the West* (Lanham, MD: Rowman & Littlefield, 2005).

Williams, Ian G. 'Relics and Baraka: Devotion to the Prophet Muhammad among Sufis in Nottingham, UK', in Elisabeth Arweck and Peter Collina (eds), *Reading Religion in Text and Context: Reflections of Faith and Practice in Religious Materials* (Aldershot: Ashgate, 2006), pp. 65–82.

Wilson, Scott and Al Kamen. '"Global War on Terror" Is Given New Name', *Washington Post*, 25 March 2009, http://www.washingtonpost.com/wp-dyn/content/article/2009/03/24/AR2009032402818.html, last accessed 20 March 2015.

Wong, Siu-Lun. *Emigrant Entrepreneurs: Shanghai Industrialists in Hong Kong* (Hong Kong: Oxford University Press, 1988).

Yale, William. *The Near East: A Modern History* (Ann Arbor, MI: Michigan University Press, 1953).

Yeor, Bat, Miriam Kochan and David Littman. *Islam and Dhimmitude: Where Civilizations Collide* (Madison, NJ: Fairleigh Dickinson University Press, 2002).

Young, Robert. *Colonial Desire: Hybridity in Theory, Culture and Race* (London: Routledge, 1995).

Zahid, Mohammed. *The Muslim Brotherhood and Egypt's Succession Crisis: The Politics of Liberalisation and Reform in the Middle East* (New York: I.B. Tauris, 2010).

Zaki, Moheb. *Civil Society & Democratisation in Egypt* (Cairo: Konrad Adenauer Stiftung - Ibn Khaldoun Center, 1995).

Zaman, Muhammad Qasim. *The Ulama in Contemporary Islam: Custodians of Change* (Princeton, NJ: Princeton University Press, 2002).

Zawahiri, Ayman. 'Knights under the Prophet's Banner', in *His Own Words: Translation and Analysis of the Writings of Dr. Ayman Al Zawahiri* (Old Tappan, NJ: TLG Publications, 2006), pp. 19–225.

Zielonka, Jan. *Europe as Empire: The Nature of the Enlarged European Union* (Oxford: Oxford University Press, 2006).

Žižek, Slavoj. 'Eastern Europe's Republics of Gilead', *New Left Review*, 1/183 (1990): 50–62.

Žižek, Slavoj. *The Plague of Fantasies* (London: Verso, 1997).

Žižek, Slavoj. *The Ticklish Subject: The Absent Centre of Political Ontology* (London: Verso, 2000).

Žižek, Slavoj. *The Parallax View* (Cambridge, MA: MIT Press, 2006).

Index

9/11 terrorist attacks 2, 4, 175, 188

'Abduh, Muhammad
    brand of reformism 38
    influence on al-Banna 101, 128
    notion of *maslaha* 121
Abbasid dynasty 36, 59, 69, 205
Abu Sayyaf Group (The Philippines) 173
Afghanistan 1, 5, 173–6, 190, 208
Al-Afghani, Jamal ad-Din 55–6
    brand of reformism 38, 101, 128
al-Aqsa Mosque 180, 181 n.29
al-Azhar mosque-university 98–100, 119, 207
al-Baghdadi, Abu Bakr 204, 206
al-Banna, Hasan
    bibliography 103–4
    compared with bin Laden 168, 178–9, 183, 191
    compared with Qutb 131–2, 136, 138, 140–141, 155
    discursive frame 97–8
    early writings
        early engagements with nationalism 111–113
        Islamic revival 114
        Islamisation from below 105
        negative dialectic and the East 110
        tradition and brotherhood 108–9
        views on sovereignty and shari'ah 106–7
    enduring influence 194–202, 213
    immediate heritage 128–9
    late 1930s
        irredentism 119–120
        multidimensional model of identity (concentric circles) 115–117
        orientalism and Europe 117; *see also* Occidentalism
    relation to modernism 29, 39
    the 1940s
        Islamic government 121–3
        Nationalism and orientalism 124–5
al-Jabri, Mohammed Abed 37–38
al-Muhajiroun 164, 202–4, 208
al-Nahda (Tunisia) 2–3, 128, 207
al-Qaeda 3–4, 167, 173, 175, 179, 186–7, 203–4, 207; *see also* bin Laden
al-Qaradawi, Yusuf 207
al-Razik, Ali Abd 98
al-Sadat, Anwar 8, 169, 172
al-Sarakhsi, Muhammad ibn Ahmad 57–8, 64
al-Turabi, Hasan 5, 128
al-Wahhab, Muhammad Ibn Abd 170
al-Zawahiri, Ayman 173, 180 n.28
Anglo-Egyptian Treaty (1936) 114
Arab League 169 n.6
Arab Socialist Union (ASU) 169
Arab spring 2–3, 8
Arab-Israeli War (1948) 103
Arabism *see* nationalism
Armed Islamic Group (Algeria) 173
asabiyyah (tribal kinship) 68
Asad, Talal 37, 42, 69
Atatürk, Mustafa Kemal 70–1
atomism 41, 43–4, 80–82
Awakening movement (Da'wa)
Azadpur, Muhammad 215
Azzam, Abdullah 175

Badiou, Alain 6, 214
Baudrillard, Jean
    hypertelia 80–81

virtualism and hyperreality 90–91
bay'a (oath of loyalty) 108, 207
bid'a (innovation) 170
bin Laden
    al-Qaeda and global jihadism 174–7
    compared with al-Banna 168, 178–9, 183, 191
    compared with Qutb 168, 179–180, 182–3, 185–6
    dar al-Islam and global antagonism 183–4
    discursive frame 167–8, 171
    influence 202–4, 211
    jihad as an individual duty 178–80
    negotiation 190–192
    pragmatism and rhetorics 188–9
    reciprocity and the language of terror 181–2
    relation to globalism and transmodernity 89, 94, 138
    vanguardism 185–7
Bosnia 174, 177, 208
Britain 54 n.66, 98, 184
Bush, George W. 1, 184–5

Caliban 213
caliphate
    abolition 70–71, 97
    reference by al-Banna 106, 121
    reference by DAIISH and Hizb ut-Tahrir 201–8
    reinvention of and enduring influence 36, 39, 57, 65-6, 69–70, 73
Camp David treaty (1978) 8, 169, 172
Castells, Manuel 87, 89
chain of equivalence 25, 29
clash of civilisation 167, 184–5, 192
Cold War 1, 76, 85, 167, 174
colonialism 15, 22, 28, 41, 46, 52, 67, 71, 77, 84, 97, 110, 114, 138, 194
Computer-mediated Communication (CMC) *see* Informatisation
Constant, Benjamin 43
Council of Guardians 198
court system 107, 122

crusades 66-67
cyberspace 78–9, 88, 91; *see also* virtuality, Informatisation

DAIISH 3, 4
    as ISIS 185, 204–7
dar al-'ahd 59–60, 63, 66, 121, 152–3, 163, 189
dar al-harb
    in relation to bin Laden 180, 182–3, 185, 189, 191–2
    in relation to Islamic universalism 58–9, 61–4, 66, 214
    in relation to Qutb 146–55, 162–3
dar al-Islam
    in relation to bin Laden 176, 180, 182–4, 189, 192
    in relation to Islamic universalism 57–71, 205, 214, 216
    in relation to Qutb 144, 146–7, 149–53, 155–61, 163–4
da'wa (Islamic call) 58, 105, 111, 178
dawla 26, 70, 205–6
Debord, Guy 80
deprivatisation of religion 32–3, 41
desedimentation
    as a concept 22, 24, 28
    effect of colonialism 35, 39, 70–71, 97, 107, 138
    effect of globalisation 74, 77, 79, 82, 84, 88, 170, 210, 212
dhimmi 151–2, 154, 156, 196
discourse
    theory and concept 17–29
dualism 27 n.32, 41, 62, 159, 193

effendia 100–101, 100 n.12
Egypt
    British control 97–8, 114–115
    Egyptian Revolution (1952) 101–3
    Egyptian Revolution (2011) 2, 196–7
    relevance for Islamism 7–8, 118–119, 124
    under Nasser and Sadat 134–5, 168–9, 171–3

Enduring Freedom (2001 US Operation) 5
Eurocentrism 214; *see also* orientalism

Faraj, Mohammed Abd al-Salam 172–3, 178
Farouk, king 102
First World War 54, 71, 98
Foucault, Michel 16–7, 20, 39, 51
fragmentation
    as a desedimenting factor 74, 79–82, 84, 91–3, 114, 209–210
    political fragmentation 65, 70, 169
Free Officers 102, 133
fundamentalism
    as distinct from Islamism 13
    neo-fundamentalism 4 n.7, 93, 208

Gamaat Islamiya (Egypt) 173
Gellner, Ernest 53
Ghannuchi, Rachid 128, 207
Ghazali, Muhammad 100
global jihadi movement 132, 167, 171, 173–5, 191
globalism 88–9, 175, 193
globalisation
    desedimenting process 73–7, 210–211
    as distinct from universalism 211
    g-localisation 92–3
    reconfiguration of space and time 77–9

hadith 177 n.20
hākimiyya 106–7, 140
Hamas (Islamic Resistance Movement) 128, 199–202
Hanbalism 59, 171
Hardt, Michael and Antonio Negri 45, 50–51, 75, 80, 86, 94
Harvey, David 77, 93
hegemony 21, 168, 183
hijra 58, 67
hip hop 211–212
Hizb ut-Tahrir 164, 202–4, 207–8
Hobbes, Thomas 47–8, 50, 179
Hong Kong 33
Huntington, Samuel 184

Husain, Taha 98
Husserl, Edmund 22
hybridity 73, 85, 88, 93
hyperreality 90
hypertelia 81, 83

Ibn Khaldun 68
Ibn Taymiyyah 179
ijtihad 38
imperialism 52–3, 108, 110–111, 208
inclusivity 9, 27 n.32, 44, 62, 89, 144, 148
individualism 41–4, 80, 82, 84, 123, 133
Indonesia 173, 186
informatisation 76–82, 90, 92, 171, 174; *see also* Internet
Internet 78–9, 91, 211
Iran 5, 129, 171, 198–9, 206, 208
ISIS (or ISIL, ISI, IS) *see* DAIISH
Islam
    as a master signifier 23–6
    objectification of 209–210
    progressive Islam 211–212
    reference to orientalism 16
    self-sufficiency of Islam 106, 113
Islamic Action Front (Jordan) 128
Islamic Jihad (Egypt) 172–3
Islamic order 42, 65, 122
Islamic punk 211–212
Islamic Salvation Front (Algeria) 173
Islamic state 128, 141, 172–3, 195, 198–200, 202; *see also* DAIISH
Islamic universalism *see* universalism
Israel 169, 172, 174, 176, 177 n.20, 181, 184, 189, 199–200

jahiliyyah 114, 136, 142 n.30, 153–64, 172, 180, 183, 185–6, 202, 204, 208, *see also* Qutb
jamaat-e-Islami (Pakistan) 134
jemaah islamiyah (Indonesia) 173
jihad
    in relation to al-Banna 105, 118, 120
    in relation to bin Laden 167, 171–5, 177–83, 191
    in relation to Hizb ut-Tahrir 203–4

in relation to tradition 39, 58–61, 90
in relation to Qutb 136, 152, 160, 163

Kepel, Gilles 4–5, 134
Khadduri, Majid 59, 63–4
Khamanei, Ali 198
Khomeini, Ruhollah Mousavi 5, 8, 198
Knight, Michael Muhammad 212
Kuwait 174

Lacan, Jacques 18–19, 24
Laclau, Ernesto 8, 17–23, 27
Lebanon 54 n.66, 177, 181
Libya 3
List for Change and Reform (C&R) 200–201

Mandate system 54 n.66
maslaha 59, 121
master signifier 23–26, 47, 57, 71, 97, 111, 113, 123, 146, 150
Mawdudi, Syed Abul A'ala 154–5
Mecca 67, 170, 181
Medina 67, 170
Migration 58–9, 67
millet system 152, 153 n.50,
Möbius strip 62–3, 148–9, 158
modernism
    Egyptian modernists 27, 29, 97
    modernist perspectives on Islamism 14, 34, 99, 115
    modernist theories 14, 31 n.2, 31–3, 35, 37, 41, 73, 127
modernity
    colonialism and political discourse 45–7
    discourse-centred reading of 39–42
    as a historical and sociological time 31–4
    Islamisation of modernity 36
    modernisation of Islam 35
    modernisation 40, 55, 76–7
    as a symbolic scenario 27–9
Morocco 128
Morsi, Mohamed 194–7

Motahhari, Morteza 8
Mubarak, Hosni 196–7
mujahideen 173–5, 187, 208
multitude 45, 50–1, 68, 88–90, 93, 216
Muslim Brotherhood (al-Ikhwān al-Muslimūn, Muslim Brothers)
    1954 abolition of 133–4
    2011 January Revolution 196–7
    Arab Spring 2–3
    early rise and consolidation 100–103
    historical context 97
    later developments 194–6
    literature on 98–9
Muxlim 211–212

Nasser, Jamal Abdel 55, 102, 133–4, 164, 168–9, 172
National Islamic Front (Sudan) 5, 128
nationalism
    Arab nationalism, Arabism, pan-Arabism 53–5, 134, 168–70
    discursive structure of 47–53
    Egyptian nationalism 98, 112–113, 124, 134, 169–70
    Kemalism 26, 71
    Nasserism 134
Negri, Antonio *see* Hardt, Michael
neo-fundamentalism 4 n.7, 93, 135, 208
neo-orientalism 6, 16; *see also* orientalism
Nietzsche, Friedrich Wilhelm 61 n.87
nodal point *see* master signifier

Obama, Barack 1, 184–5
Occidentalism 110–111, 117, 126–7, 133, *see also* Orientalism
October War (1973) 169
Oedipus complex, 83
Orientalism 14–16, 23–5, 46–7, 110, 126–7
Oslo Accords (1993) 200
Ottoman Empire, 36, 54–6, 70–71, 100 n.15, 119, 152–3, 205, 208
Ottoman-Mamluk War 100 n.15
over-development 74, 81–84

Pahlavi, Mohammad Reza 171, 198
Pakistan 173, 177, 186, 191
Palestine 54 n.66, 103, 128, 176–7, 181 n.29, 182, 188, 199–202
Palestinian Legislative Council elections (2006) 200
Palestinian Liberation Organisation (PLO) 200
pan-Arabism *see* nationalism
pan-Islamism *see* universalism
paradigm 27 n.32
Parvin, Manoucher and Maurie Sommer 57, 60, 66–7
paternal Law *see* Oedipus complex
people
    concept of national 48–51
point de capiton 19, 26, *see also* master signifier
post-colonialism, post-coloniality 45 n.34, 84, 132, 134–5, 165, 169, 194, 216
post-fordism 76 n.6
postmodernism, postmodernity 16, 83–8, 93–4, *see also* transmodernity
post-nationality, post-Westphalian 73–6, 94, 135
pro-Palestinian campaign (1936) 103
progressive Islam *see* Islam
psychasthenia 88–89

Qana 177 n.20, 181
Qur'an 38, 57, 67–8, 106, 109, 118, 126, 132, 136, 177 n.20, 201
Qutb, Sayyid
    compared with al-Banna 131–2, 136, 138, 140–141, 155
    compared with bin Laden 168, 179–180, 182–3, 185–6
    dar al-Islam and Islamic space 146–53
    heritage 164–5, 202, 204, 207–8
    historical context 133–6
    Islamic sovereignty and shari'ah 140–143
    jahiliyyah 154–9
    on modern discourses 137–8
    necessity and universalism of Islam 144–6
    on prophecy and universalism 215
    revivalism and jihad 159–61
    virtuality and vanguardism 161–3

reformist movement 38, 56, 98–9, 101, 121, 128
relativism 41, 86
religious courts 107
revivalism *see* fundamentalism
Rida, Muhammad Rashid 38, 98
Roy, Olivier 4–5, 93, 208–9
Ruthven, Malise 5, 206

Said, Edward 15–16
salafism 38, 171, 186
Sartre, Jean-Paul 110
Saudi Arabia 135, 169–70, 173, 176, 208
Saussure, Ferdinand de 18–19
Sayyid, Bobby 15, 23–6
Second World War 120, 126
secularisation, secularism 31–2, 34, 41–2, 48, 69, 105, 183
shari'ah
    in the context of the Islamic Republic of Iran 198
    as part of tradition 39
    in relation to al-Banna 106–107, 111, 121–2, 128
    in relation to bin Laden 172
    in relation to Qutb 140–142, 149, 151–2
Shariati, Ali 8
Six-Day War (1967 Arab–Israeli War) 8, 55, 168–9
social networks 206, 211; *see also* informatisation, internet
Sommer, Maurie *see* Parvin, Manoucher
sovereignty
    sovereignty of God 64, 66–7, 106–7, 140–143
    theories of national sovereignty 45–8, 50–53, 73, 75, 94, 122

spatial displacement 75–9, 88–9, 93, 209–210
Sudan 5, 98, 128, 176
Suez Canal 98, 105
    Suez Crisis (1956) 134
sufism 108, nn.33–34, 170
Sultan Abdul Hamid II 55–6, 70
Sunna 38, 68 n.95, 176, 177 n.20, 184
Sykes-Picot agreement (1916) and border 206
symbolic scenario 7–8, 28, 35, 39, 82–3, 97, 122, 129, 132, 164, 193, 206, 213
Syria 3, 54 n.66, 112, 128, 168, 204–6

Tablighi Jama'at 93, 209–210
tajdid (renewal) 38
Takfir w-al-Hijra 172
Taliban 2, 5, 93
Tamarod movement 197
taqlid (imitation) 38, 99
territory
    concept of national territory 51–3
terrorism, as self defence, support for 181–2, 184–5, 203–4
topology 62, 148
tradition
    discourse-centred reading of 35–7
    Islamic tradition, *turāth* 37–9
    modernist perspective 31–4
    as a symbolic scenario 27–9
transmodernity
    context 73–4
    discourse-centred reading of 82–4, 87–8, 90
    relation with modernity and tradition 92–4
    as a symbolic scenario 27–9
    Tunisia 2–3, 128
turāth see tradition, Islamic tradition
Turkey 3, 71, 129

ulama
    authority, changing role 99 n.8, 101
    criticism by the Muslim Brotherhood 100–101

ummah
    as compared with the national people 51
    concept in Islamic tradition 67–71
    virtual ummah 211–212
United Arab Republic (UAR) 55, 169
United Nations (UN) 178, 181
United States 133, 143, 174, 181–2, 190, 203
universalism
    comparison between Pauline and Islamic universalism 213–216
    Islamic universalism
        contribution to tradition 29
        discourse of 56–71
        political movement 55–6
    universalism and transmodernity 89–90, 93–4

vanguardism 162–4, 185–6, 192, 208–210
virtuality
    discourse of virtualism and virtual communities 90–2
    effect of globalisation 78–9
    virtual ummah and virtual reality 211–212
    virtualisation of the Islamic society 157, 159–60, 208

Wafd (Delegation Party) 98, 100, 112, 119–120, 122
Wahhabism 170–171
wilayat al-faqih al-mutlaqa (absolute mandate of the jurist) 198–9
World Islamic Front 176
World Trade Centre attacks 189

Young Turks 70 n.104, 97

Zionism, Zionist American alliance 180, 184, 200
Žižek, Slavoj 16, 24, 83, 212–214